PROJECT: PATRON ™

STEVE ORLANDO

PATRICK PIAZZALUNGA

CARLOS LOPEZ

HASSAN OTSMANE-ELHAOU

THOMAS MAUER

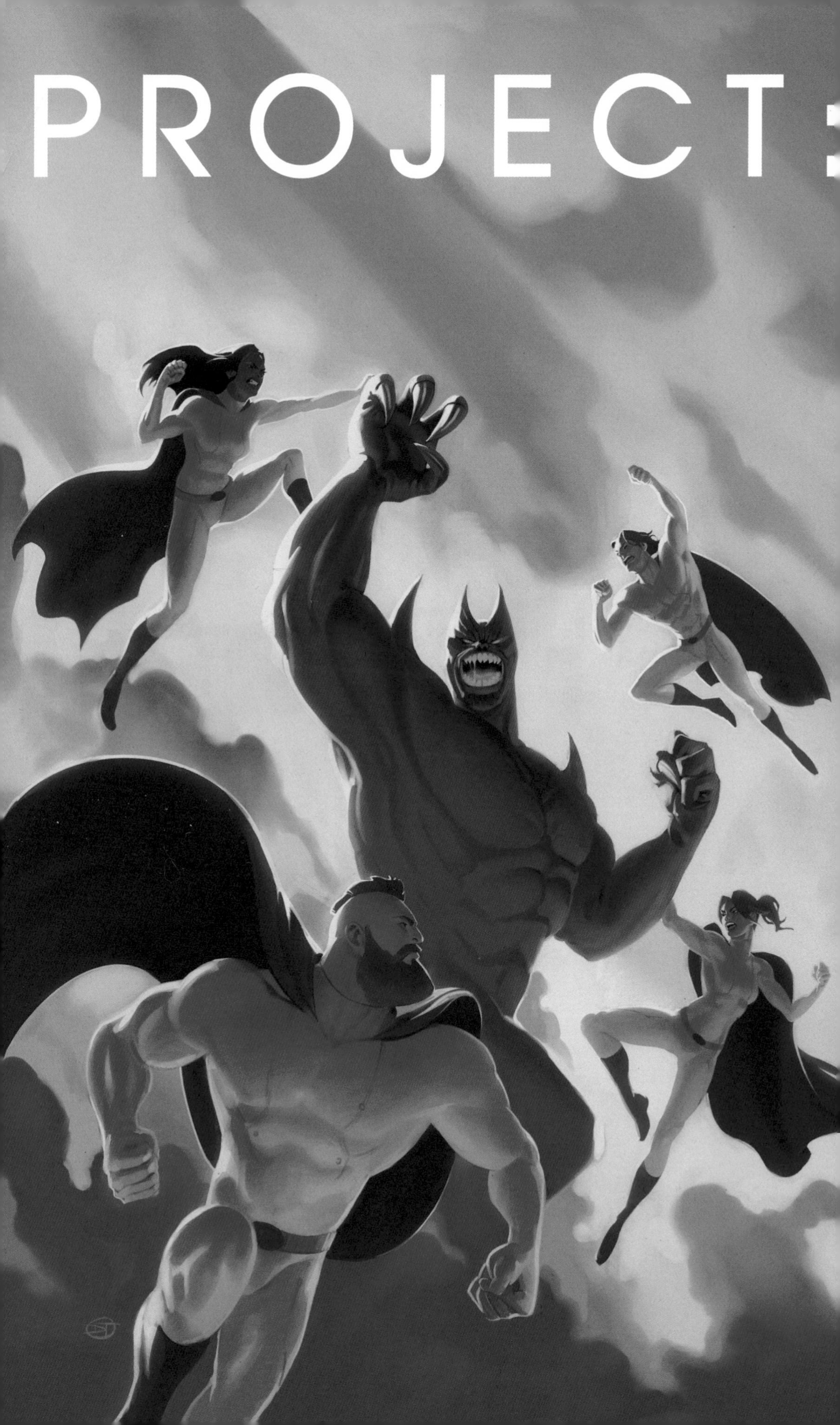
PROJECT:

PATRON

STEVE ORLANDO writer

PATRICK PIAZZALUNGA artist

CARLOS LOPEZ colorist

HASSAN OTSMANE-ELHAOU & **THOMAS MAUER** letterers

DAVID TALASKI front & original covers

TONY HARRIS & **AARON LOPRESTI** variant covers

TOM MULLER logo designer

CHARLES PRITCHETT issue #1 backmatter designer

COREY BREEN book designer

MIKE MARTS editor

created by **STEVE ORLANDO** & **PATRICK PIAZZALUNGA**

AFTERSHOCK™

MIKE MARTS - Editor-in-Chief • JOE PRUETT - Publisher/CCO • LEE KRAMER - President • JON KRAMER - Chief Executive Officer
STEVE ROTTERDAM - SVP, Sales & Marketing • DAN SHIRES - VP, Film & Television UK • CHRISTINA HARRINGTON - Managing Editor
MARC HAMMOND - Sr. Retail Sales Development Manager • RUTHANN THOMPSON - Sr. Retailer Relations Manager
KATHERINE JAMISON - Marketing Manager • KELLY DIODATI - Ambassador Outreach Manager • BLAKE STOCKER - VP, Finance
AARON MARION - Publicist • LISA MOODY - Finance • RYAN CARROLL - Director, Comics/Film/TV Liaison • JAWAD QURESHI - Technology Advisor/Strategist
RACHEL PINNELAS - Social Community Manager • CHARLES PRITCHETT - Design & Production Manager • COREY BREEN - Collections Production
TEODORO LEO - Associate Editor • STEPHANIE CASEBIER & SARAH PRUETT - Publishing Assistants

AfterShock Logo Design by COMICRAFT
Publicity: contact AARON MARION (aaron@publichausagency.com) & RYAN CROY (ryan@publichausagency.com) at PUBLICHAUS
Special thanks to: ATOM! FREEMAN, IRA KURGAN, MARINE KSADZHIKYAN, KEITH MANZELLA, ANTHONY MILITANO, ANTONIA LIANOS, STEPHAN NILSON & ED ZAREMBA

AFTERSHOCKCOMICS.COM Follow us on social media 𝕏 📷 f

I N T R O D U C T I O N

PROJECT: PATRON was an idea that kept fighting to the top of my mind, screaming for attention, screaming to be fully realized, even as the world outside my head kept making it more and more relevant. It was always just a matter of time until those two factors reached critical mass and my head yet again split open, Zeus-style, to let a comic spill out.

Is rewarding our faith and belief more important than the truth? That's the question we ask in these pages. What if the death of the world's greatest superhero was, in fact, a work? What if years ago, an alien hero from the stars battled a primordial destroyer, and both fell in battle; if what the world saw when the hero rose days later was secretly a replacement? This is the social calculus of the powers at the top of the world engaged within PROJECT: PATRON. But that was thirty years ago. And now, three decades after The Patron died, three decades in a conspiracy to help people believe their hero would always be with them, the secret is heavier than ever. And what's worse, the longer it lasts, the more nuclear and dangerous it becomes.

So, we've got your big blockbuster super heroics. We've got your intense interpersonal dramas between expert pilots operating under the most seismic pressure in the world. We've got wild villains that you could only find in the pages of the pop culture creature known as the comic book. And all of this is coming to you via the incredible work of Patrick Piazzalunga, Carlos Lopez, Thomas Mauer and Hassan Otsmane-Elhaou.

But that's just the skin and the plumage.

Pulsing beneath that is the heart: a story about faith and facts, that digs deep into just how much we believe in ourselves as a society and as a species. Thirty years ago, those in power thought we couldn't handle the truth, but here, now, today...that truth is back with a vengeance. In their desperation to save the world, have its masters actually made it into an even bigger powder keg than ever before? And laid the fuse with the biggest con job in modern history?

Read on, my friends, and know you're appreciated for it...

STEVE ORLANDO
August 2021

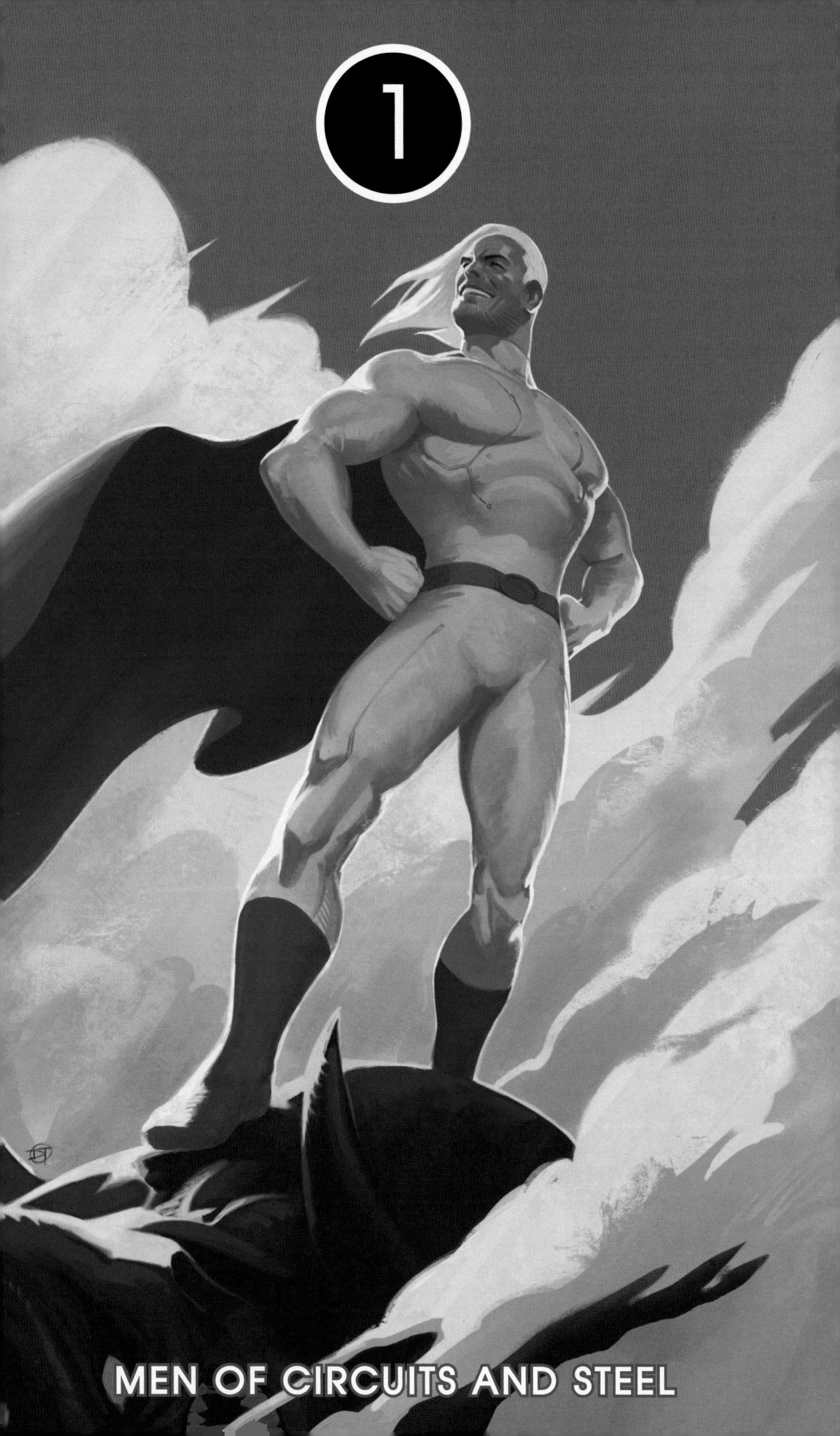

1

MEN OF CIRCUITS AND STEEL

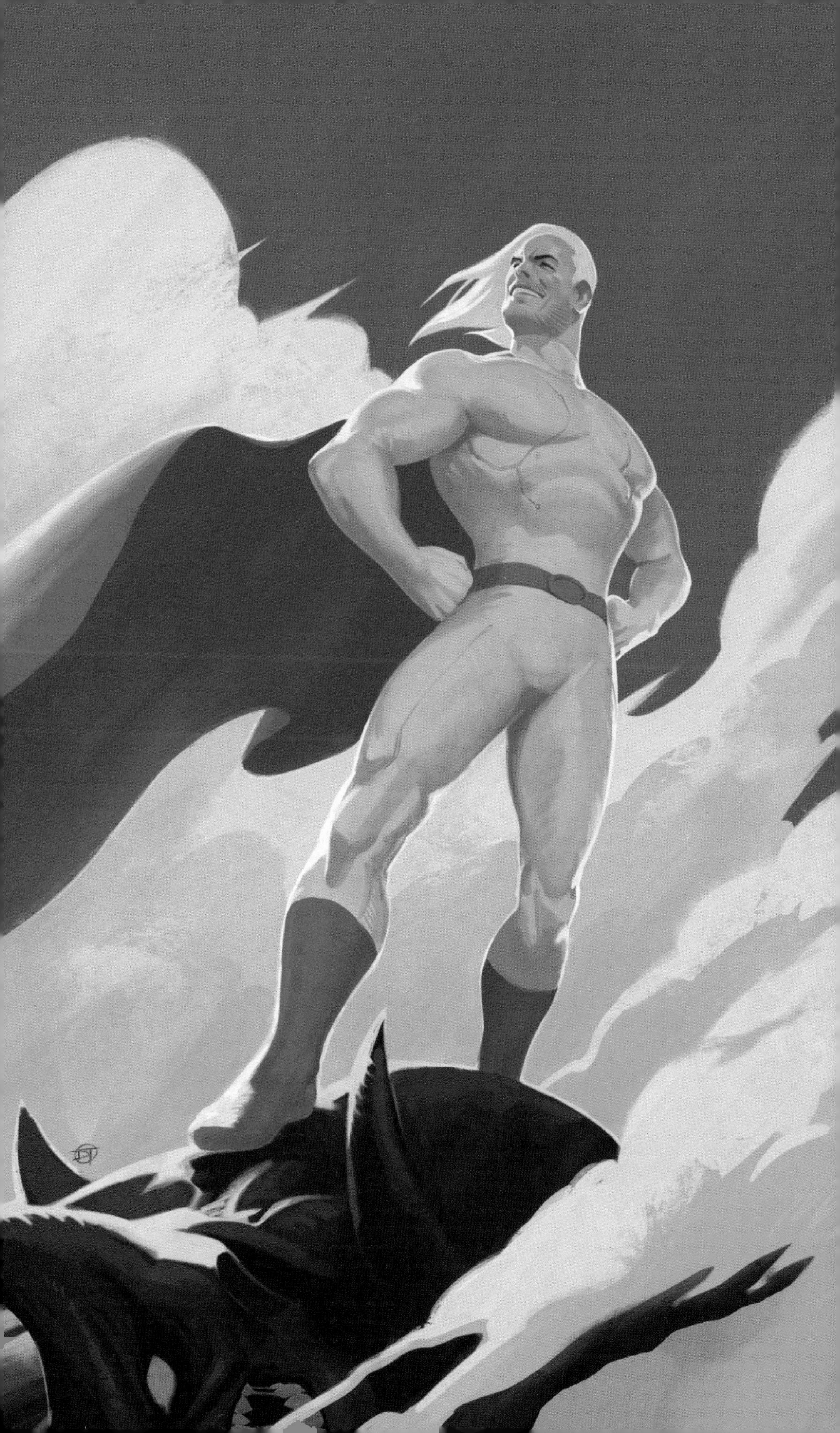

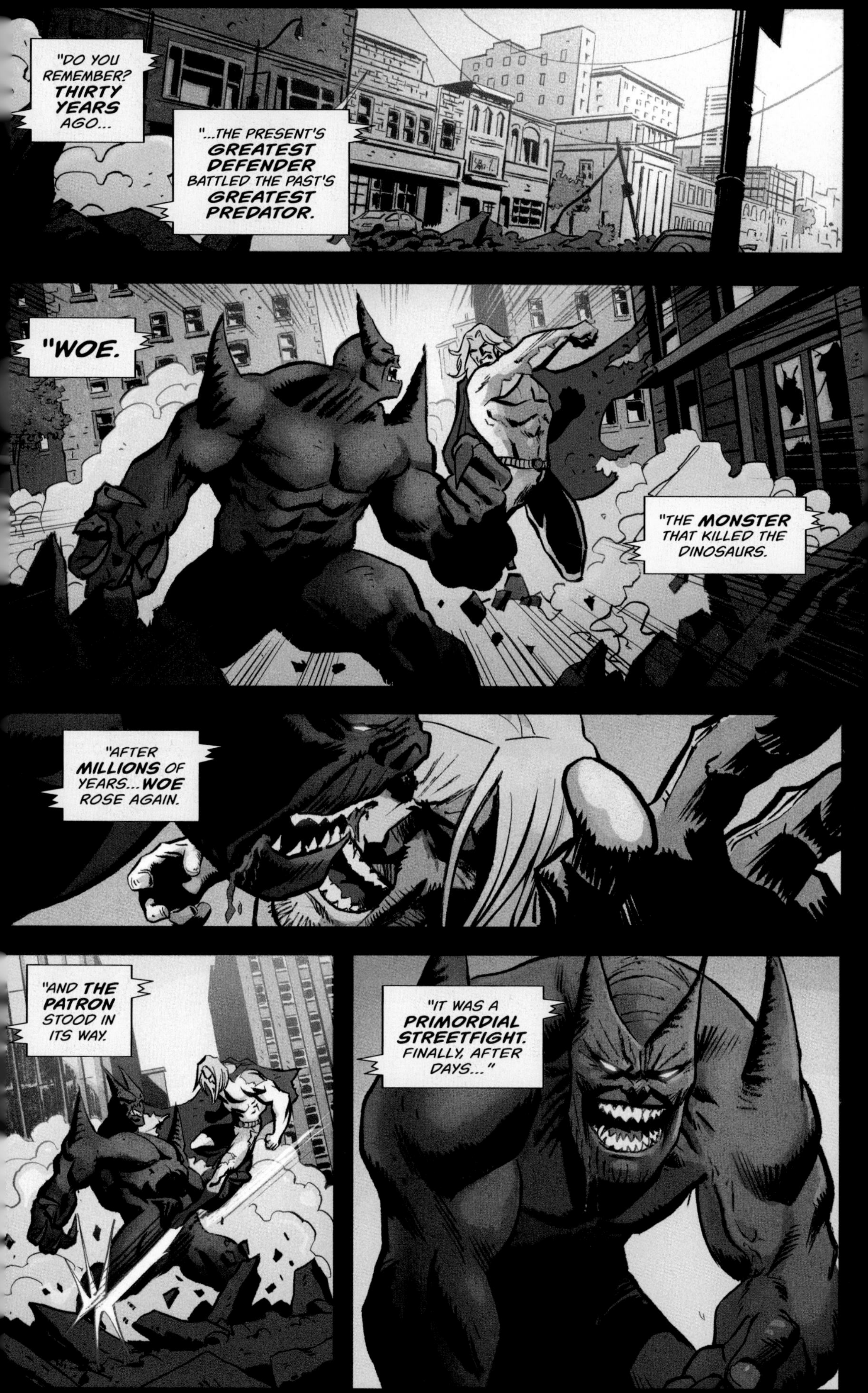
"DO YOU REMEMBER? THIRTY YEARS AGO...
"...THE PRESENT'S GREATEST DEFENDER BATTLED THE PAST'S GREATEST PREDATOR.
"WOE.
"THE MONSTER THAT KILLED THE DINOSAURS.
"AFTER MILLIONS OF YEARS...WOE ROSE AGAIN.
"AND THE PATRON STOOD IN ITS WAY.
"IT WAS A PRIMORDIAL STREETFIGHT. FINALLY, AFTER DAYS..."

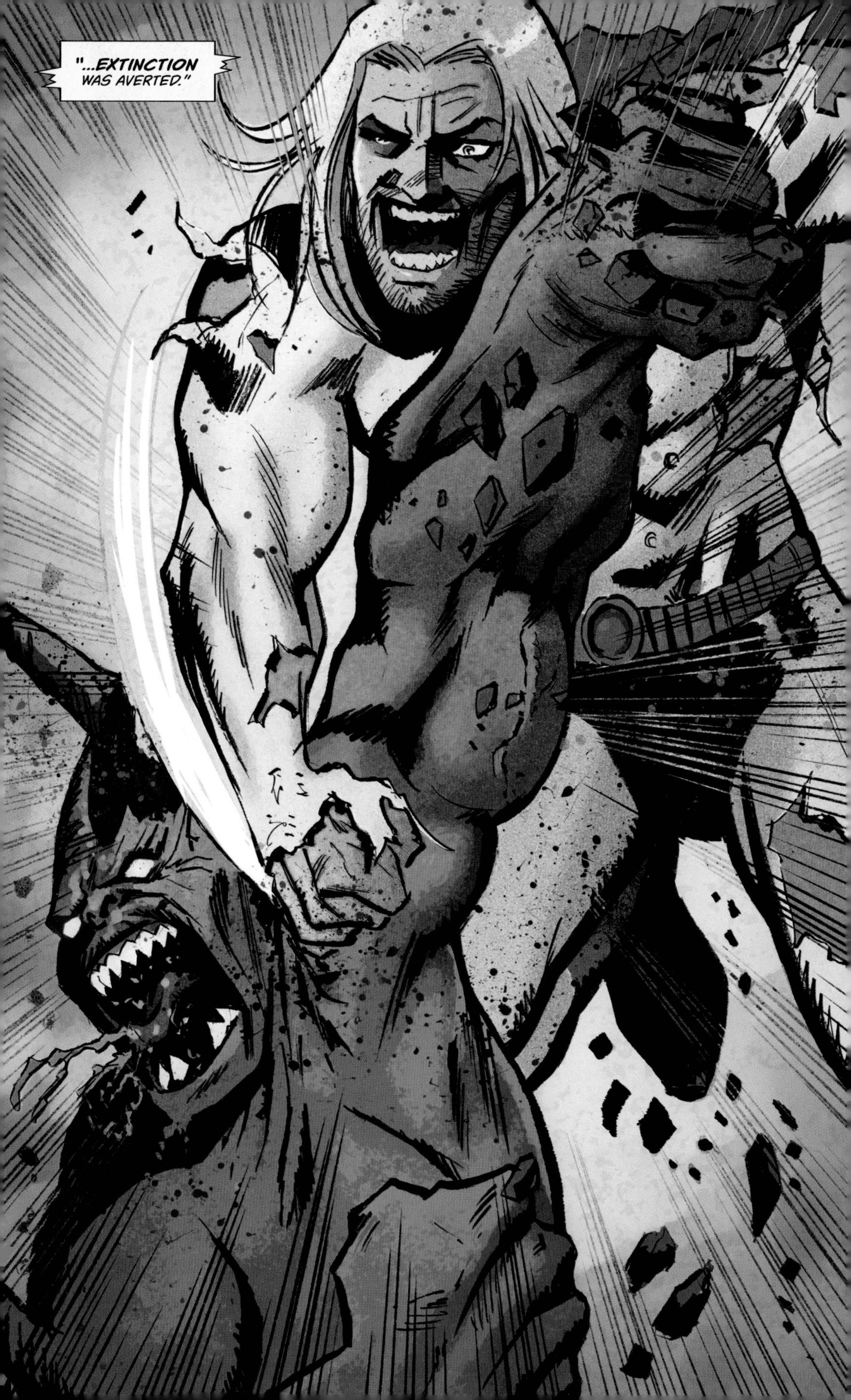
"...EXTINCTION WAS AVERTED."

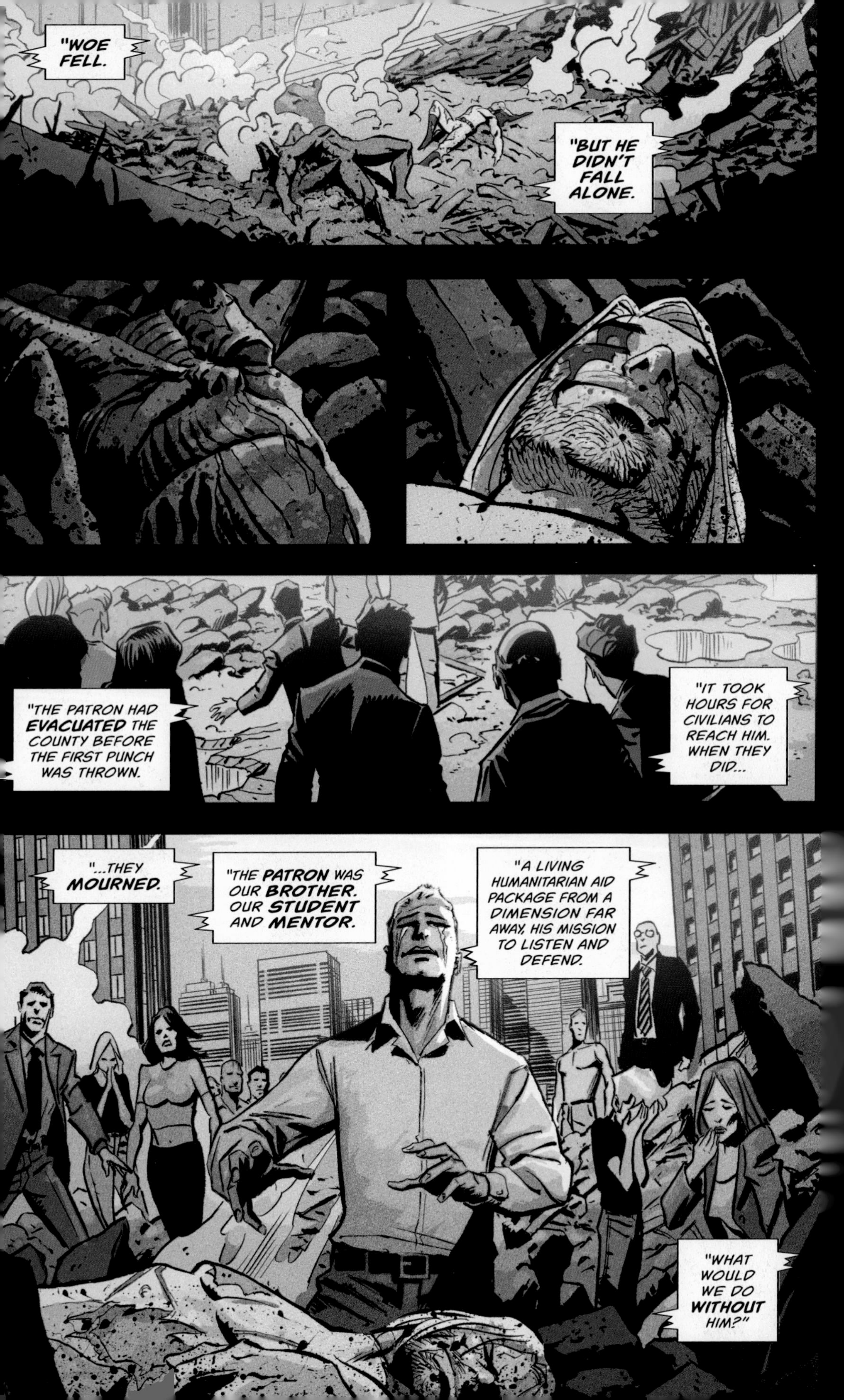

"WOE FELL.
"BUT HE DIDN'T FALL ALONE.
"THE PATRON HAD EVACUATED THE COUNTY BEFORE THE FIRST PUNCH WAS THROWN.
"IT TOOK HOURS FOR CIVILIANS TO REACH HIM. WHEN THEY DID...
"...THEY MOURNED.
"THE PATRON WAS OUR BROTHER. OUR STUDENT AND MENTOR.
"A LIVING HUMANITARIAN AID PACKAGE FROM A DIMENSION FAR AWAY, HIS MISSION TO LISTEN AND DEFEND.
"WHAT WOULD WE DO WITHOUT HIM?"

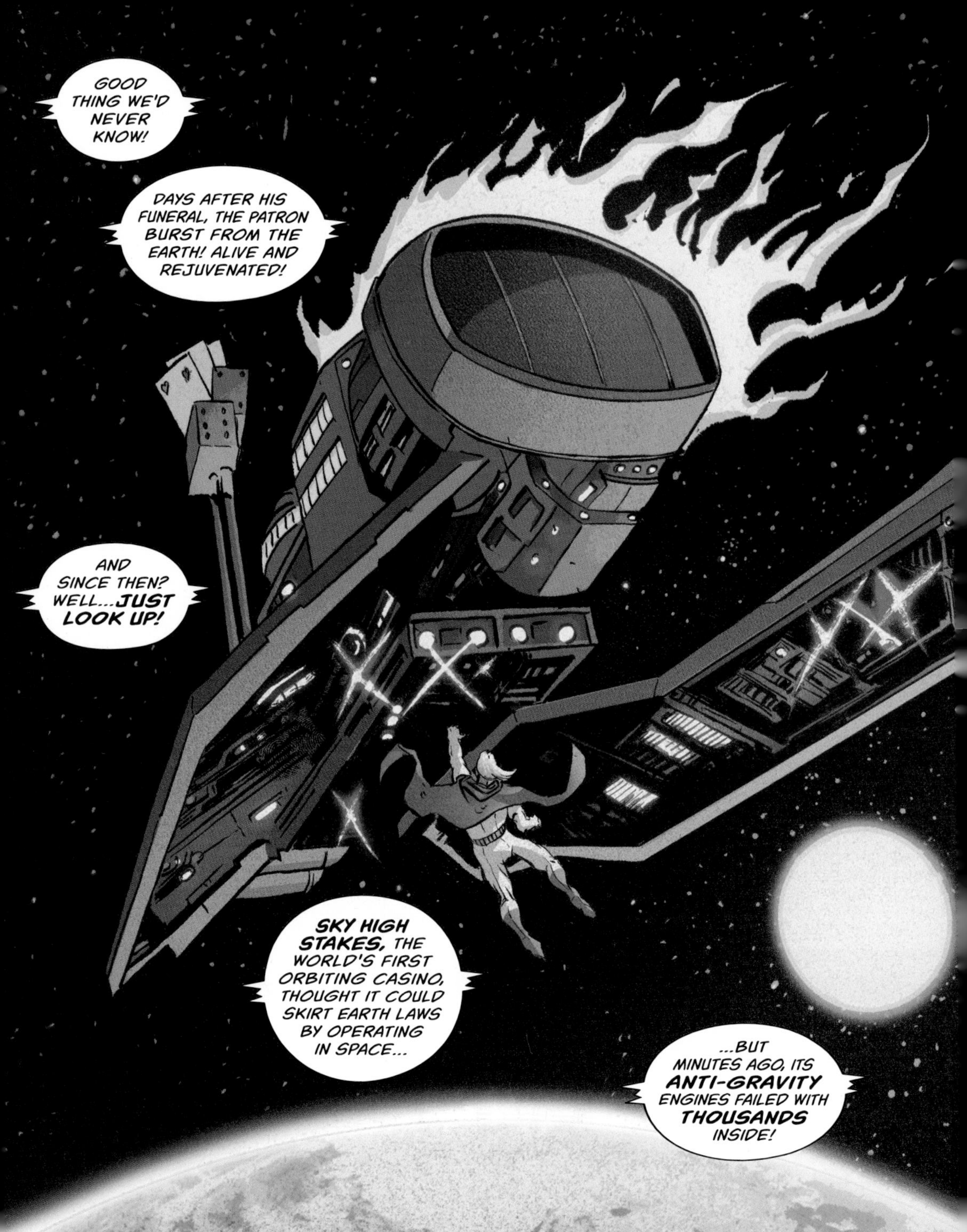
GOOD THING WE'D NEVER KNOW!
DAYS AFTER HIS FUNERAL, THE PATRON BURST FROM THE EARTH! ALIVE AND REJUVENATED!
AND SINCE THEN? WELL... **JUST LOOK UP!**
SKY HIGH STAKES, THE WORLD'S FIRST ORBITING CASINO, THOUGHT IT COULD SKIRT EARTH LAWS BY OPERATING IN SPACE...
...BUT MINUTES AGO, ITS **ANTI-GRAVITY** ENGINES FAILED WITH **THOUSANDS** INSIDE!

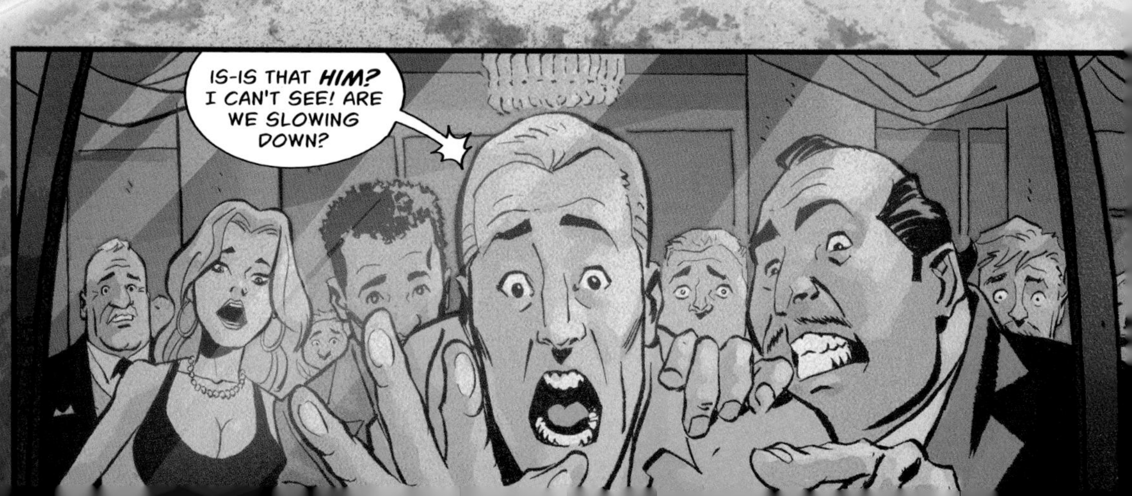
IS-IS THAT ***HIM?*** I CAN'T SEE! ARE WE SLOWING DOWN?

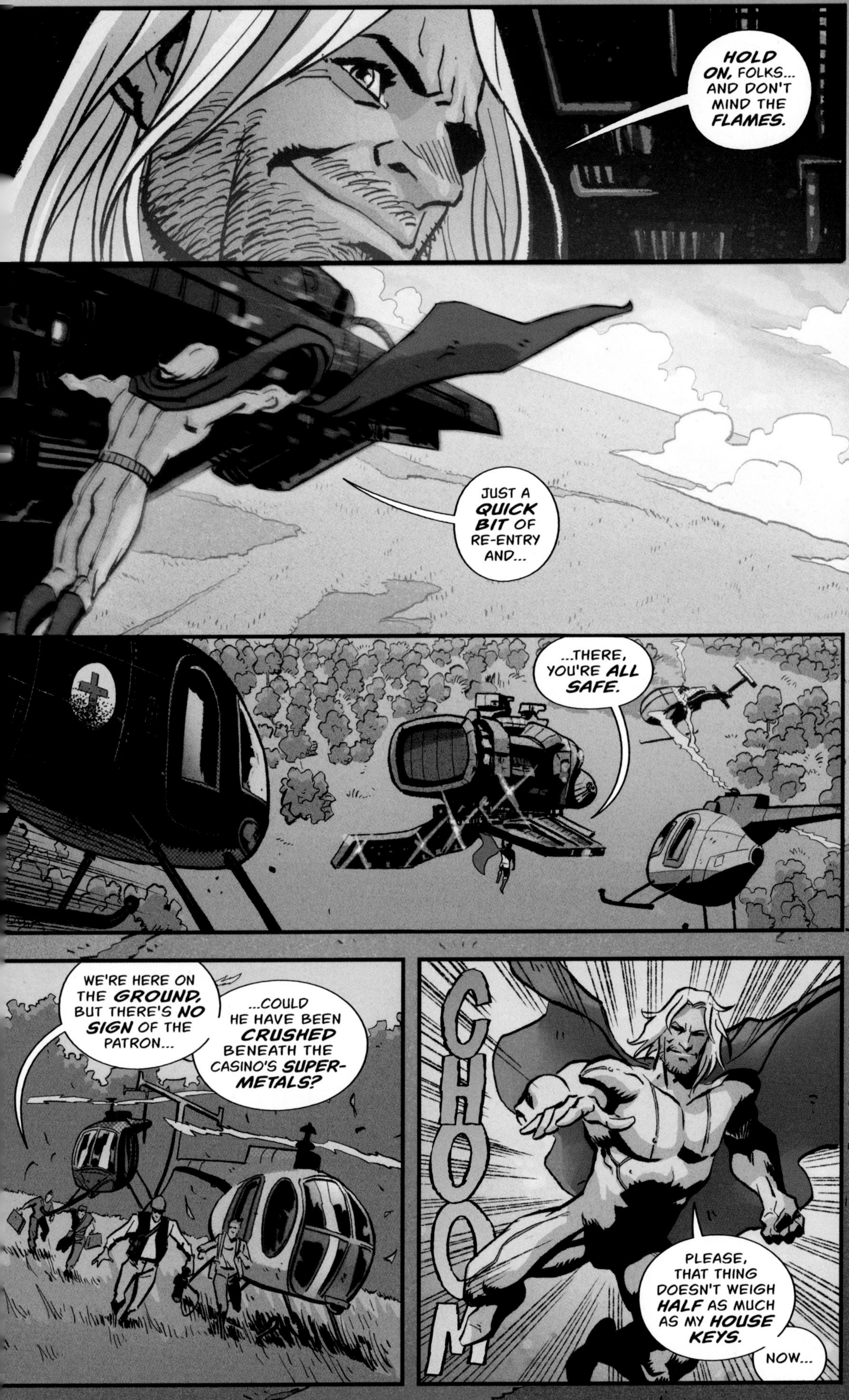
HOLD ON, FOLKS... AND DON'T MIND THE FLAMES.
JUST A QUICK BIT OF RE-ENTRY AND...
...THERE, YOU'RE ALL SAFE.
WE'RE HERE ON THE GROUND, BUT THERE'S NO SIGN OF THE PATRON...
...COULD HE HAVE BEEN CRUSHED BENEATH THE CASINO'S SUPER-METALS?
CHOOM
PLEASE, THAT THING DOESN'T WEIGH HALF AS MUCH AS MY HOUSE KEYS.
NOW...

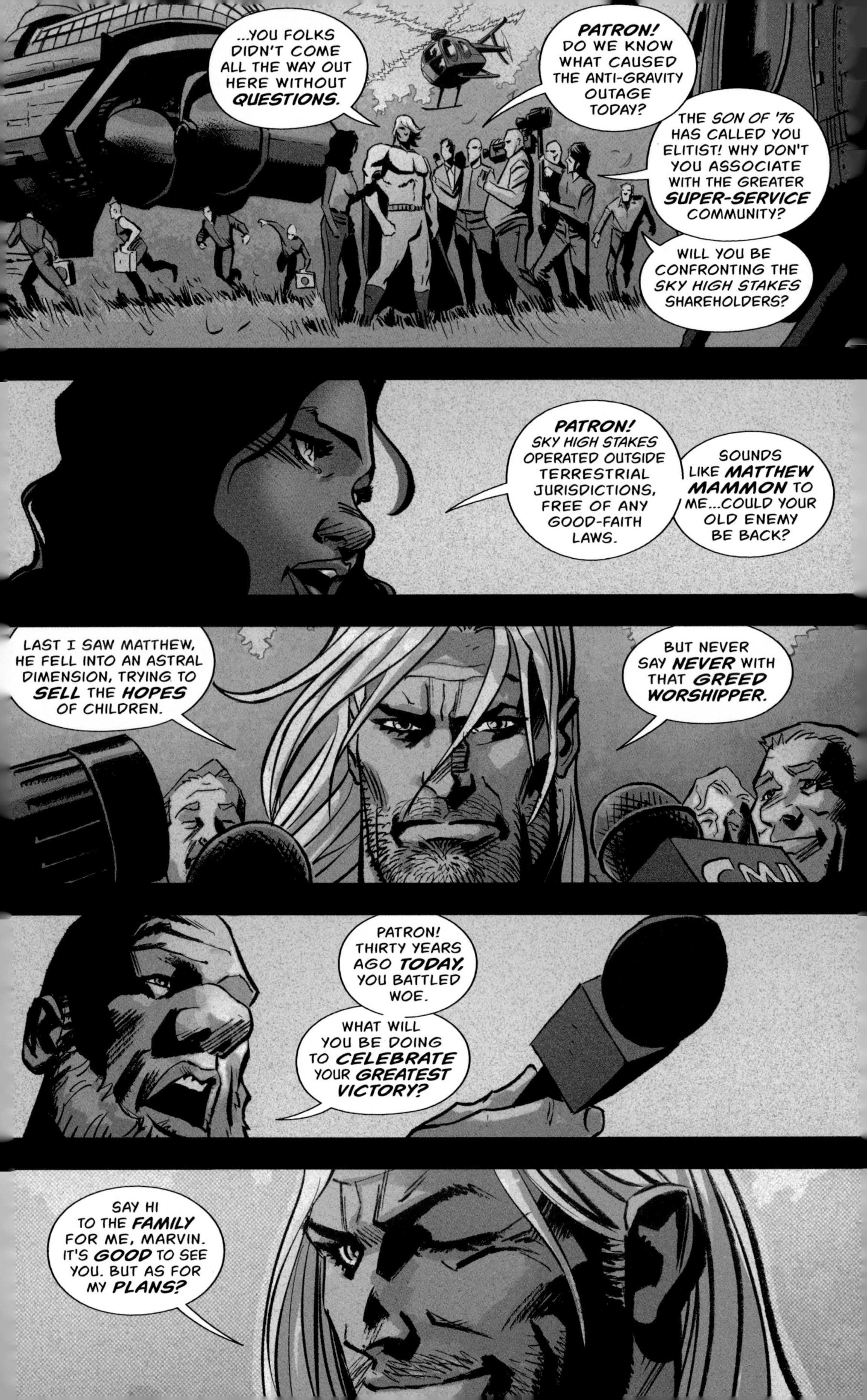
...YOU FOLKS DIDN'T COME ALL THE WAY OUT HERE WITHOUT QUESTIONS.
PATRON! DO WE KNOW WHAT CAUSED THE ANTI-GRAVITY OUTAGE TODAY?
THE SON OF '76 HAS CALLED YOU ELITIST! WHY DON'T YOU ASSOCIATE WITH THE GREATER SUPER-SERVICE COMMUNITY?
WILL YOU BE CONFRONTING THE SKY HIGH STAKES SHAREHOLDERS?
PATRON! SKY HIGH STAKES OPERATED OUTSIDE TERRESTRIAL JURISDICTIONS, FREE OF ANY GOOD-FAITH LAWS.
SOUNDS LIKE MATTHEW MAMMON TO ME...COULD YOUR OLD ENEMY BE BACK?
LAST I SAW MATTHEW, HE FELL INTO AN ASTRAL DIMENSION, TRYING TO SELL THE HOPES OF CHILDREN.
BUT NEVER SAY NEVER WITH THAT GREED WORSHIPPER.
PATRON! THIRTY YEARS AGO TODAY, YOU BATTLED WOE.
WHAT WILL YOU BE DOING TO CELEBRATE YOUR GREATEST VICTORY?
SAY HI TO THE FAMILY FOR ME, MARVIN. IT'S GOOD TO SEE YOU. BUT AS FOR MY PLANS?

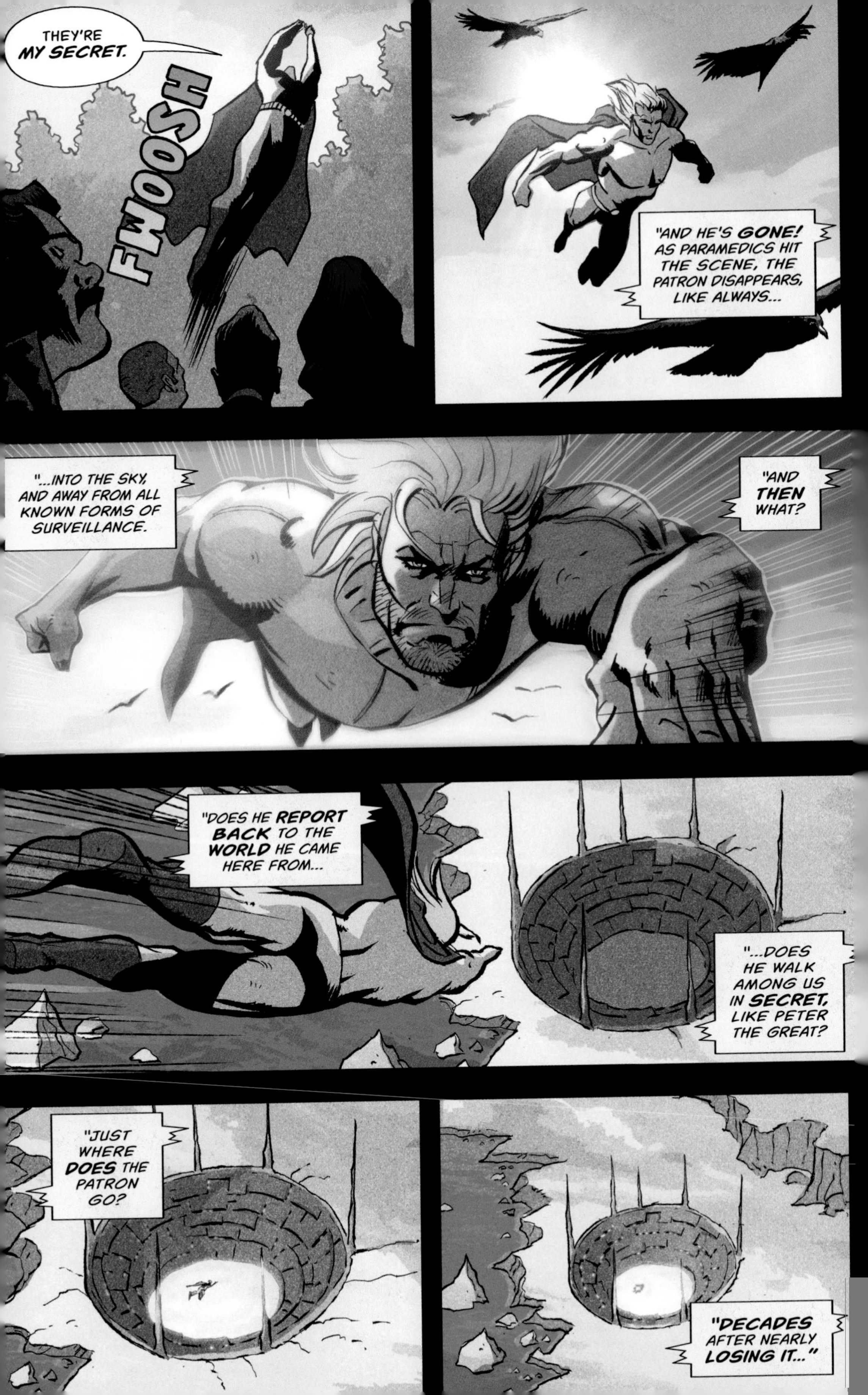
THEY'RE MY SECRET.
FWOOSH
"AND HE'S GONE! AS PARAMEDICS HIT THE SCENE, THE PATRON DISAPPEARS, LIKE ALWAYS...
"...INTO THE SKY, AND AWAY FROM ALL KNOWN FORMS OF SURVEILLANCE.
"AND THEN WHAT?
"DOES HE REPORT BACK TO THE WORLD HE CAME HERE FROM...
"...DOES HE WALK AMONG US IN SECRET, LIKE PETER THE GREAT?
"JUST WHERE DOES THE PATRON GO?
"DECADES AFTER NEARLY LOSING IT..."

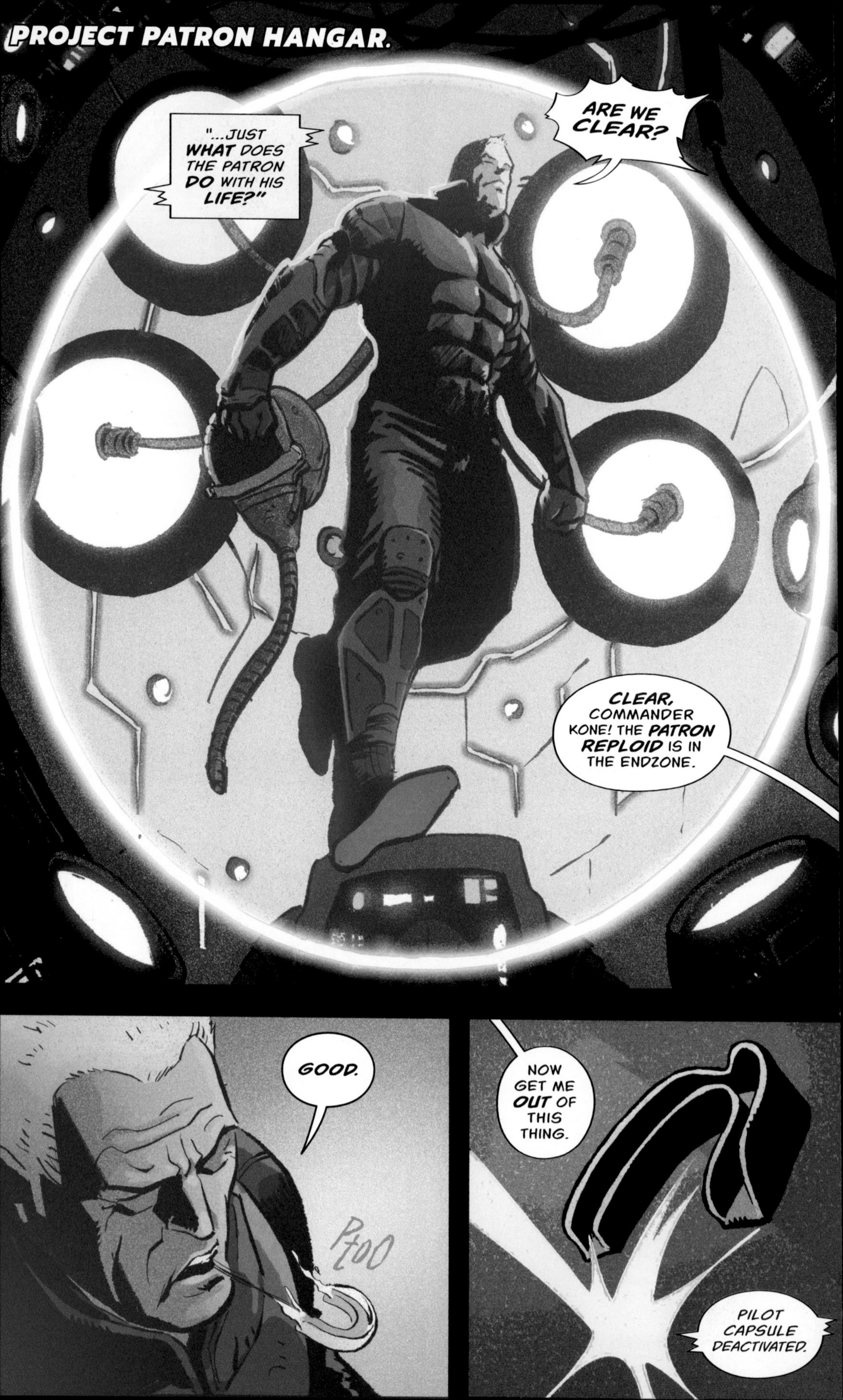
PROJECT PATRON HANGAR.
"...JUST WHAT DOES THE PATRON DO WITH HIS LIFE?"
ARE WE CLEAR?
CLEAR, COMMANDER KONE! THE PATRON REPLOID IS IN THE ENDZONE.
GOOD.
PTOO
NOW GET ME OUT OF THIS THING.
PILOT CAPSULE DEACTIVATED.

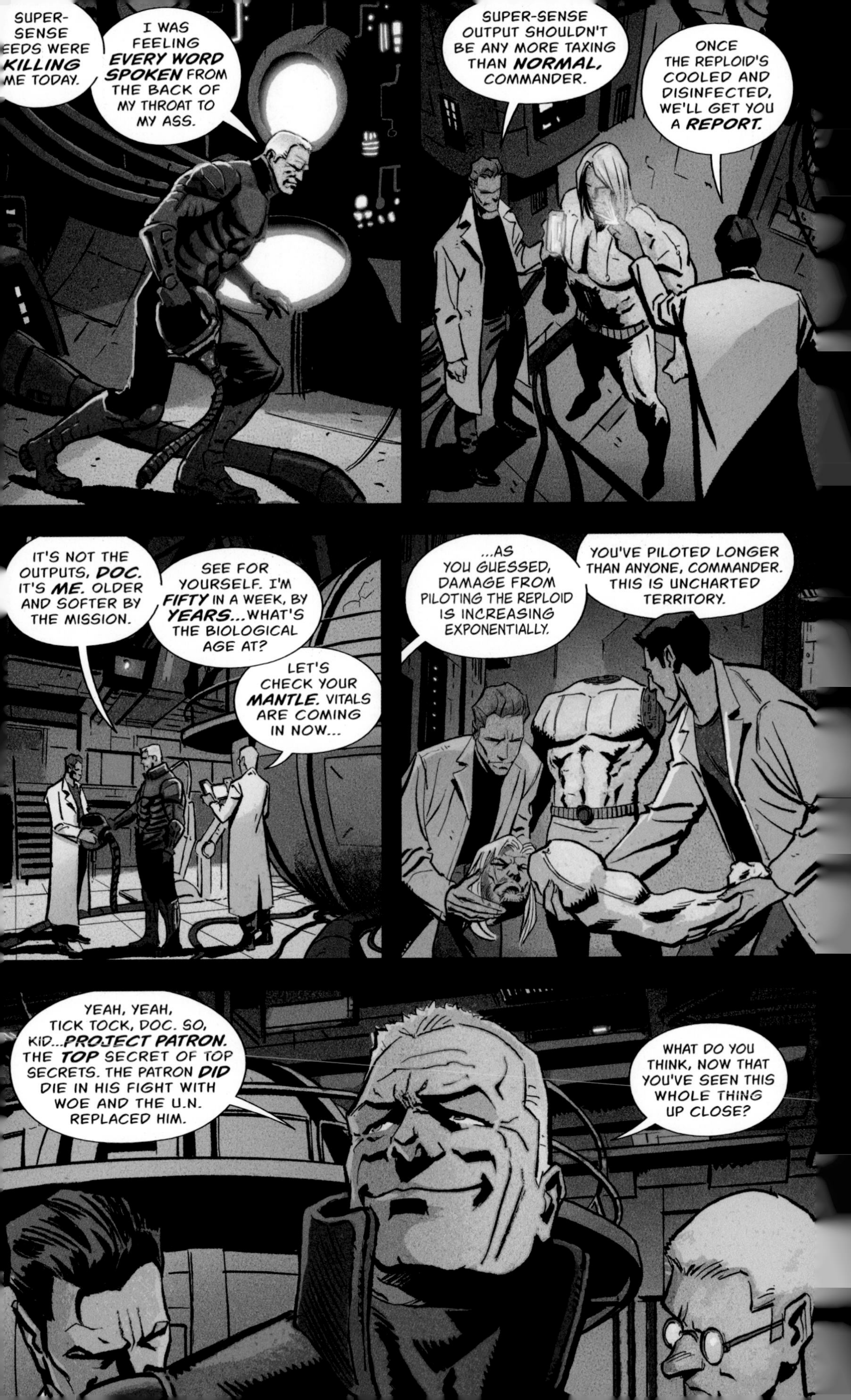
SUPER-SENSE EEDS WERE KILLING ME TODAY.
I WAS FEELING EVERY WORD SPOKEN FROM THE BACK OF MY THROAT TO MY ASS.
SUPER-SENSE OUTPUT SHOULDN'T BE ANY MORE TAXING THAN NORMAL, COMMANDER.
ONCE THE REPLOID'S COOLED AND DISINFECTED, WE'LL GET YOU A REPORT.
IT'S NOT THE OUTPUTS, DOC. IT'S ME. OLDER AND SOFTER BY THE MISSION.
SEE FOR YOURSELF. I'M FIFTY IN A WEEK, BY YEARS...WHAT'S THE BIOLOGICAL AGE AT?
LET'S CHECK YOUR MANTLE. VITALS ARE COMING IN NOW...
...AS YOU GUESSED, DAMAGE FROM PILOTING THE REPLOID IS INCREASING EXPONENTIALLY.
YOU'VE PILOTED LONGER THAN ANYONE, COMMANDER. THIS IS UNCHARTED TERRITORY.
YEAH, YEAH, TICK TOCK, DOC. SO, KID...PROJECT PATRON. THE TOP SECRET OF TOP SECRETS. THE PATRON DID DIE IN HIS FIGHT WITH WOE AND THE U.N. REPLACED HIM.
WHAT DO YOU THINK, NOW THAT YOU'VE SEEN THIS WHOLE THING UP CLOSE?

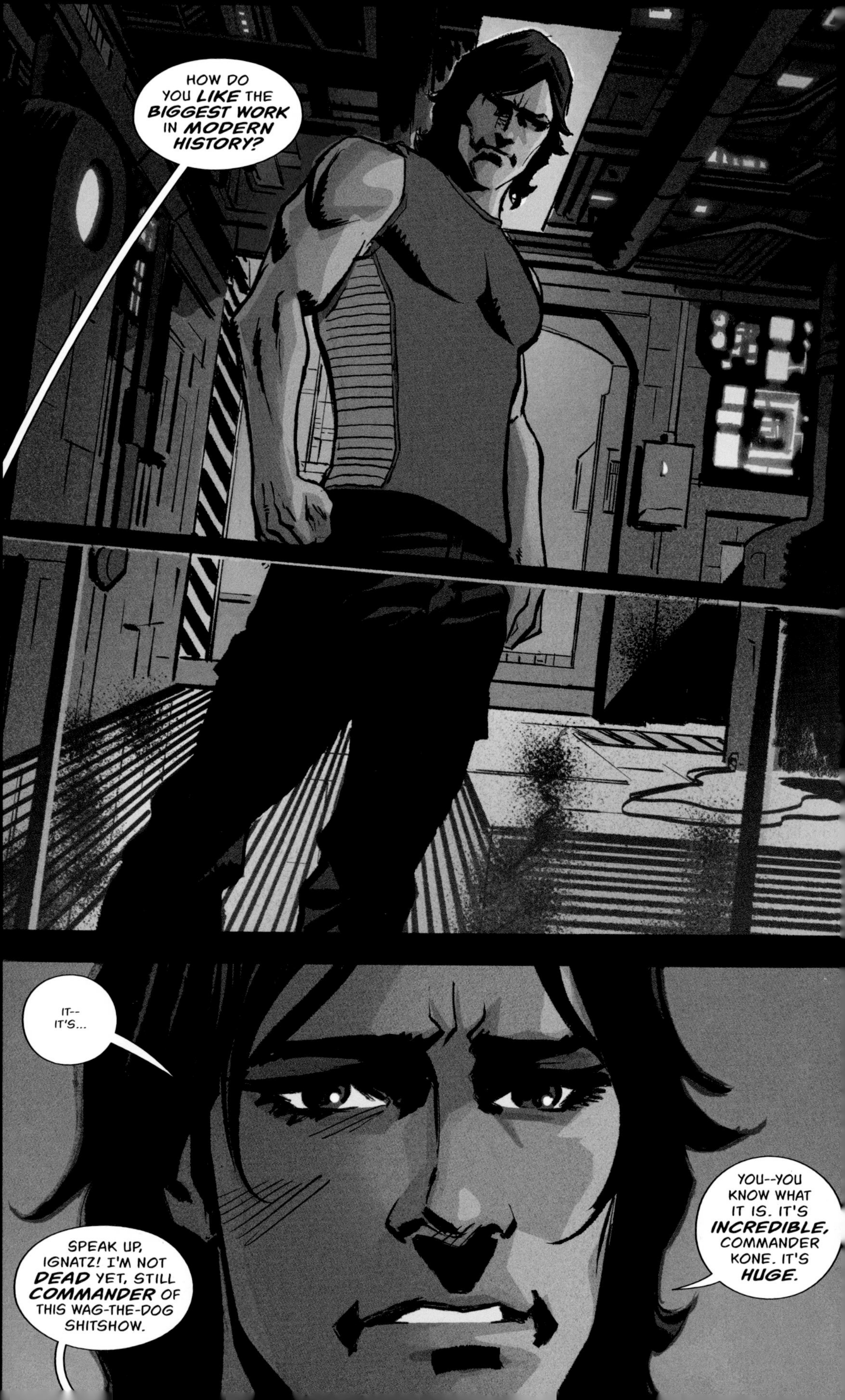
HOW DO YOU LIKE THE BIGGEST WORK IN MODERN HISTORY?
IT-- IT'S...
SPEAK UP, IGNATZ! I'M NOT DEAD YET, STILL COMMANDER OF THIS WAG-THE-DOG SHITSHOW.
YOU--YOU KNOW WHAT IT IS. IT'S INCREDIBLE, COMMANDER KONE. IT'S HUGE.

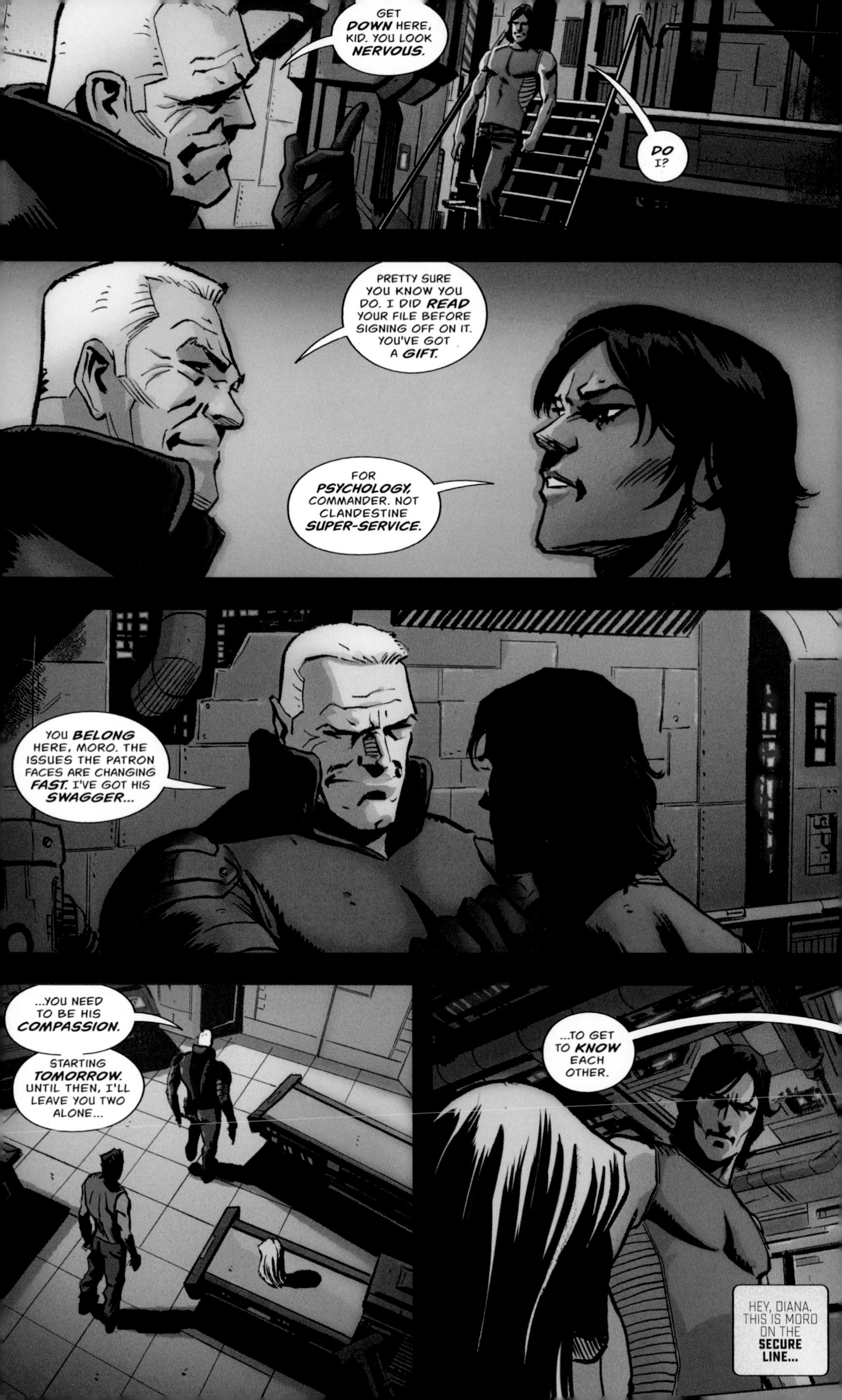
GET DOWN HERE, KID. YOU LOOK NERVOUS.
DO I?
PRETTY SURE YOU KNOW YOU DO. I DID READ YOUR FILE BEFORE SIGNING OFF ON IT. YOU'VE GOT A GIFT.
FOR PSYCHOLOGY, COMMANDER. NOT CLANDESTINE SUPER-SERVICE.
YOU BELONG HERE, MORO. THE ISSUES THE PATRON FACES ARE CHANGING FAST. I'VE GOT HIS SWAGGER...
...YOU NEED TO BE HIS COMPASSION.
STARTING TOMORROW. UNTIL THEN, I'LL LEAVE YOU TWO ALONE...
...TO GET TO KNOW EACH OTHER.
HEY, DIANA. THIS IS MORO ON THE SECURE LINE...

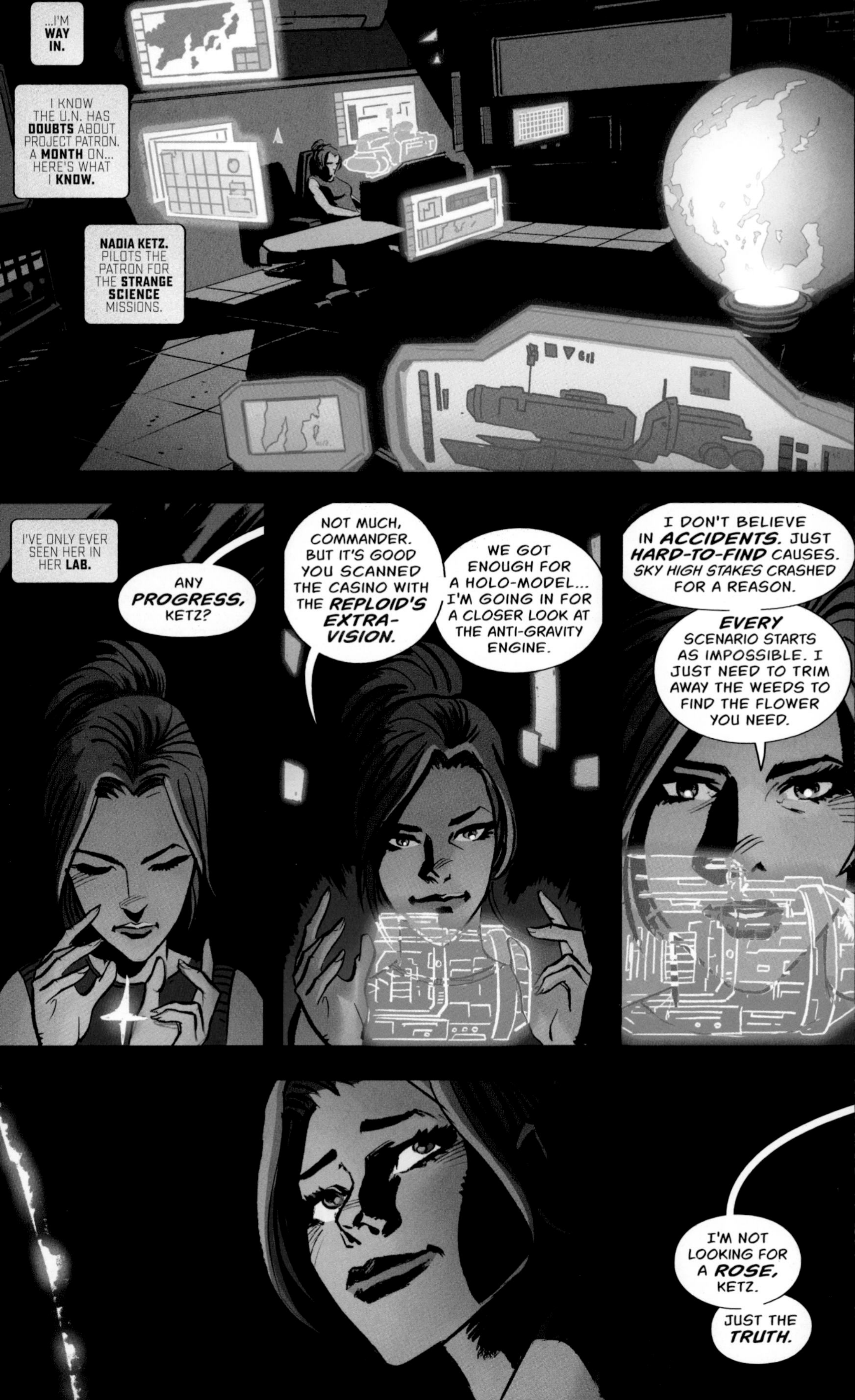

...I'M WAY IN.
I KNOW THE U.N. HAS DOUBTS ABOUT PROJECT PATRON. A MONTH ON... HERE'S WHAT I KNOW.
NADIA KETZ. PILOTS THE PATRON FOR THE STRANGE SCIENCE MISSIONS.
I'VE ONLY EVER SEEN HER IN HER LAB.
ANY PROGRESS, KETZ?
NOT MUCH, COMMANDER. BUT IT'S GOOD YOU SCANNED THE CASINO WITH THE REPLOID'S EXTRA-VISION.
WE GOT ENOUGH FOR A HOLO-MODEL... I'M GOING IN FOR A CLOSER LOOK AT THE ANTI-GRAVITY ENGINE.
I DON'T BELIEVE IN ACCIDENTS. JUST HARD-TO-FIND CAUSES. SKY HIGH STAKES CRASHED FOR A REASON.
EVERY SCENARIO STARTS AS IMPOSSIBLE. I JUST NEED TO TRIM AWAY THE WEEDS TO FIND THE FLOWER YOU NEED.
I'M NOT LOOKING FOR A ROSE, KETZ.
JUST THE TRUTH.

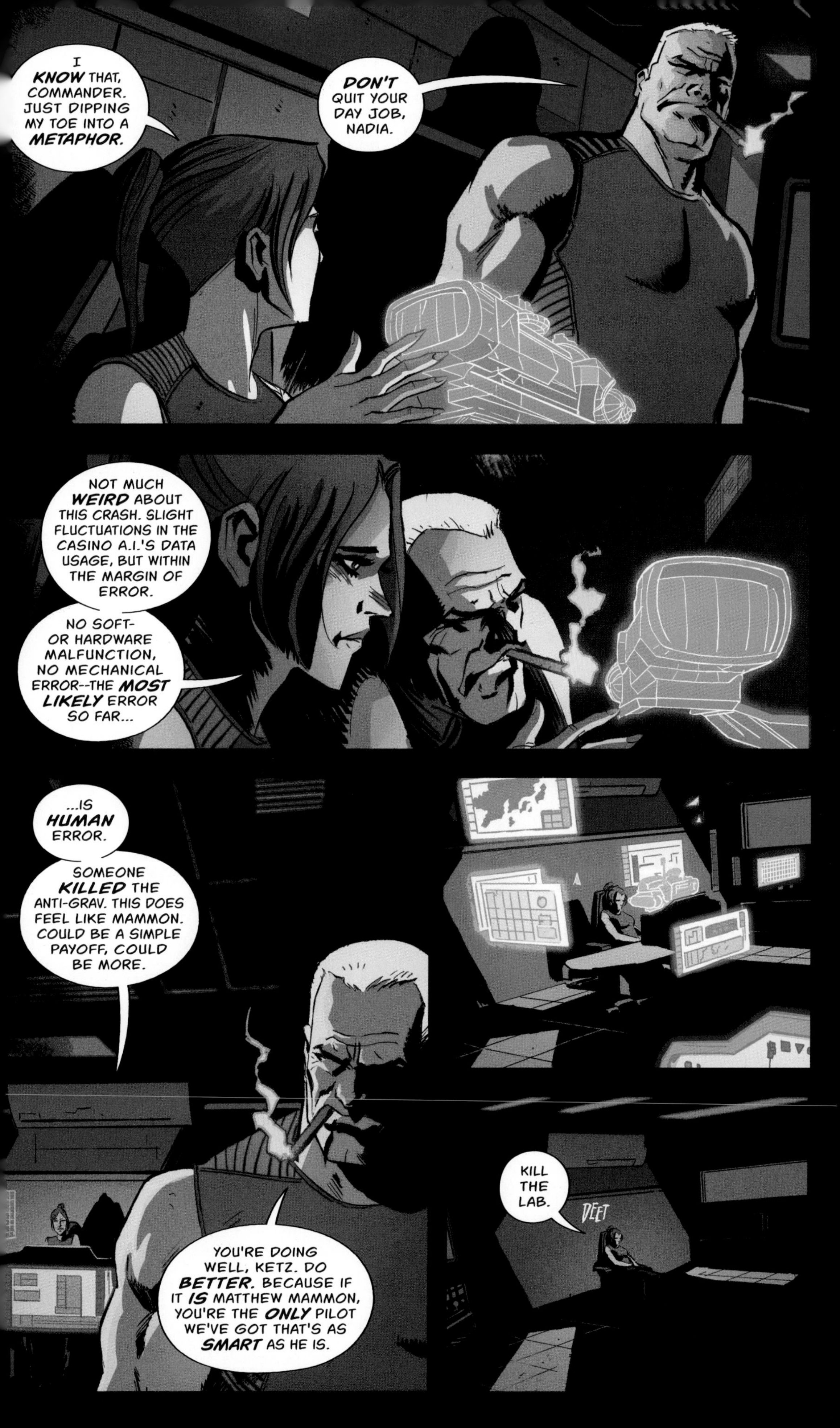
I KNOW THAT, COMMANDER. JUST DIPPING MY TOE INTO A METAPHOR.
DON'T QUIT YOUR DAY JOB, NADIA.
NOT MUCH WEIRD ABOUT THIS CRASH. SLIGHT FLUCTUATIONS IN THE CASINO A.I.'S DATA USAGE, BUT WITHIN THE MARGIN OF ERROR.
NO SOFT- OR HARDWARE MALFUNCTION, NO MECHANICAL ERROR--THE MOST LIKELY ERROR SO FAR...
...IS HUMAN ERROR.
SOMEONE KILLED THE ANTI-GRAV. THIS DOES FEEL LIKE MAMMON. COULD BE A SIMPLE PAYOFF, COULD BE MORE.
YOU'RE DOING WELL, KETZ. DO BETTER. BECAUSE IF IT IS MATTHEW MAMMON, YOU'RE THE ONLY PILOT WE'VE GOT THAT'S AS SMART AS HE IS.
KILL THE LAB.
DEET

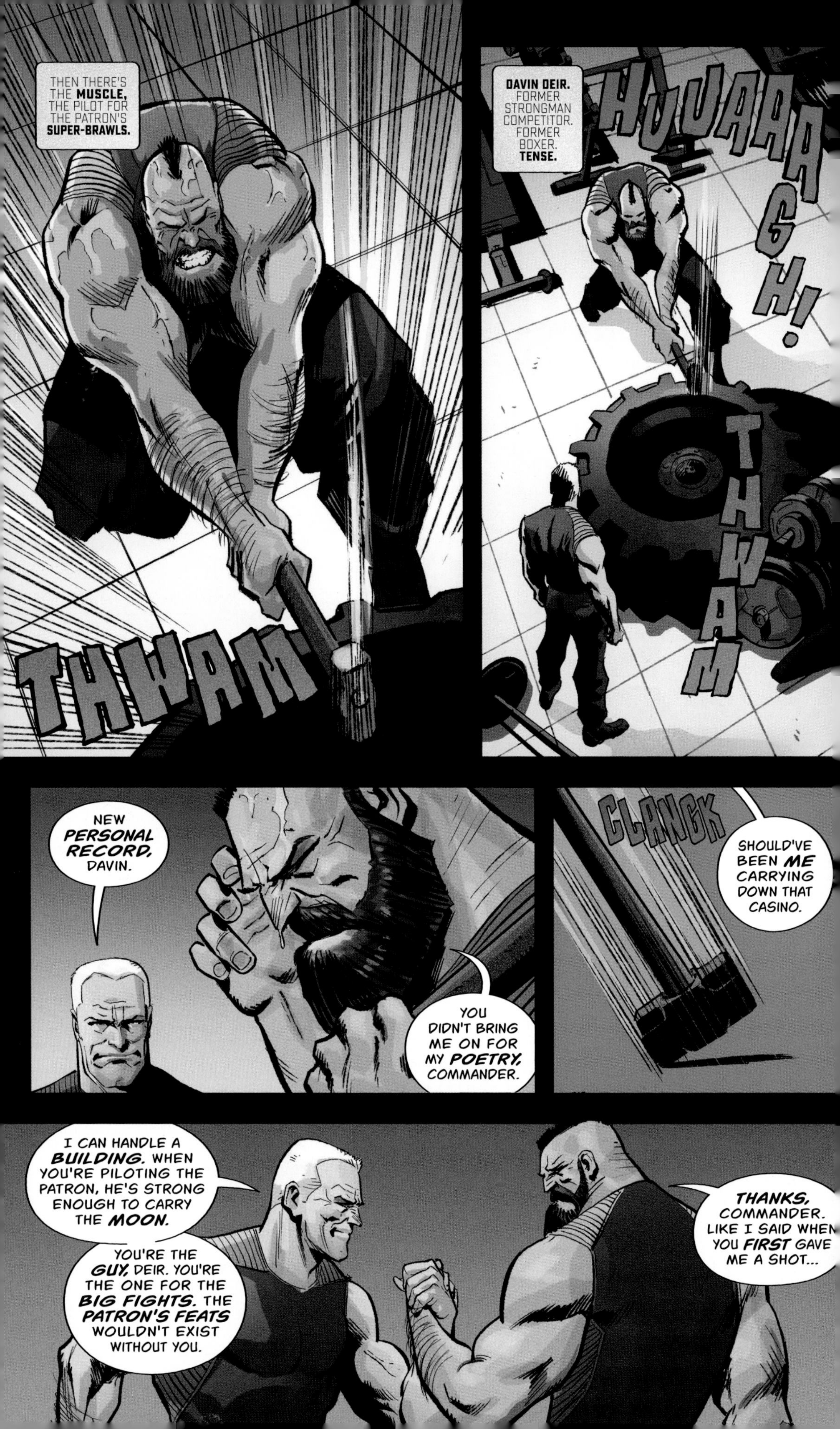
THEN THERE'S THE **MUSCLE**, THE PILOT FOR THE PATRON'S **SUPER-BRAWLS.**
THWAM
DAVIN DEIR. FORMER STRONGMAN COMPETITOR. FORMER BOXER. **TENSE.**
HUUAAARGH!
THWAM
NEW *PERSONAL RECORD,* DAVIN.
YOU DIDN'T BRING ME ON FOR MY *POETRY,* COMMANDER.
CLANGK
SHOULD'VE BEEN *ME* CARRYING DOWN THAT CASINO.
I CAN HANDLE A *BUILDING.* WHEN YOU'RE PILOTING THE PATRON, HE'S STRONG ENOUGH TO CARRY THE *MOON.*
YOU'RE THE *GUY,* DEIR. YOU'RE THE ONE FOR THE *BIG FIGHTS.* THE *PATRON'S FEATS* WOULDN'T EXIST WITHOUT YOU.
THANKS, COMMANDER. LIKE I SAID WHEN YOU *FIRST* GAVE ME A SHOT...

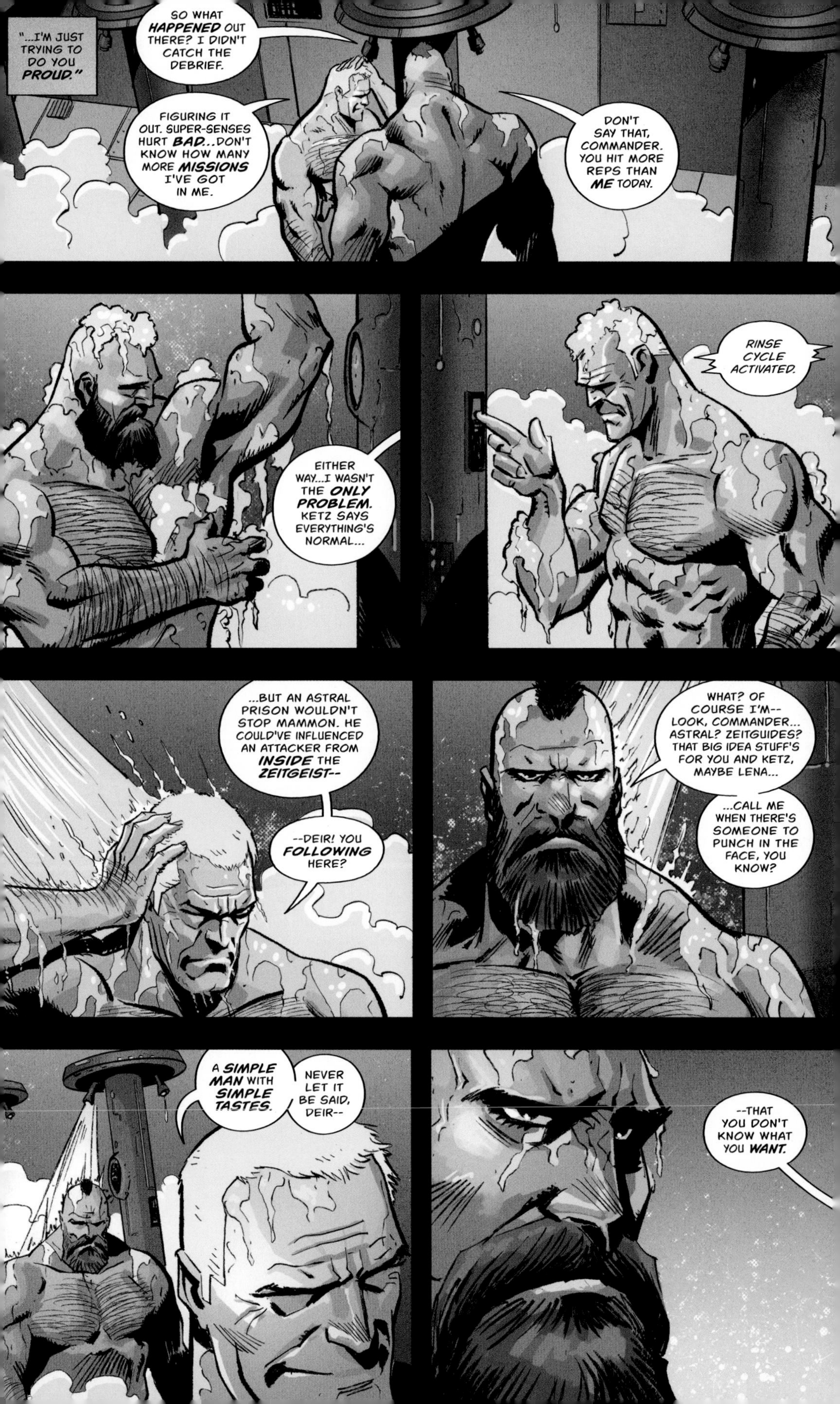
"...I'M JUST TRYING TO DO YOU PROUD."
SO WHAT HAPPENED OUT THERE? I DIDN'T CATCH THE DEBRIEF.
FIGURING IT OUT. SUPER-SENSES HURT BAD...DON'T KNOW HOW MANY MORE MISSIONS I'VE GOT IN ME.
DON'T SAY THAT, COMMANDER. YOU HIT MORE REPS THAN ME TODAY.
EITHER WAY...I WASN'T THE ONLY PROBLEM. KETZ SAYS EVERYTHING'S NORMAL...
RINSE CYCLE ACTIVATED.
...BUT AN ASTRAL PRISON WOULDN'T STOP MAMMON. HE COULD'VE INFLUENCED AN ATTACKER FROM INSIDE THE ZEITGEIST--
--DEIR! YOU FOLLOWING HERE?
WHAT? OF COURSE I'M-- LOOK, COMMANDER... ASTRAL? ZEITGUIDES? THAT BIG IDEA STUFF'S FOR YOU AND KETZ, MAYBE LENA...
...CALL ME WHEN THERE'S SOMEONE TO PUNCH IN THE FACE, YOU KNOW?
A SIMPLE MAN WITH SIMPLE TASTES.
NEVER LET IT BE SAID, DEIR--
--THAT YOU DON'T KNOW WHAT YOU WANT.

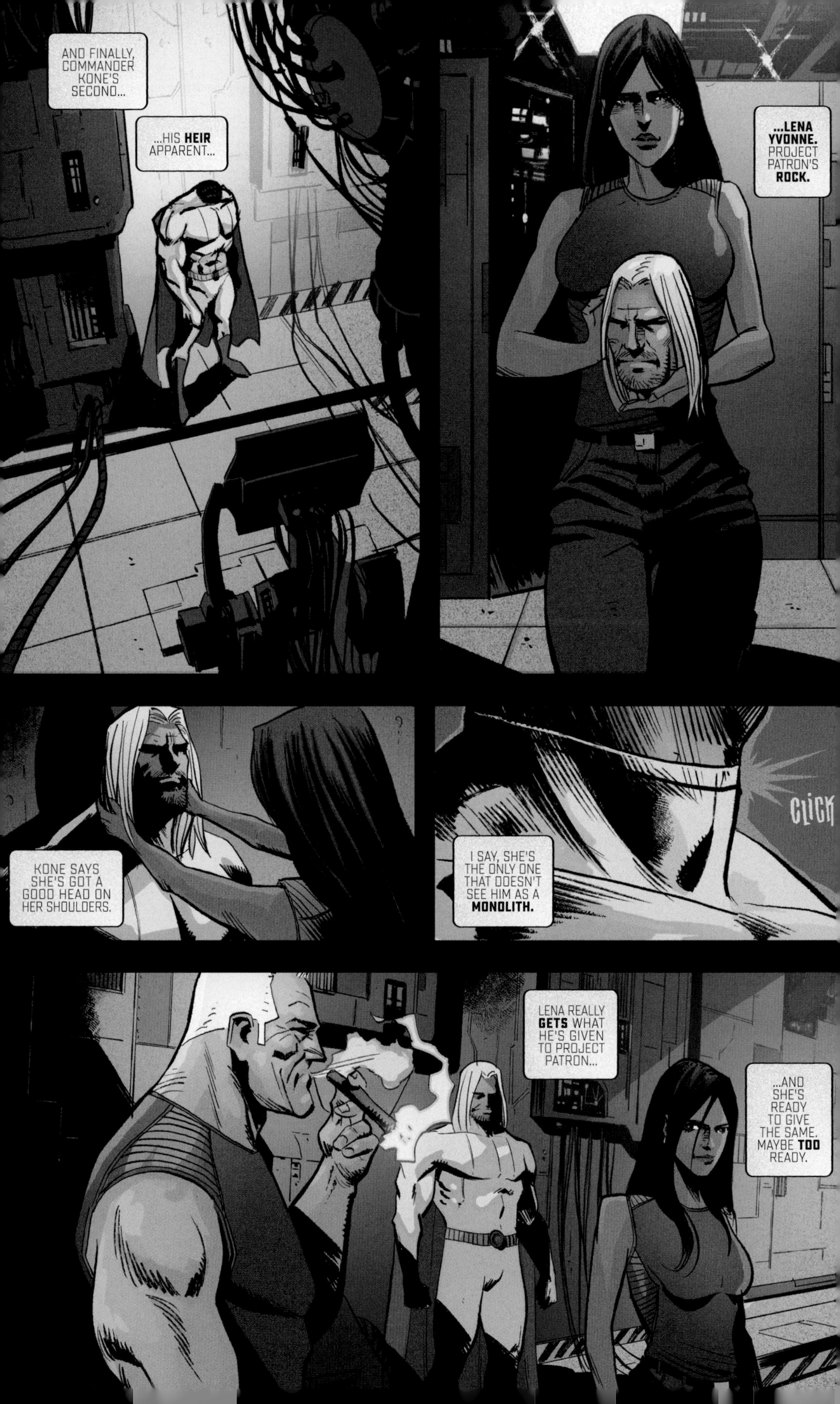
AND FINALLY, COMMANDER KONE'S SECOND...
...HIS **HEIR** APPARENT...
...LENA YVONNE. PROJECT PATRON'S **ROCK.**
KONE SAYS SHE'S GOT A GOOD HEAD ON HER SHOULDERS.
CLICK
I SAY, SHE'S THE ONLY ONE THAT DOESN'T SEE HIM AS A **MONOLITH.**
LENA REALLY **GETS** WHAT HE'S GIVEN TO PROJECT PATRON...
...AND SHE'S READY TO GIVE THE SAME. MAYBE **TOO** READY.

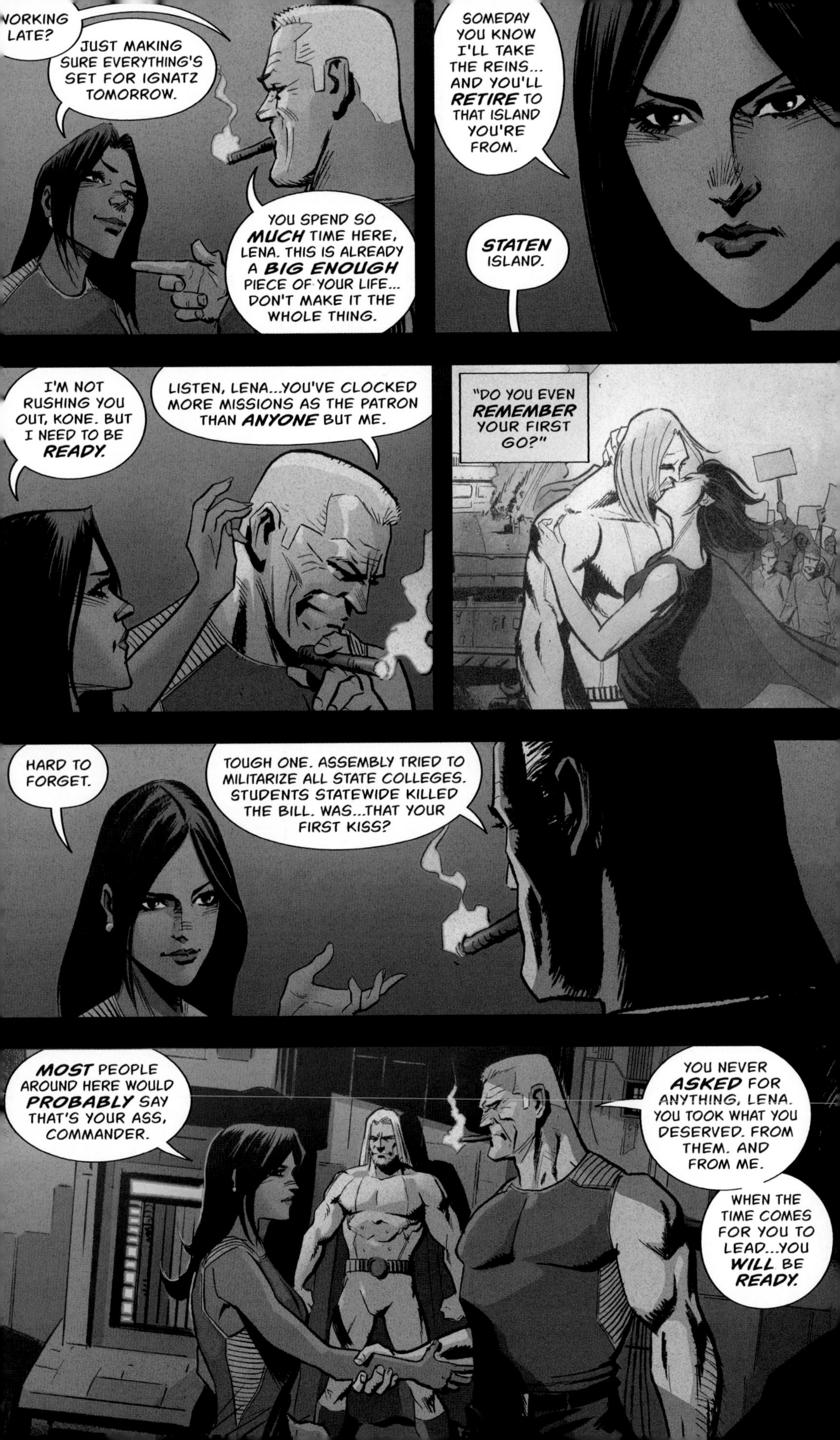
WORKING LATE?
JUST MAKING SURE EVERYTHING'S SET FOR IGNATZ TOMORROW.
YOU SPEND SO MUCH TIME HERE, LENA. THIS IS ALREADY A BIG ENOUGH PIECE OF YOUR LIFE... DON'T MAKE IT THE WHOLE THING.
SOMEDAY YOU KNOW I'LL TAKE THE REINS... AND YOU'LL RETIRE TO THAT ISLAND YOU'RE FROM.
STATEN ISLAND.
I'M NOT RUSHING YOU OUT, KONE. BUT I NEED TO BE READY.
LISTEN, LENA...YOU'VE CLOCKED MORE MISSIONS AS THE PATRON THAN ANYONE BUT ME.
"DO YOU EVEN REMEMBER YOUR FIRST GO?"
HARD TO FORGET.
TOUGH ONE. ASSEMBLY TRIED TO MILITARIZE ALL STATE COLLEGES. STUDENTS STATEWIDE KILLED THE BILL. WAS...THAT YOUR FIRST KISS?
MOST PEOPLE AROUND HERE WOULD PROBABLY SAY THAT'S YOUR ASS, COMMANDER.
YOU NEVER ASKED FOR ANYTHING, LENA. YOU TOOK WHAT YOU DESERVED. FROM THEM. AND FROM ME.
WHEN THE TIME COMES FOR YOU TO LEAD...YOU WILL BE READY.

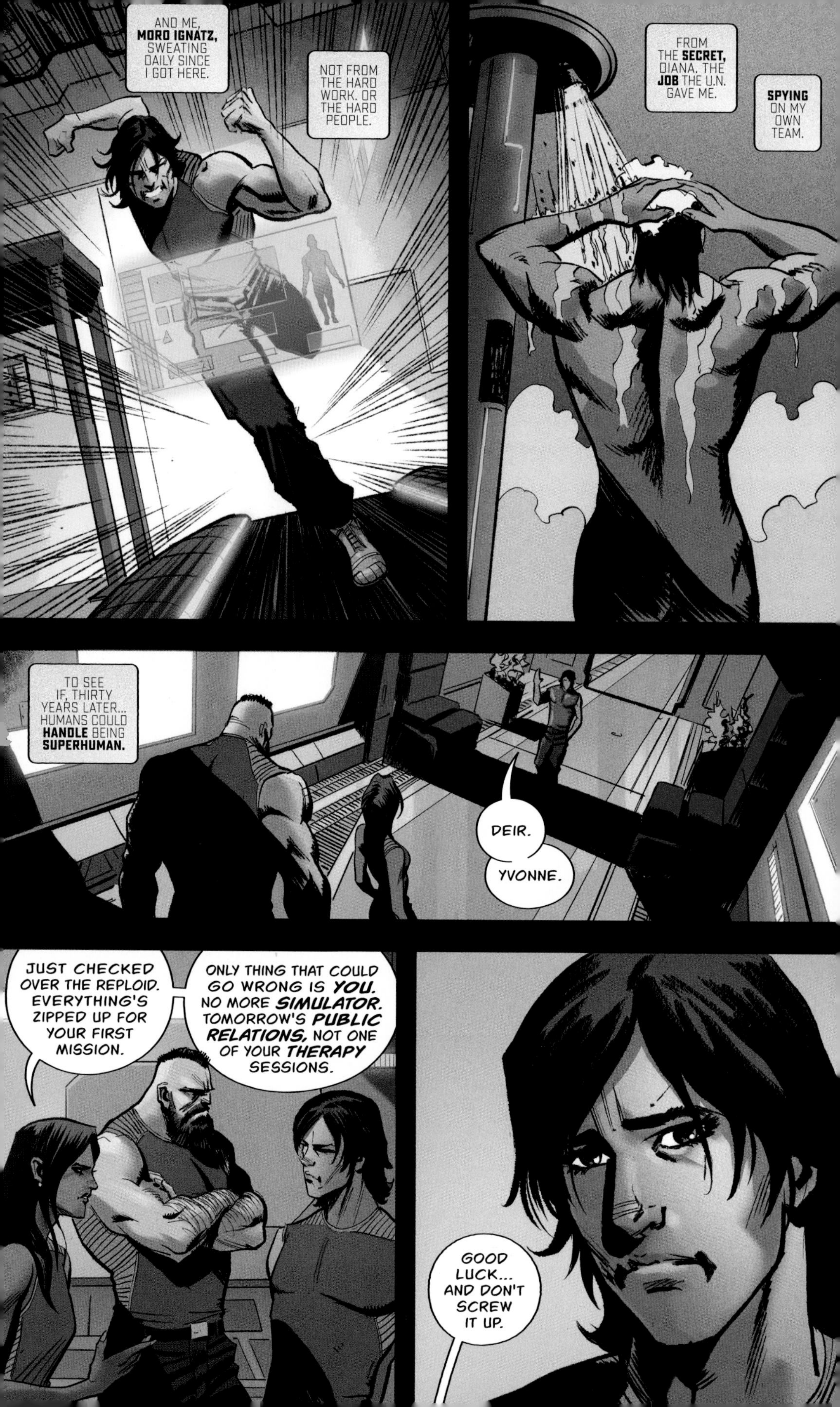
AND ME, MORO IGNATZ, SWEATING DAILY SINCE I GOT HERE.
NOT FROM THE HARD WORK. OR THE HARD PEOPLE.
FROM THE SECRET, DIANA. THE JOB THE U.N. GAVE ME.
SPYING ON MY OWN TEAM.
TO SEE IF, THIRTY YEARS LATER... HUMANS COULD HANDLE BEING SUPERHUMAN.
DEIR.
YVONNE.
JUST CHECKED OVER THE REPLOID. EVERYTHING'S ZIPPED UP FOR YOUR FIRST MISSION.
ONLY THING THAT COULD GO WRONG IS YOU. NO MORE SIMULATOR. TOMORROW'S PUBLIC RELATIONS, NOT ONE OF YOUR THERAPY SESSIONS.
GOOD LUCK... AND DON'T SCREW IT UP.

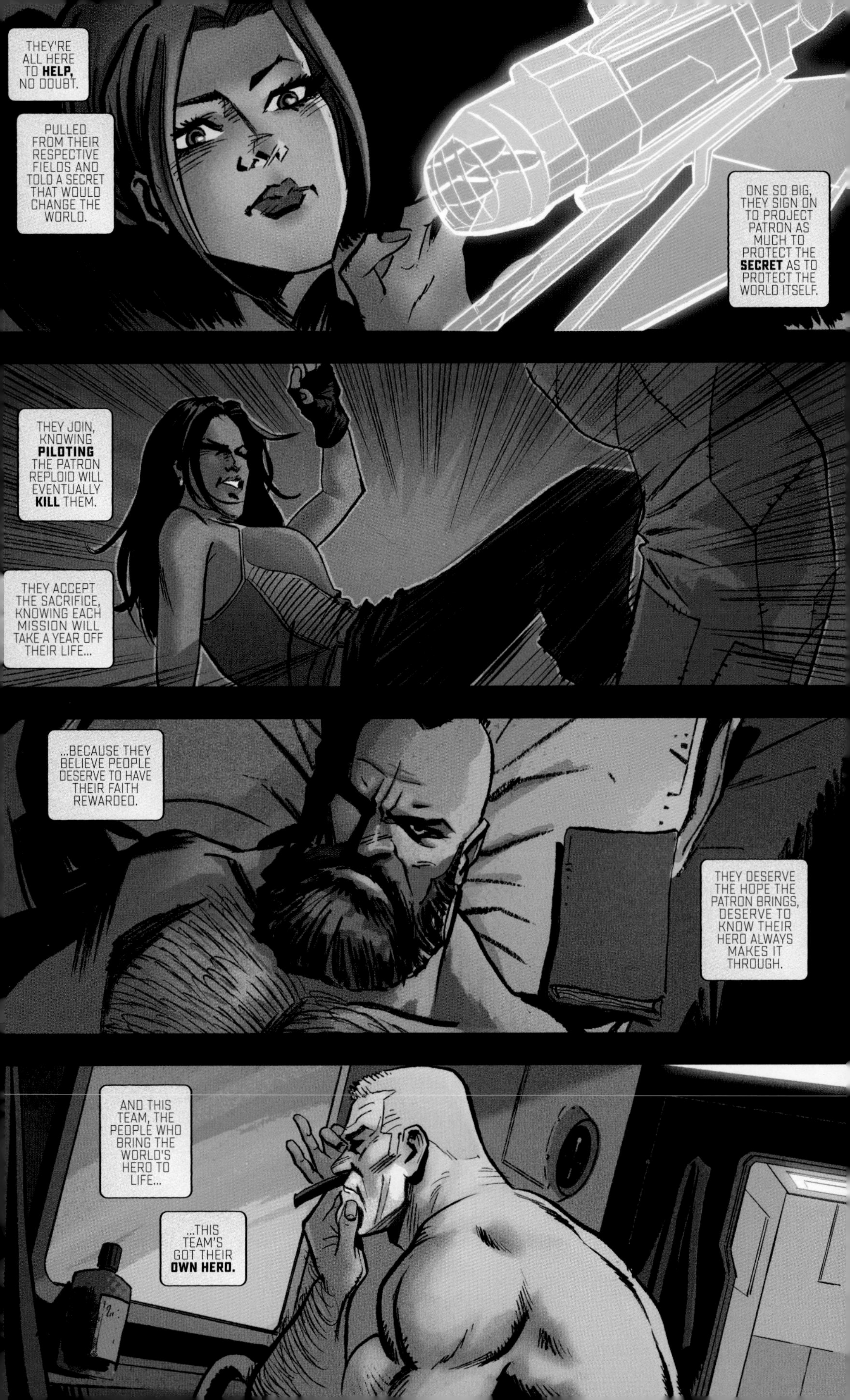
THEY'RE ALL HERE TO **HELP,** NO DOUBT.
PULLED FROM THEIR RESPECTIVE FIELDS AND TOLD A SECRET THAT WOULD CHANGE THE WORLD.
ONE SO BIG, THEY SIGN ON TO PROJECT PATRON AS MUCH TO PROTECT THE **SECRET** AS TO PROTECT THE WORLD ITSELF.
THEY JOIN, KNOWING **PILOTING** THE PATRON REPLOID WILL EVENTUALLY **KILL** THEM.
THEY ACCEPT THE SACRIFICE, KNOWING EACH MISSION WILL TAKE A YEAR OFF THEIR LIFE...
...BECAUSE THEY BELIEVE PEOPLE DESERVE TO HAVE THEIR FAITH REWARDED.
THEY DESERVE THE HOPE THE PATRON BRINGS, DESERVE TO KNOW THEIR HERO ALWAYS MAKES IT THROUGH.
AND THIS TEAM, THE PEOPLE WHO BRING THE WORLD'S HERO TO LIFE...
...THIS TEAM'S GOT THEIR **OWN HERO.**

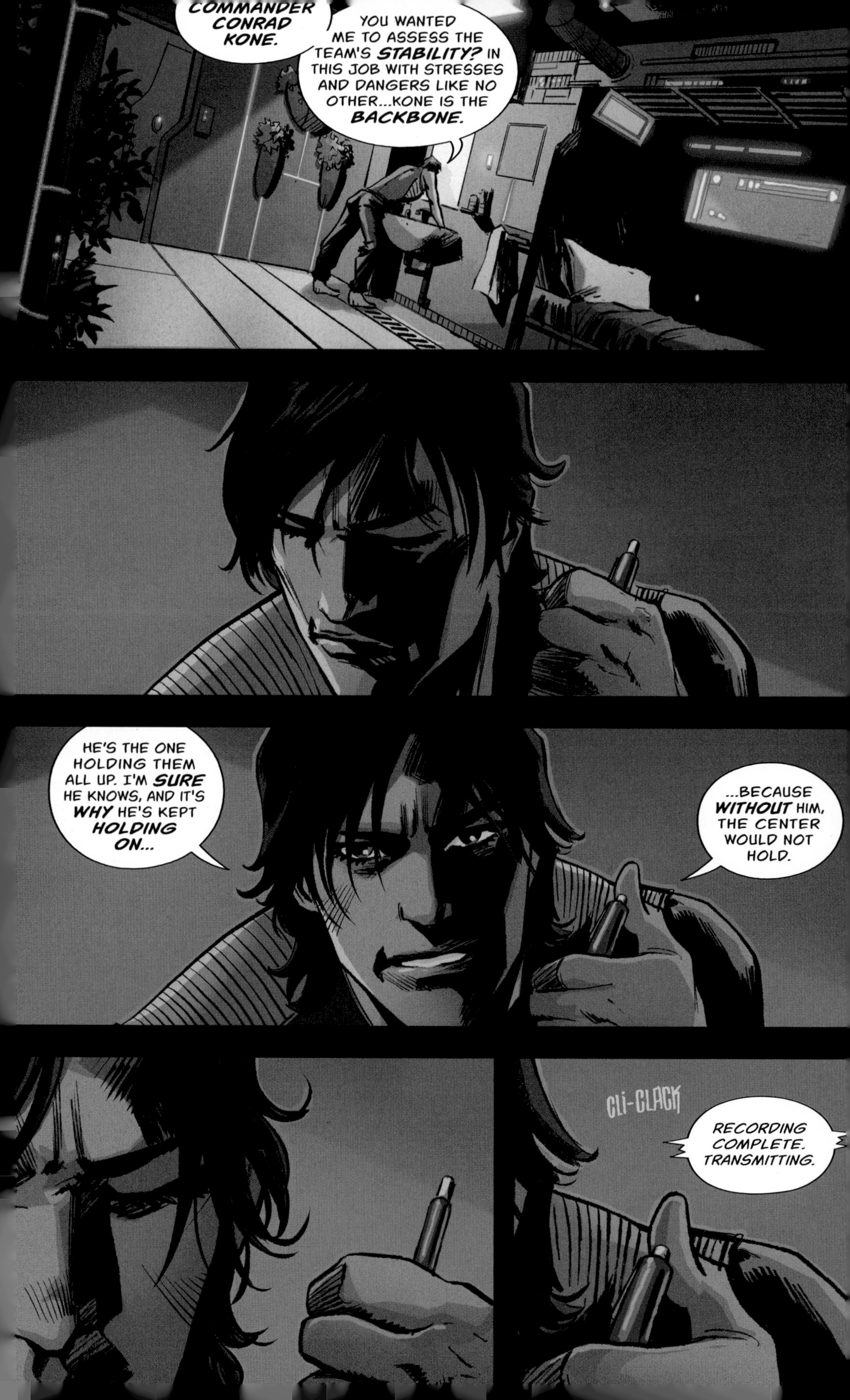
COMMANDER CONRAD KONE.
YOU WANTED ME TO ASSESS THE TEAM'S STABILITY? IN THIS JOB WITH STRESSES AND DANGERS LIKE NO OTHER...KONE IS THE BACKBONE.
HE'S THE ONE HOLDING THEM ALL UP. I'M SURE HE KNOWS, AND IT'S WHY HE'S KEPT HOLDING ON...
...BECAUSE WITHOUT HIM, THE CENTER WOULD NOT HOLD.
CLI-CLACK
RECORDING COMPLETE. TRANSMITTING.

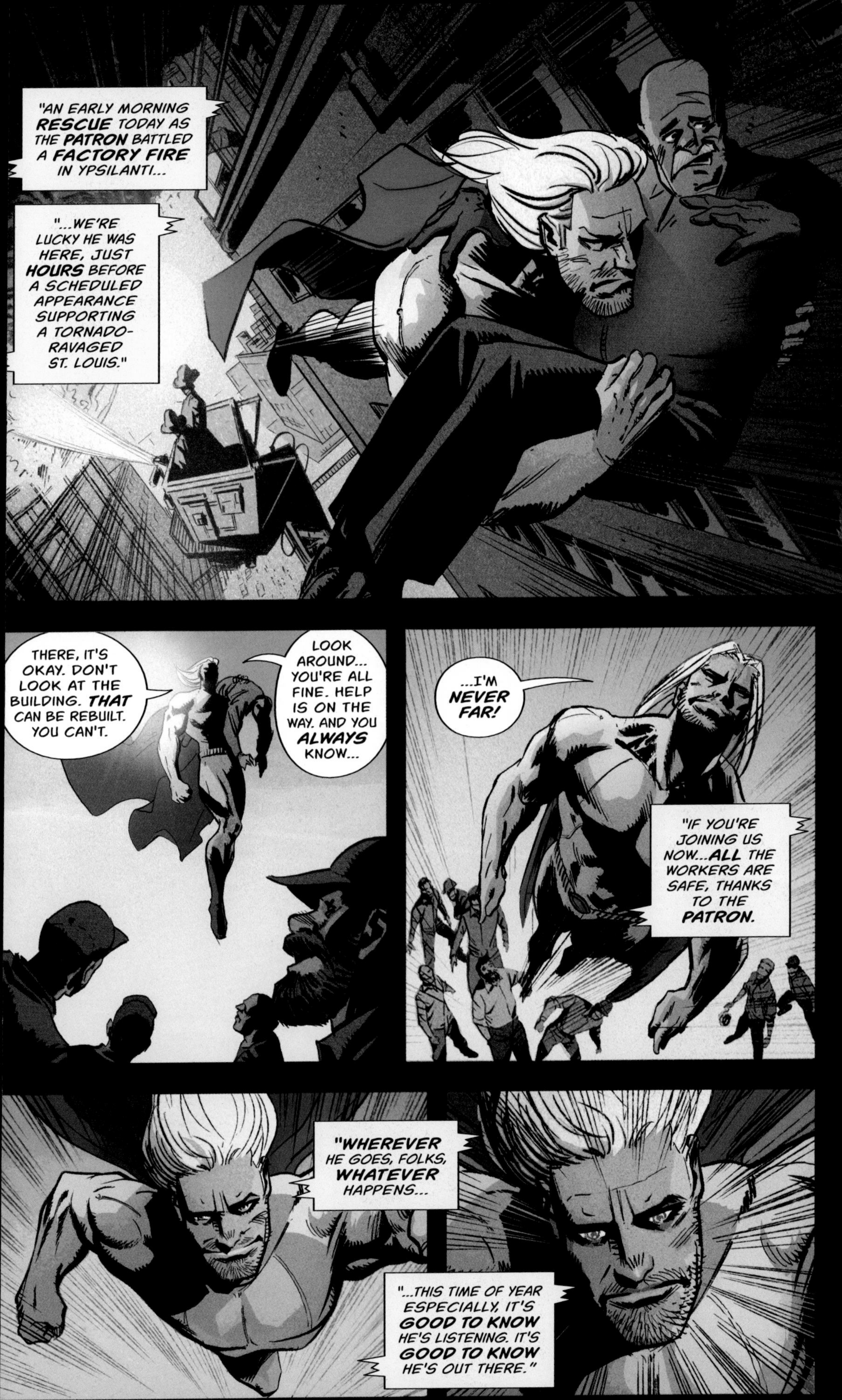
"AN EARLY MORNING RESCUE TODAY AS THE PATRON BATTLED A FACTORY FIRE IN YPSILANTI...
"...WE'RE LUCKY HE WAS HERE, JUST HOURS BEFORE A SCHEDULED APPEARANCE SUPPORTING A TORNADO-RAVAGED ST. LOUIS."
THERE, IT'S OKAY. DON'T LOOK AT THE BUILDING. THAT CAN BE REBUILT. YOU CAN'T.
LOOK AROUND... YOU'RE ALL FINE. HELP IS ON THE WAY. AND YOU ALWAYS KNOW...
...I'M NEVER FAR!
"IF YOU'RE JOINING US NOW...ALL THE WORKERS ARE SAFE, THANKS TO THE PATRON.
"WHEREVER HE GOES, FOLKS, WHATEVER HAPPENS...
"...THIS TIME OF YEAR ESPECIALLY, IT'S GOOD TO KNOW HE'S LISTENING. IT'S GOOD TO KNOW HE'S OUT THERE."

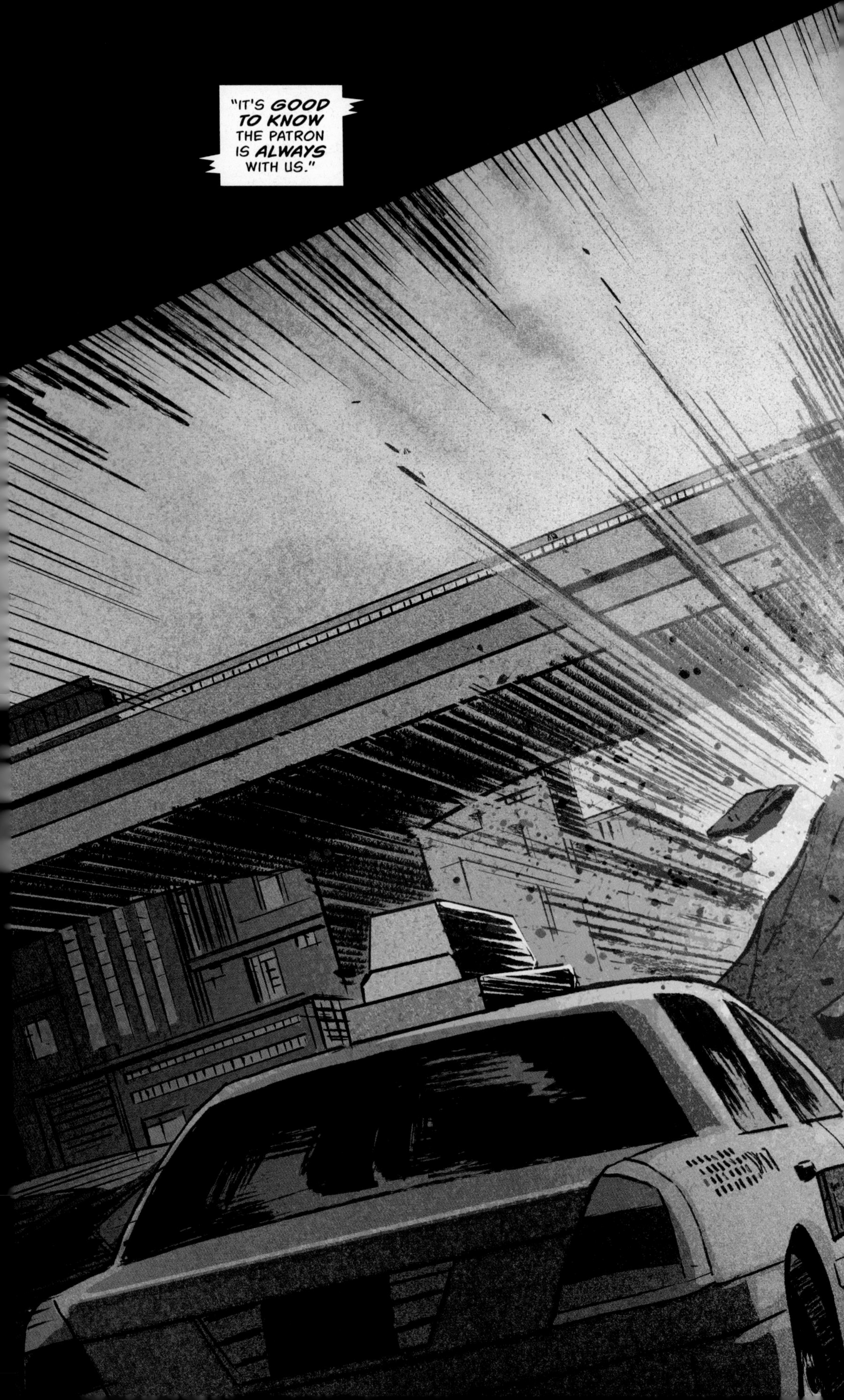
"IT'S GOOD TO KNOW THE PATRON IS ALWAYS WITH US."

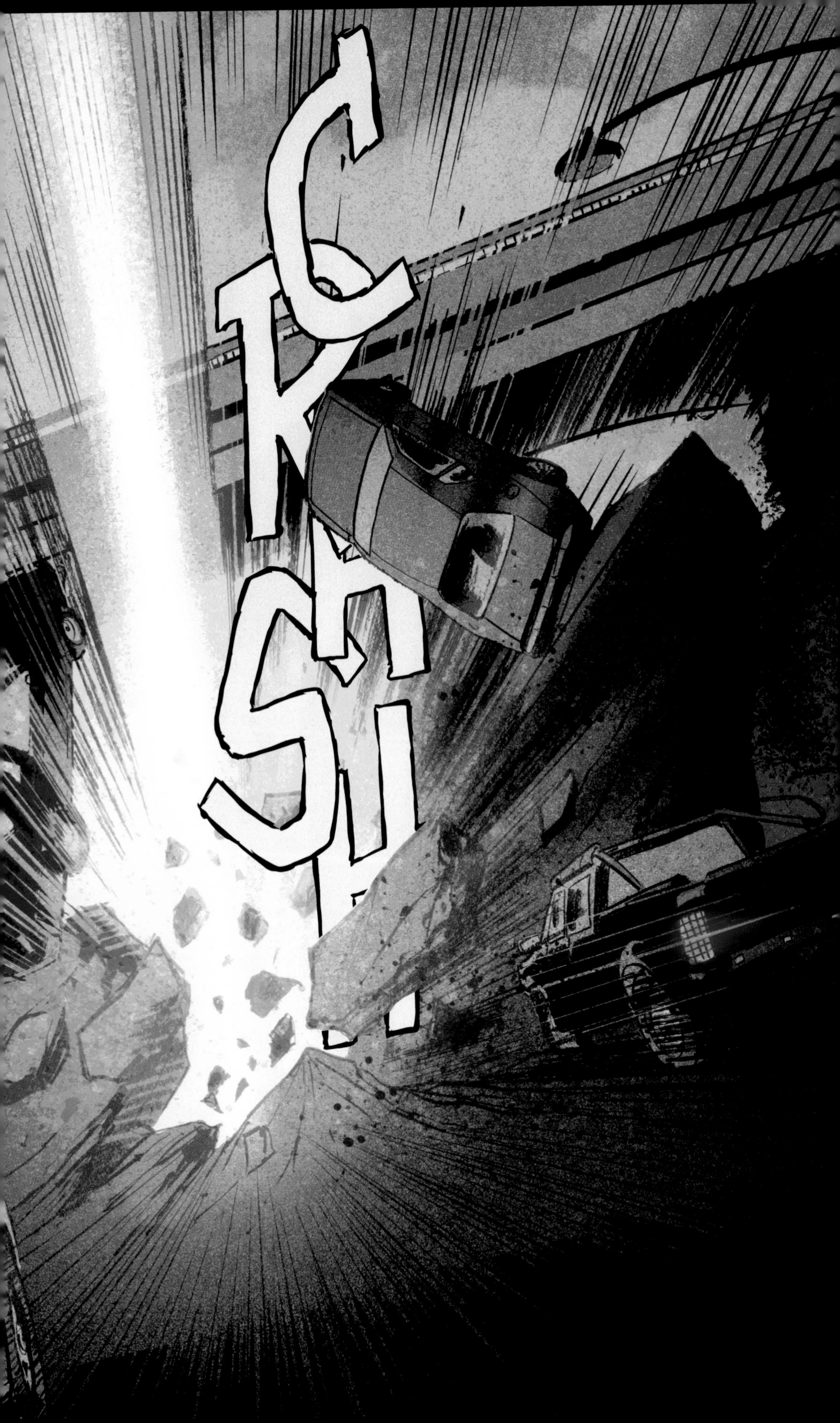
CKRSH

2

GREED AND GRIEVANCES

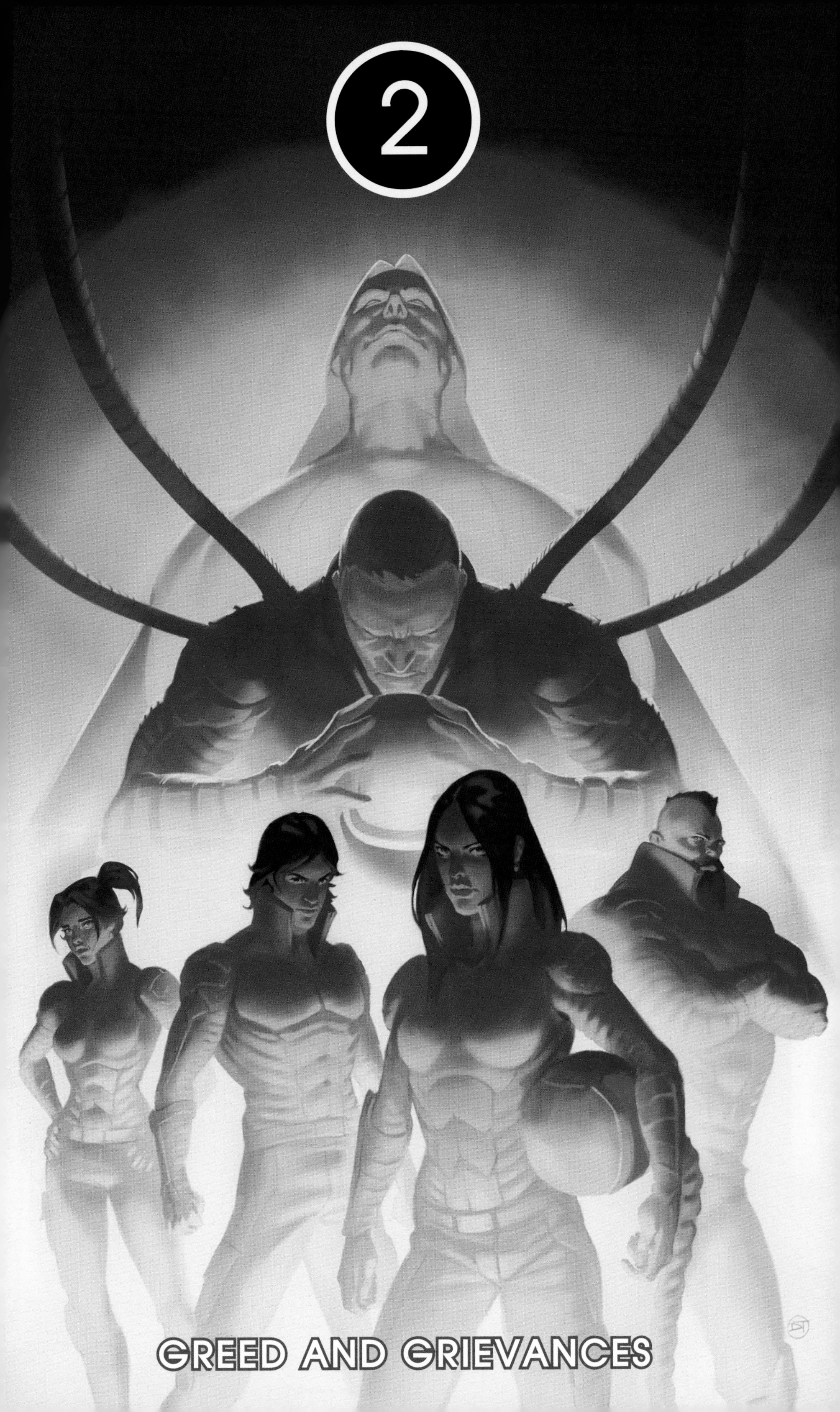

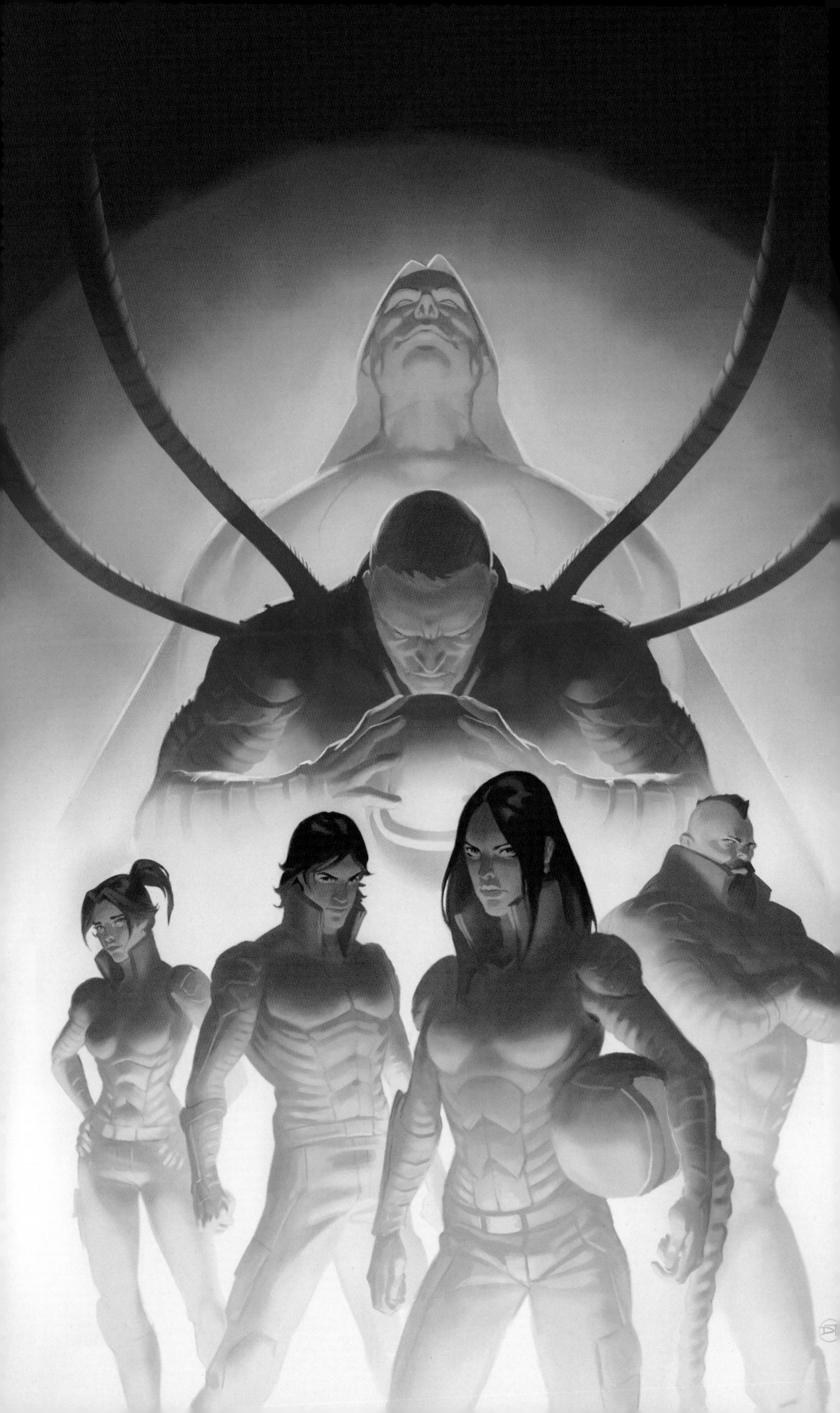

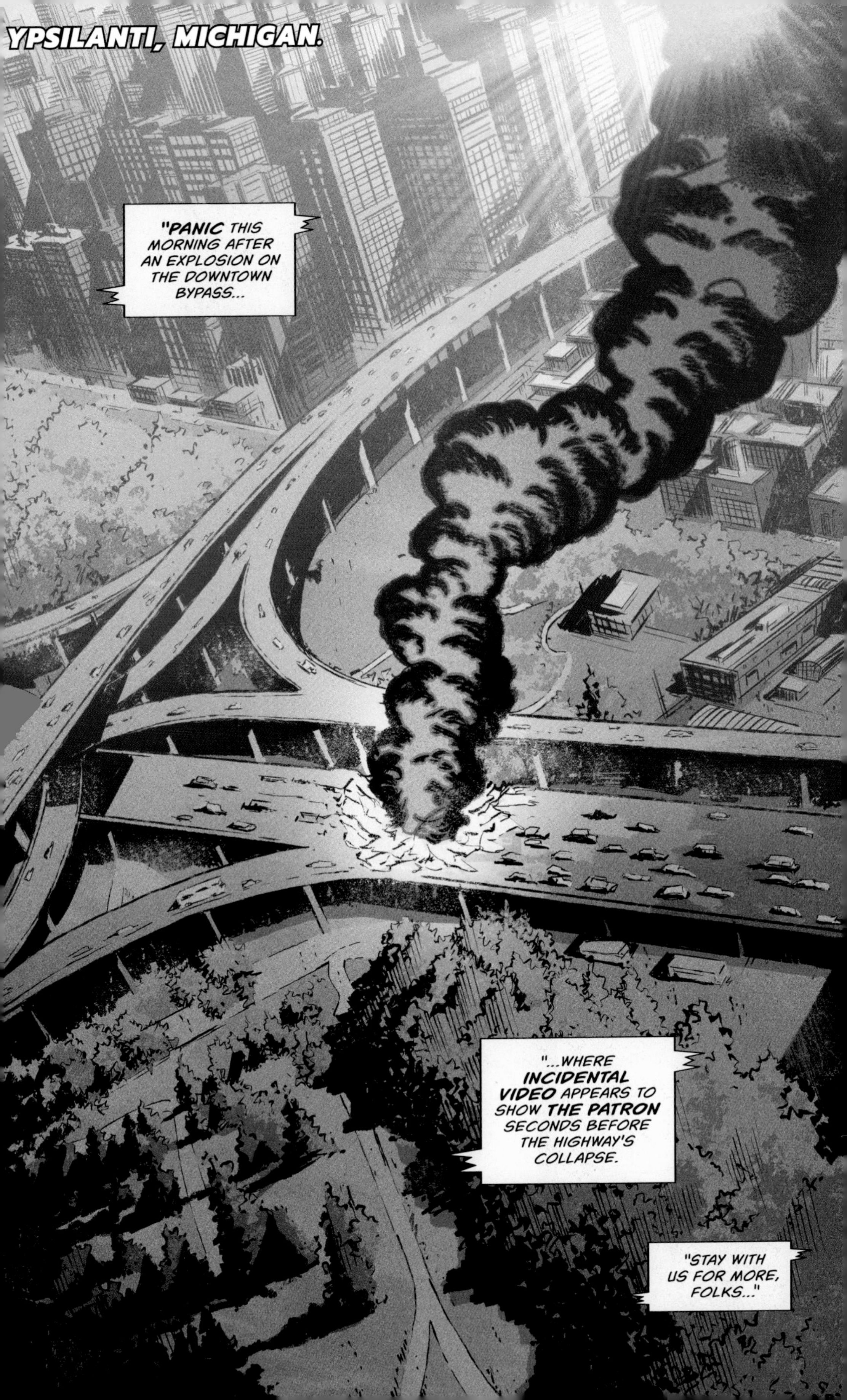
YPSILANTI, MICHIGAN.
"PANIC THIS MORNING AFTER AN EXPLOSION ON THE DOWNTOWN BYPASS...
"...WHERE INCIDENTAL VIDEO APPEARS TO SHOW THE PATRON SECONDS BEFORE THE HIGHWAY'S COLLAPSE.
"STAY WITH US FOR MORE, FOLKS..."

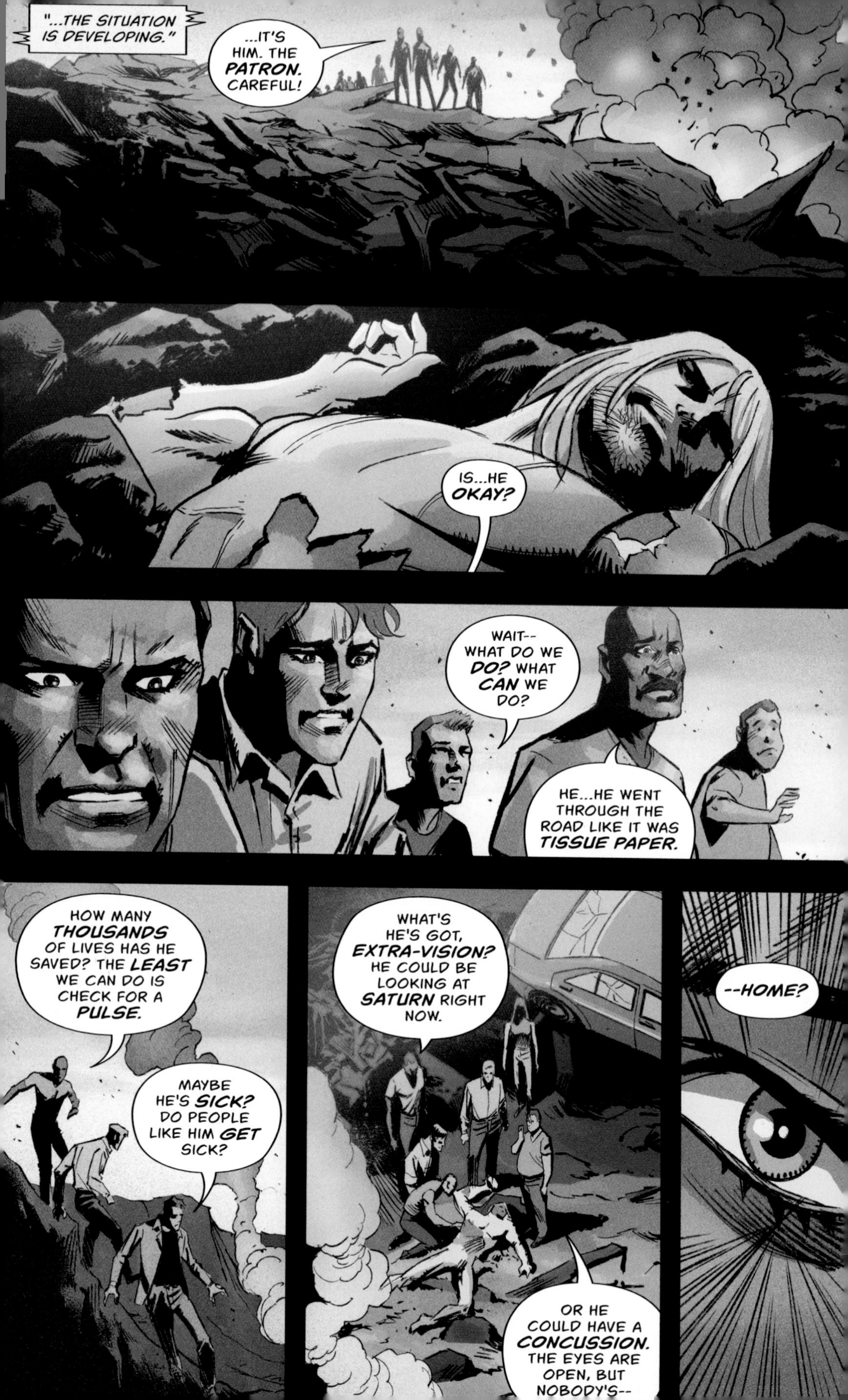
"...THE SITUATION IS DEVELOPING."
...IT'S HIM. THE PATRON. CAREFUL!
IS...HE OKAY?
WAIT-- WHAT DO WE DO? WHAT CAN WE DO?
HE...HE WENT THROUGH THE ROAD LIKE IT WAS TISSUE PAPER.
HOW MANY THOUSANDS OF LIVES HAS HE SAVED? THE LEAST WE CAN DO IS CHECK FOR A PULSE.
MAYBE HE'S SICK? DO PEOPLE LIKE HIM GET SICK?
WHAT'S HE'S GOT, EXTRA-VISION? HE COULD BE LOOKING AT SATURN RIGHT NOW.
OR HE COULD HAVE A CONCUSSION. THE EYES ARE OPEN, BUT NOBODY'S--
--HOME?

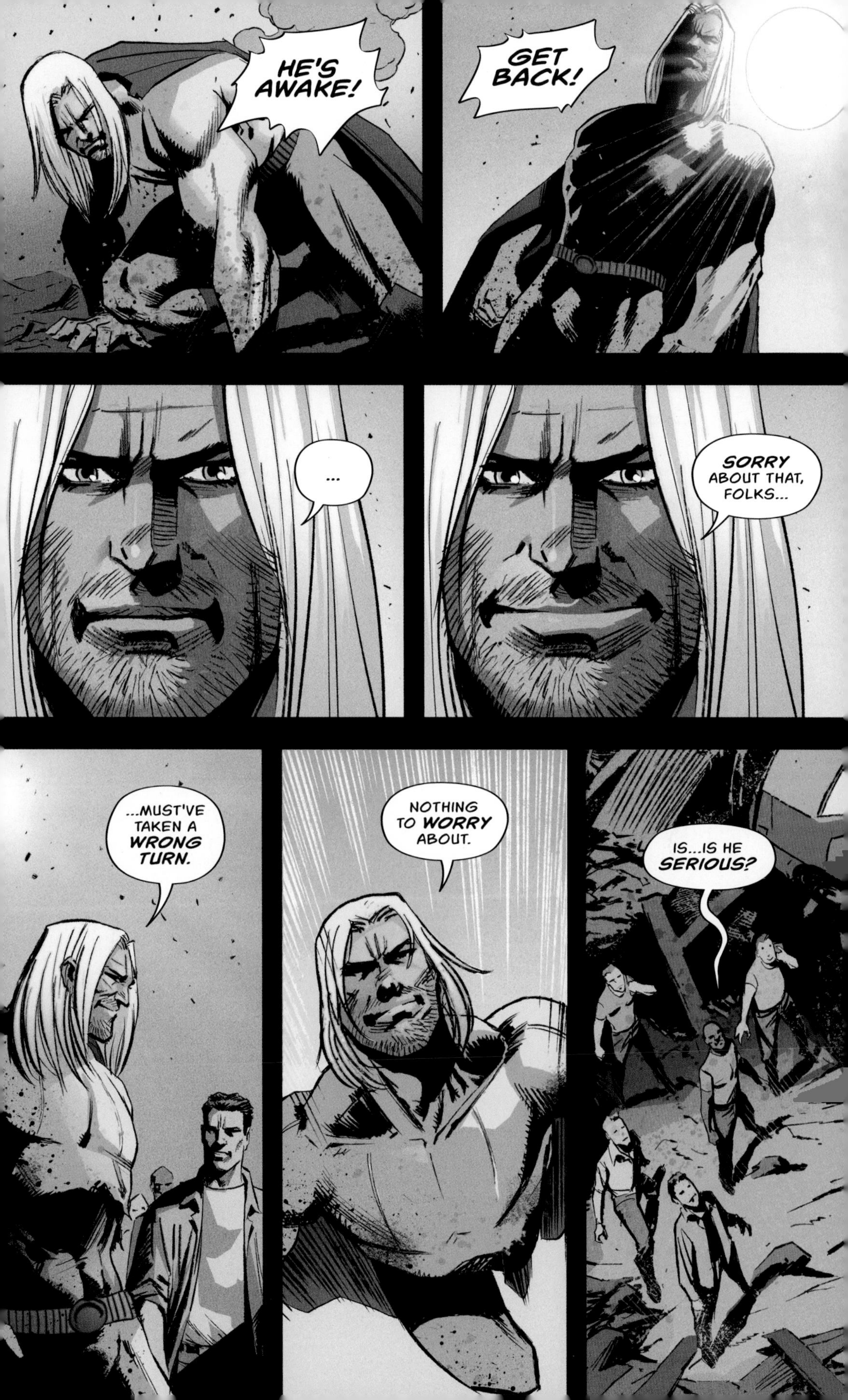
HE'S AWAKE!
GET BACK!
...
SORRY ABOUT THAT, FOLKS...
...MUST'VE TAKEN A WRONG TURN.
NOTHING TO WORRY ABOUT.
IS...IS HE SERIOUS?

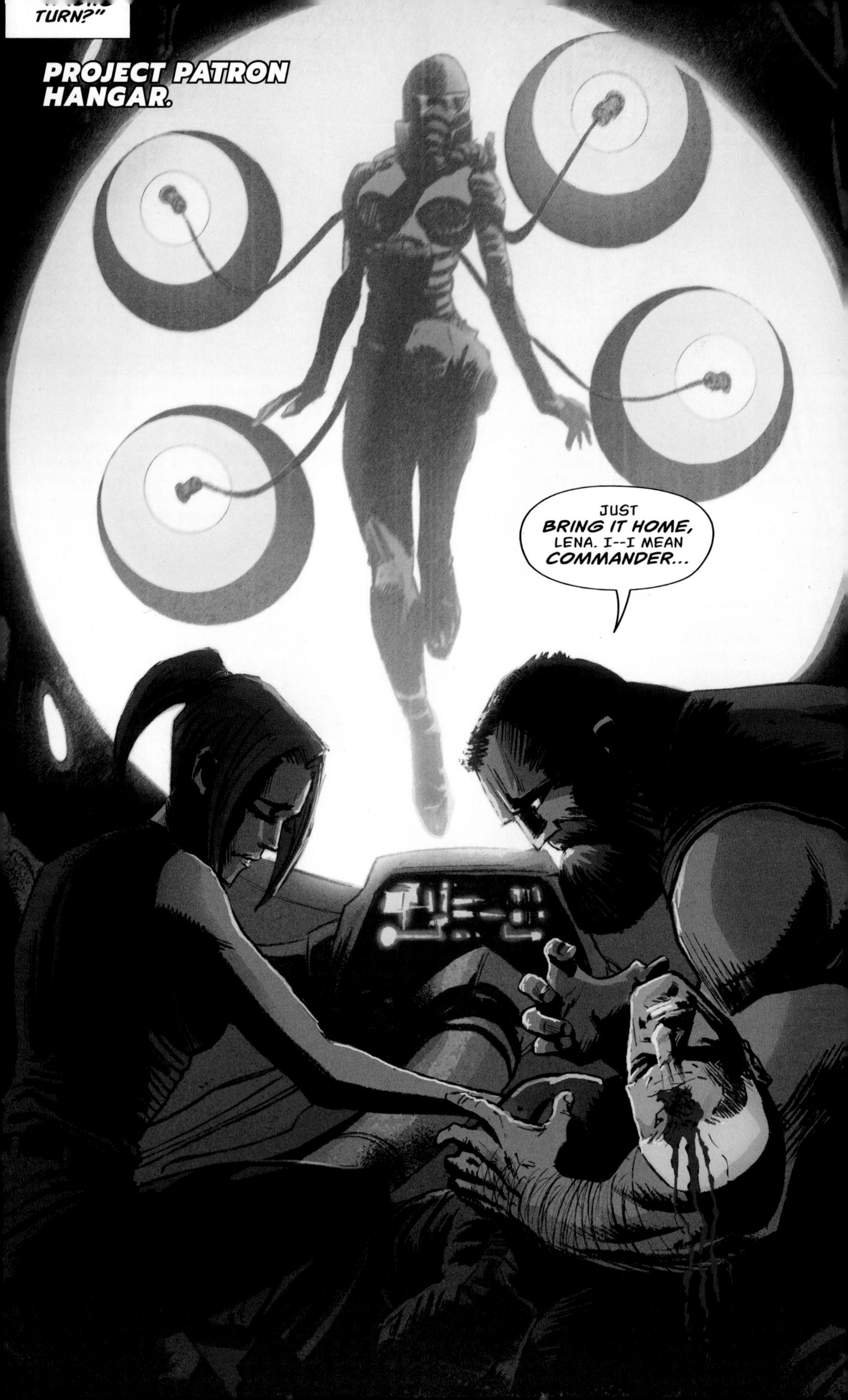
TURN?"
PROJECT PATRON HANGAR.
JUST BRING IT HOME, LENA. I--I MEAN COMMANDER...

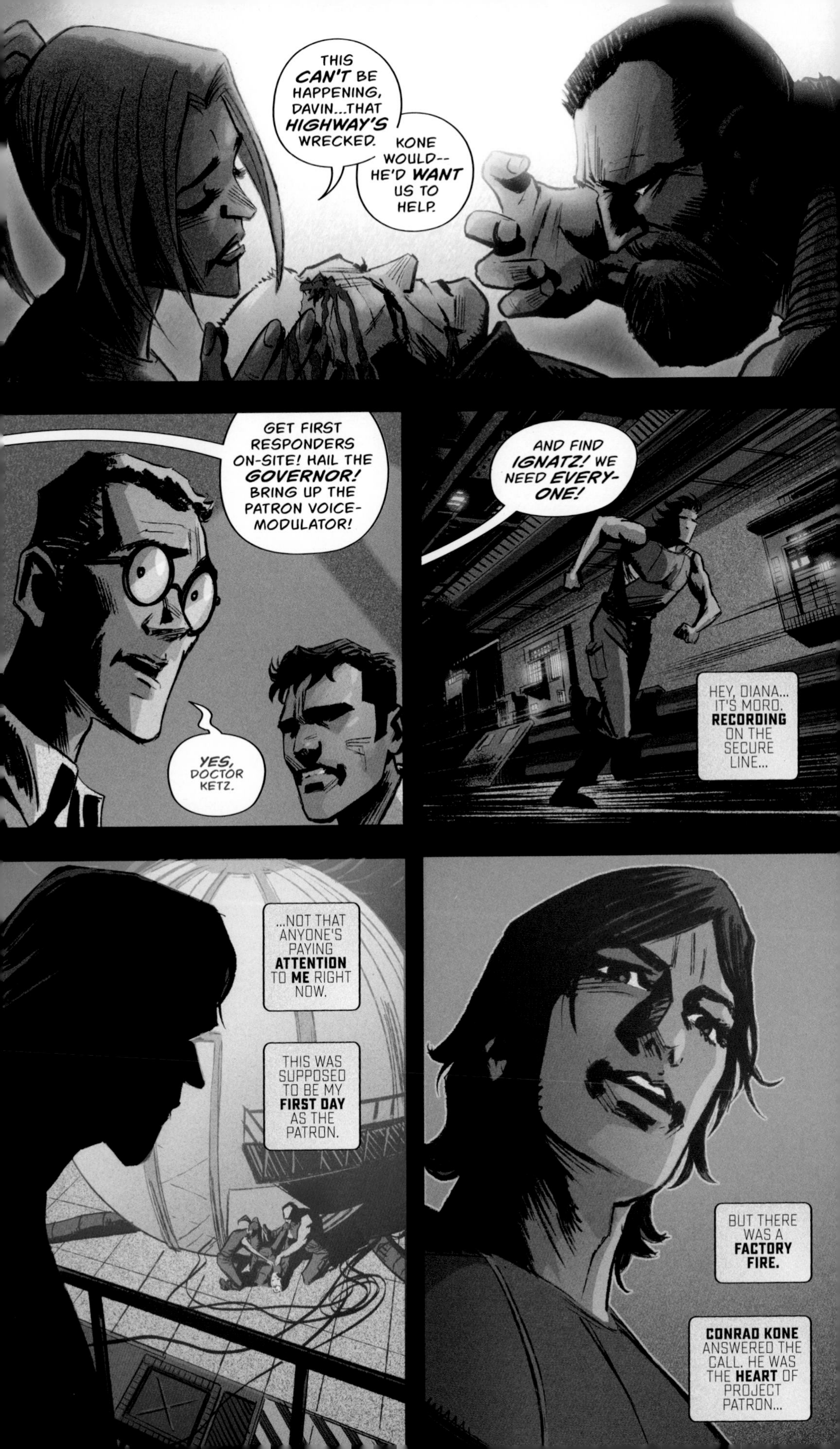
THIS CAN'T BE HAPPENING, DAVIN...THAT HIGHWAY'S WRECKED.
KONE WOULD-- HE'D WANT US TO HELP.
GET FIRST RESPONDERS ON-SITE! HAIL THE GOVERNOR! BRING UP THE PATRON VOICE-MODULATOR!
YES, DOCTOR KETZ.
AND FIND IGNATZ! WE NEED EVERY-ONE!
HEY, DIANA... IT'S MORO. RECORDING ON THE SECURE LINE...
...NOT THAT ANYONE'S PAYING ATTENTION TO ME RIGHT NOW.
THIS WAS SUPPOSED TO BE MY FIRST DAY AS THE PATRON.
BUT THERE WAS A FACTORY FIRE.
CONRAD KONE ANSWERED THE CALL. HE WAS THE HEART OF PROJECT PATRON...

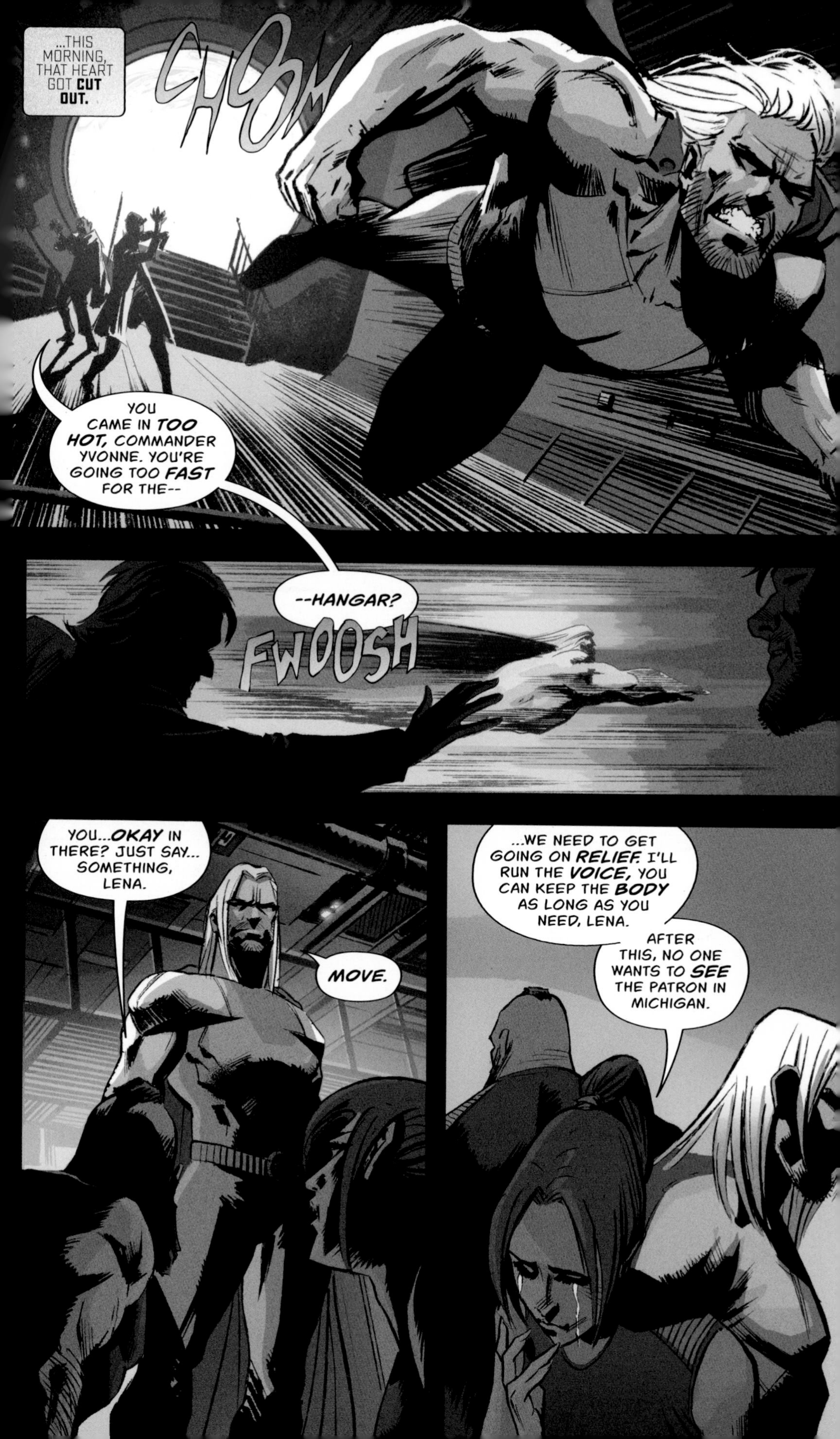
...THIS MORNING, THAT HEART GOT **CUT OUT.**
CHOOM
YOU CAME IN *TOO HOT,* COMMANDER YVONNE. YOU'RE GOING TOO *FAST* FOR THE--
--HANGAR?
FWOOSH
YOU...*OKAY* IN THERE? JUST SAY... SOMETHING, LENA.
MOVE.
...WE NEED TO GET GOING ON *RELIEF.* I'LL RUN THE *VOICE,* YOU CAN KEEP THE *BODY* AS LONG AS YOU NEED, LENA.
AFTER THIS, NO ONE WANTS TO *SEE* THE PATRON IN MICHIGAN.

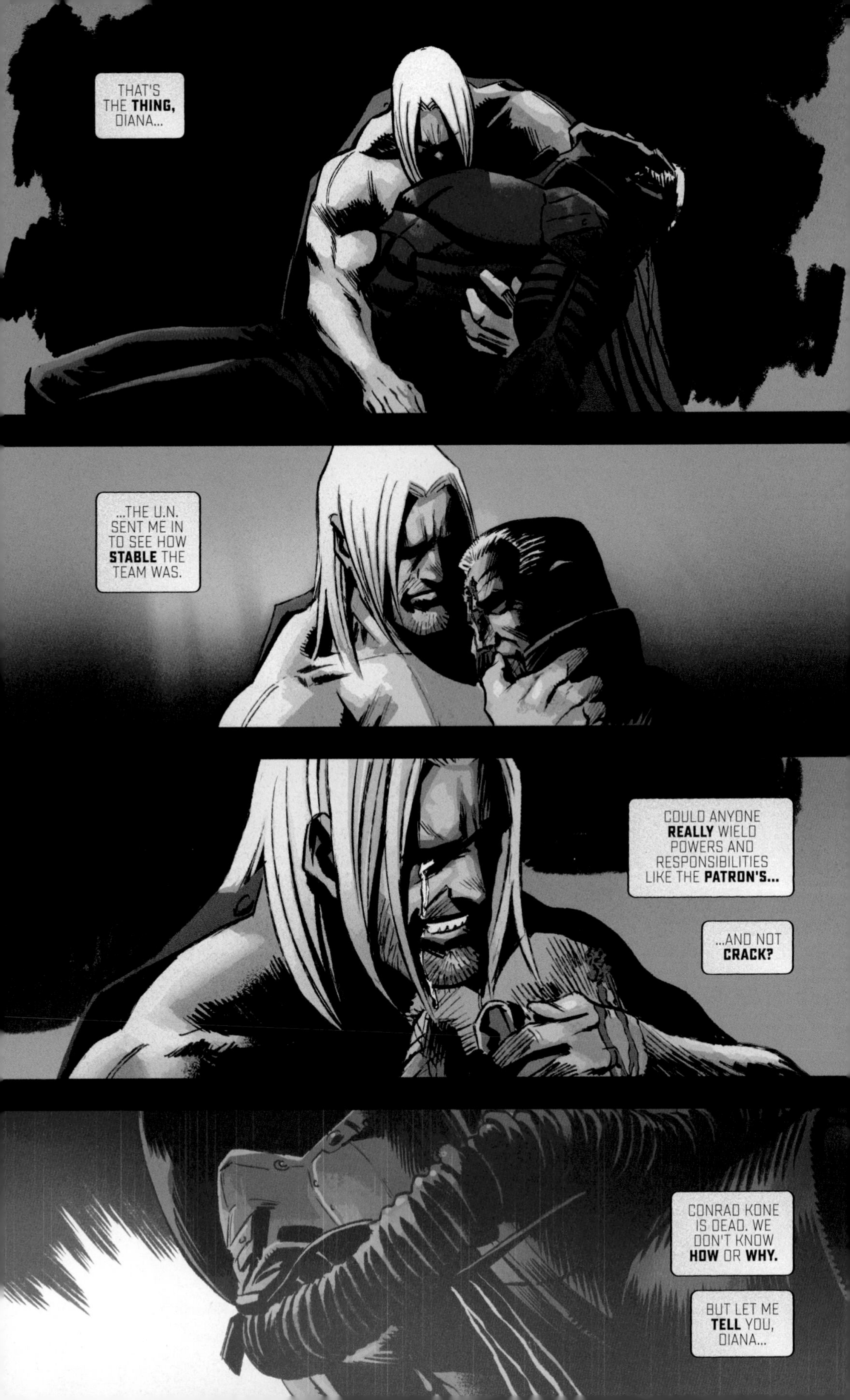

THAT'S THE **THING,** DIANA...
...THE U.N. SENT ME IN TO SEE HOW **STABLE** THE TEAM WAS.
COULD ANYONE **REALLY** WIELD POWERS AND RESPONSIBILITIES LIKE THE **PATRON'S...**
...AND NOT **CRACK?**
CONRAD KONE IS DEAD. WE DON'T KNOW **HOW** OR **WHY.**
BUT LET ME **TELL** YOU, DIANA...

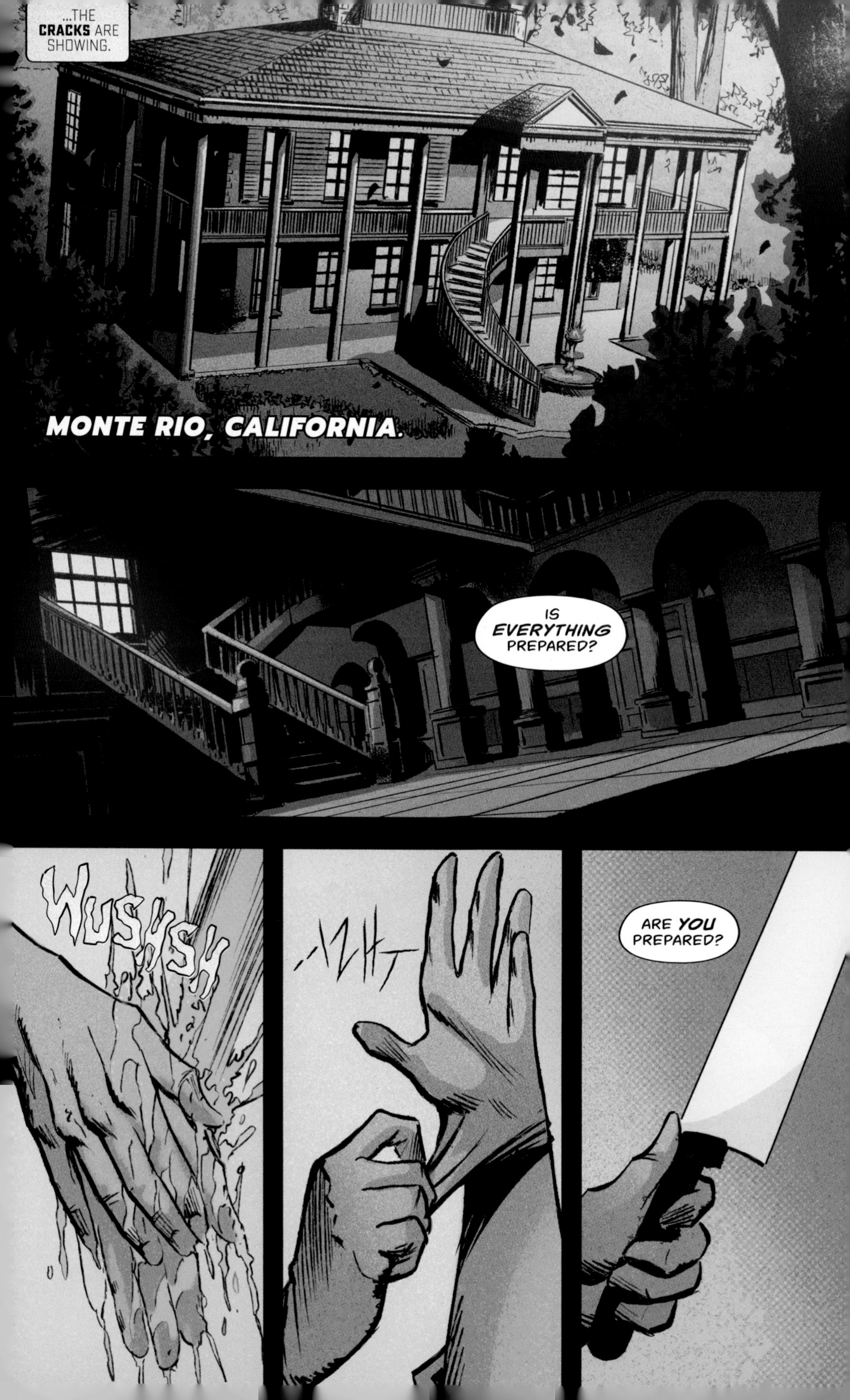
...THE CRACKS ARE SHOWING.
MONTE RIO, CALIFORNIA.
IS EVERYTHING PREPARED?
WUSHSH
-NZHT
ARE YOU PREPARED?

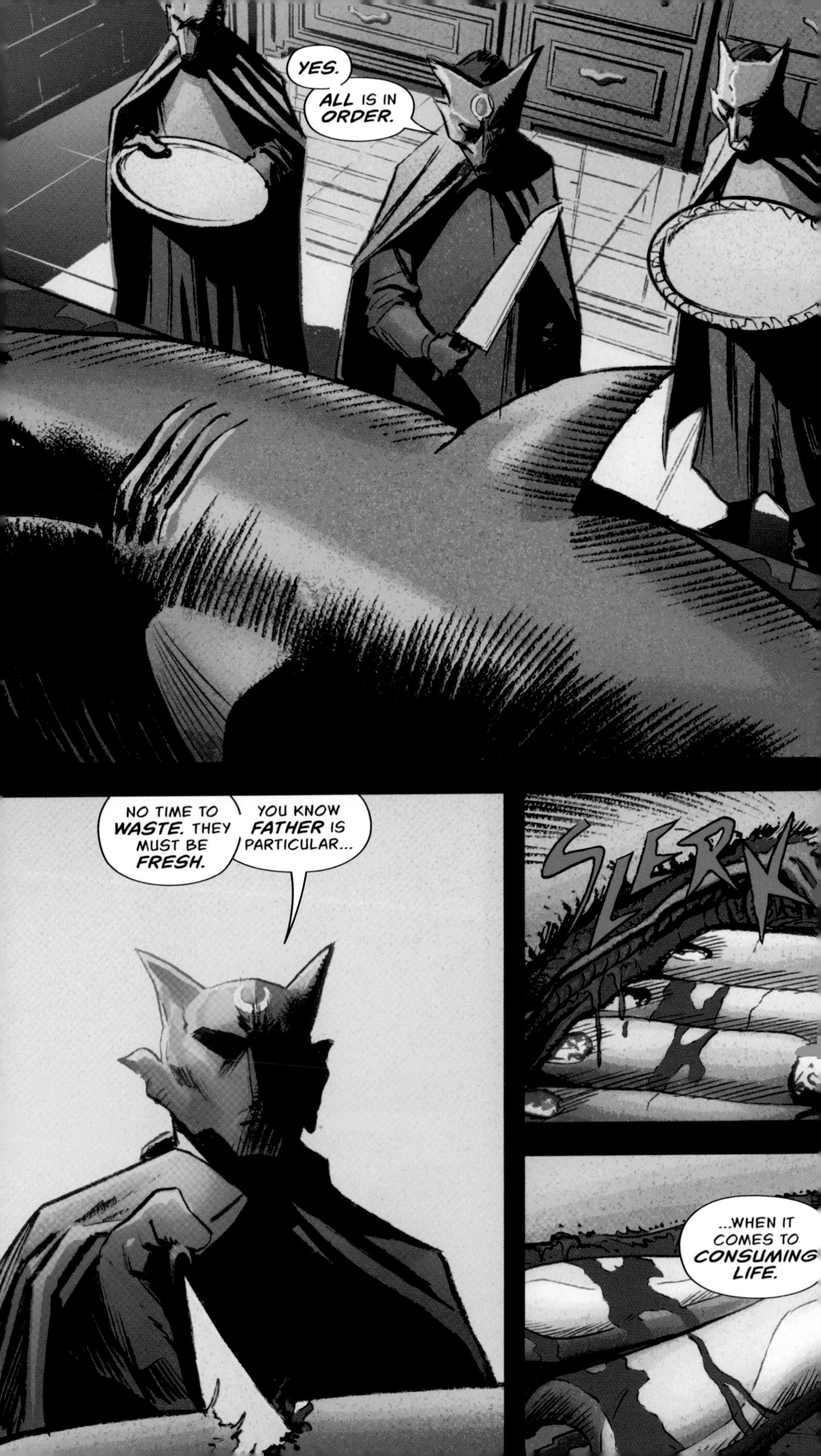
YES.
ALL IS IN ORDER.
NO TIME TO WASTE. THEY MUST BE FRESH.
YOU KNOW FATHER IS PARTICULAR...
...WHEN IT COMES TO CONSUMING LIFE.

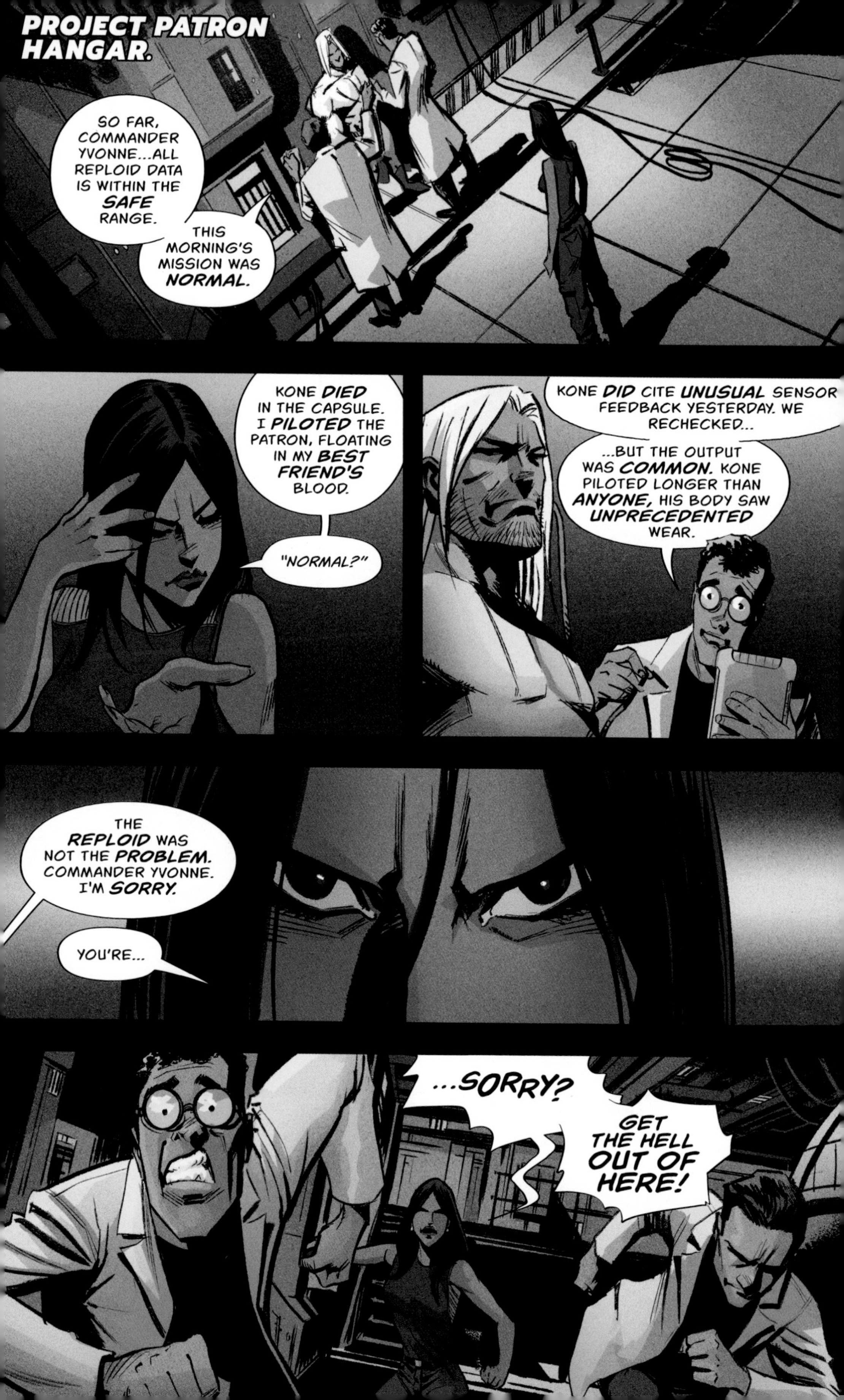
PROJECT PATRON HANGAR.
SO FAR, COMMANDER YVONNE... ALL REPLOID DATA IS WITHIN THE SAFE RANGE.
THIS MORNING'S MISSION WAS NORMAL.
KONE DIED IN THE CAPSULE. I PILOTED THE PATRON, FLOATING IN MY BEST FRIEND'S BLOOD.
"NORMAL?"
KONE DID CITE UNUSUAL SENSOR FEEDBACK YESTERDAY. WE RECHECKED...
...BUT THE OUTPUT WAS COMMON. KONE PILOTED LONGER THAN ANYONE, HIS BODY SAW UNPRECEDENTED WEAR.
THE REPLOID WAS NOT THE PROBLEM. COMMANDER YVONNE. I'M SORRY.
YOU'RE...
...SORRY?
GET THE HELL OUT OF HERE!

...YOU.

HE GAVE YOU EVERY-THING.

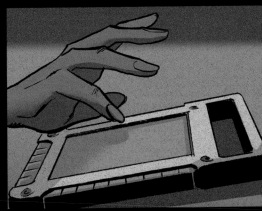

SMASH

THIS JOB'S *SUPPOSED* TO STEAL *TIME* FROM US... BUT KONE SHOULD'VE SPENT HIS *LAST YEARS* SMOKING, DRINKING AND CELEBRATING.

THIS ISN'T HOW *HE* WAS SUPPOSED TO GO.

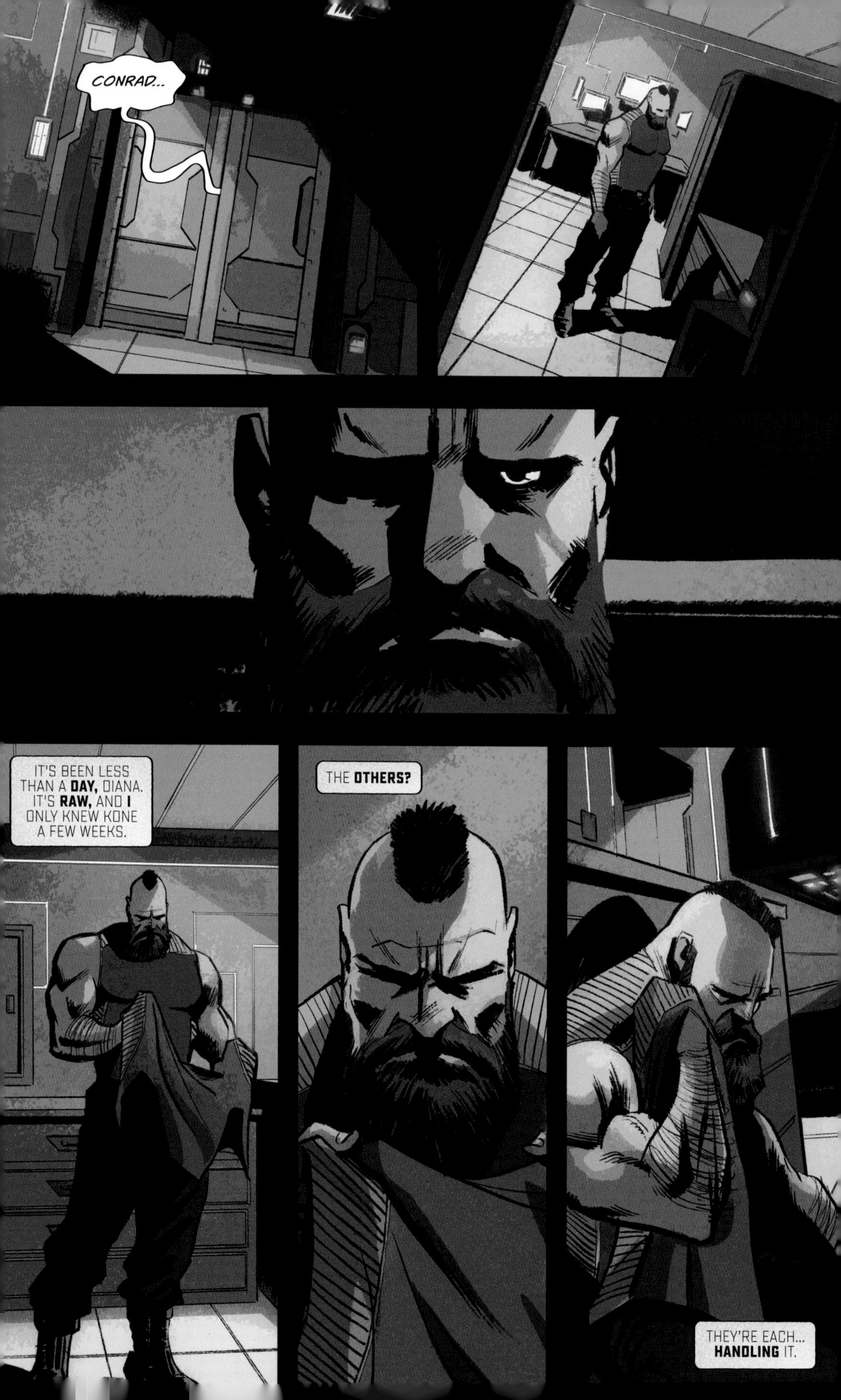
CONRAD...
IT'S BEEN LESS THAN A DAY, DIANA. IT'S RAW, AND I ONLY KNEW KONE A FEW WEEKS.
THE OTHERS?
THEY'RE EACH... HANDLING IT.

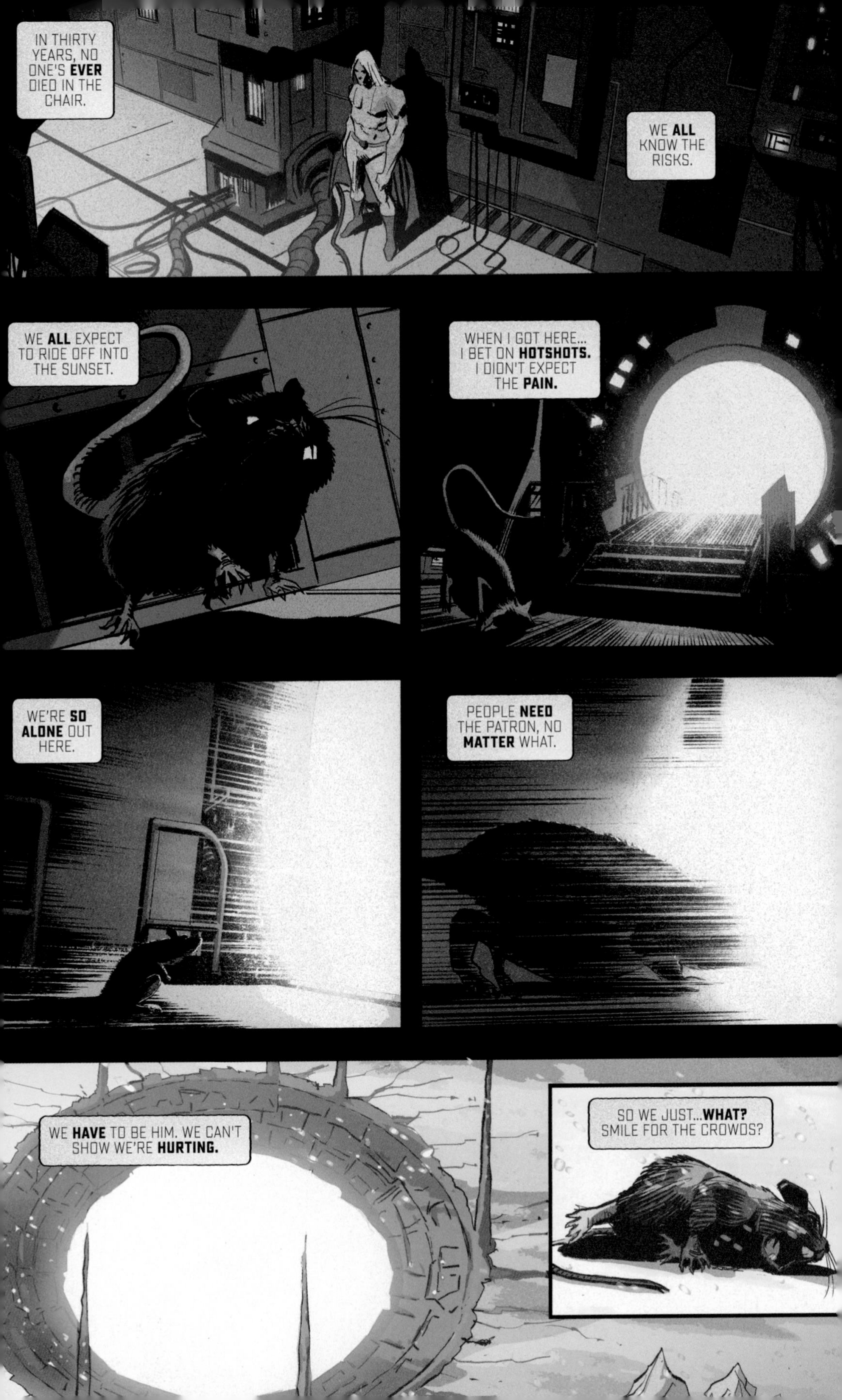
IN THIRTY YEARS, NO ONE'S **EVER** DIED IN THE CHAIR.
WE **ALL** KNOW THE RISKS.
WE **ALL** EXPECT TO RIDE OFF INTO THE SUNSET.
WHEN I GOT HERE... I BET ON **HOTSHOTS.** I DIDN'T EXPECT THE **PAIN.**
WE'RE **SO ALONE** OUT HERE.
PEOPLE **NEED** THE PATRON, NO **MATTER** WHAT.
WE **HAVE** TO BE HIM. WE CAN'T SHOW WE'RE **HURTING.**
SO WE JUST...**WHAT?** SMILE FOR THE CROWDS?

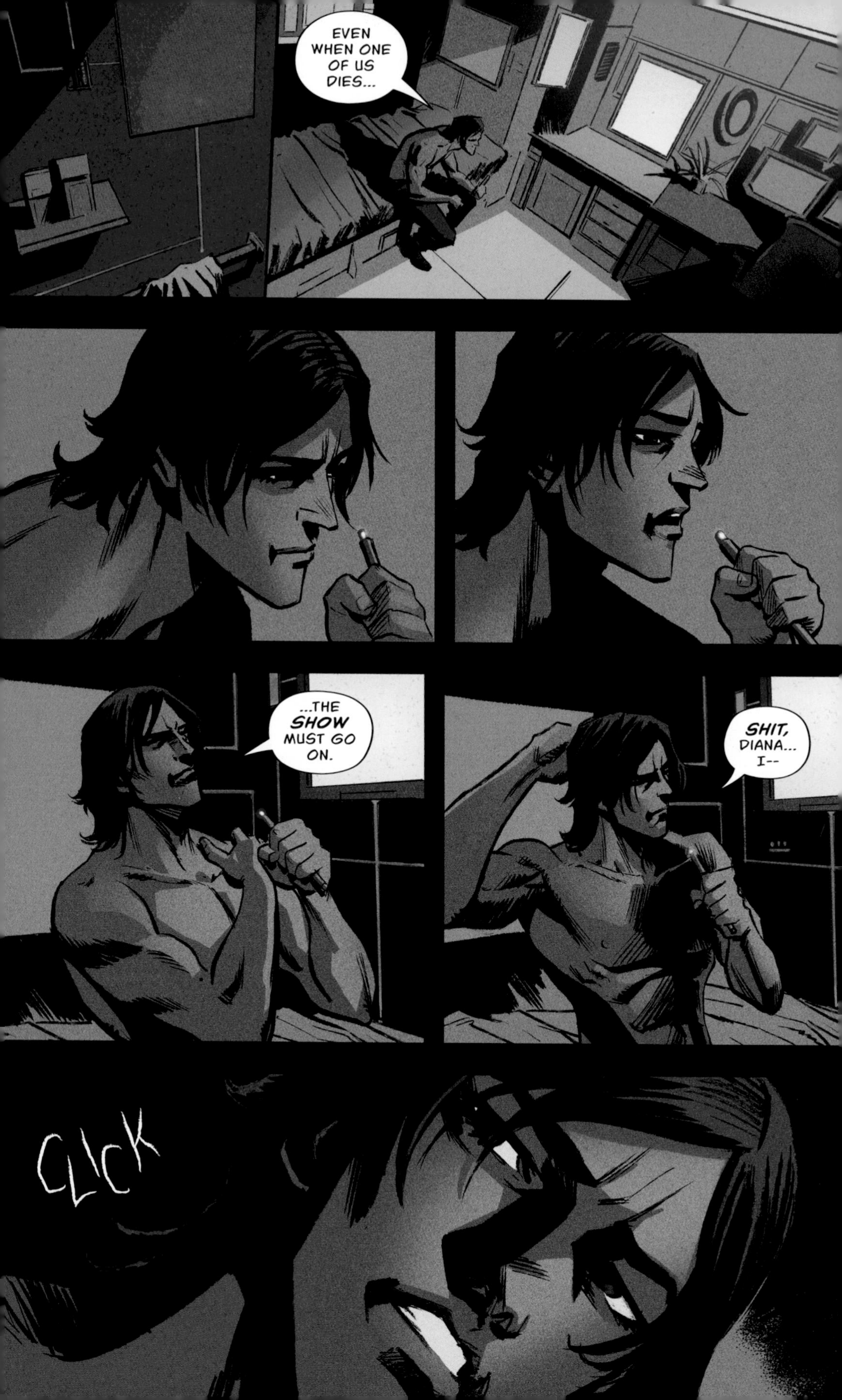
EVEN WHEN ONE OF US DIES...
...THE SHOW MUST GO ON.
SHIT, DIANA... I--
CLICK

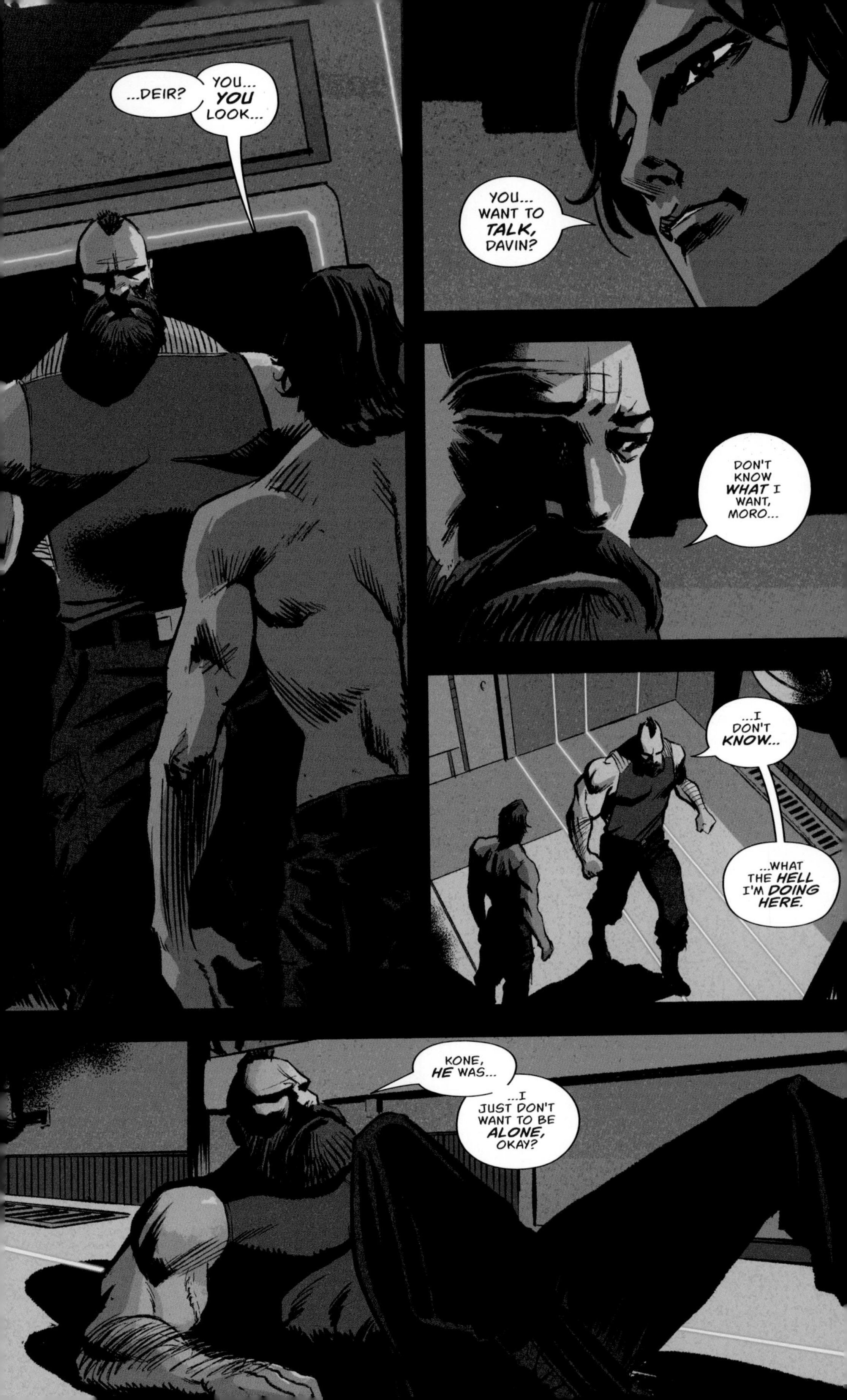
...DEIR?
YOU... YOU LOOK...
YOU... WANT TO TALK, DAVIN?
DON'T KNOW WHAT I WANT, MORO...
...I DON'T KNOW...
...WHAT THE HELL I'M DOING HERE.
KONE, HE WAS...
...I JUST DON'T WANT TO BE ALONE, OKAY?

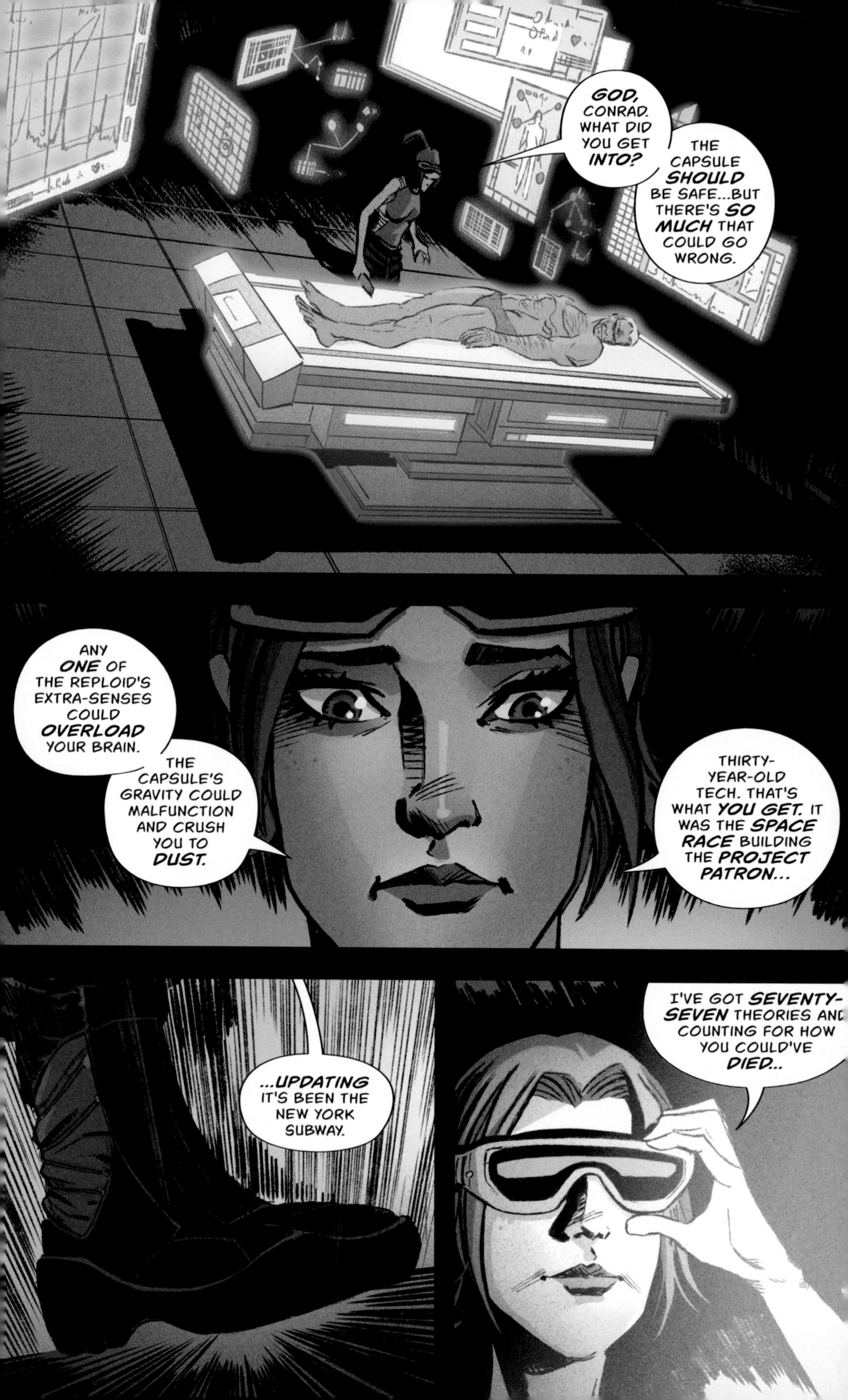
GOD, CONRAD. WHAT DID YOU GET INTO?
THE CAPSULE SHOULD BE SAFE...BUT THERE'S SO MUCH THAT COULD GO WRONG.
ANY ONE OF THE REPLOID'S EXTRA-SENSES COULD OVERLOAD YOUR BRAIN.
THE CAPSULE'S GRAVITY COULD MALFUNCTION AND CRUSH YOU TO DUST.
THIRTY-YEAR-OLD TECH. THAT'S WHAT YOU GET. IT WAS THE SPACE RACE BUILDING THE PROJECT PATRON...
...UPDATING IT'S BEEN THE NEW YORK SUBWAY.
I'VE GOT SEVENTY-SEVEN THEORIES AND COUNTING FOR HOW YOU COULD'VE DIED...

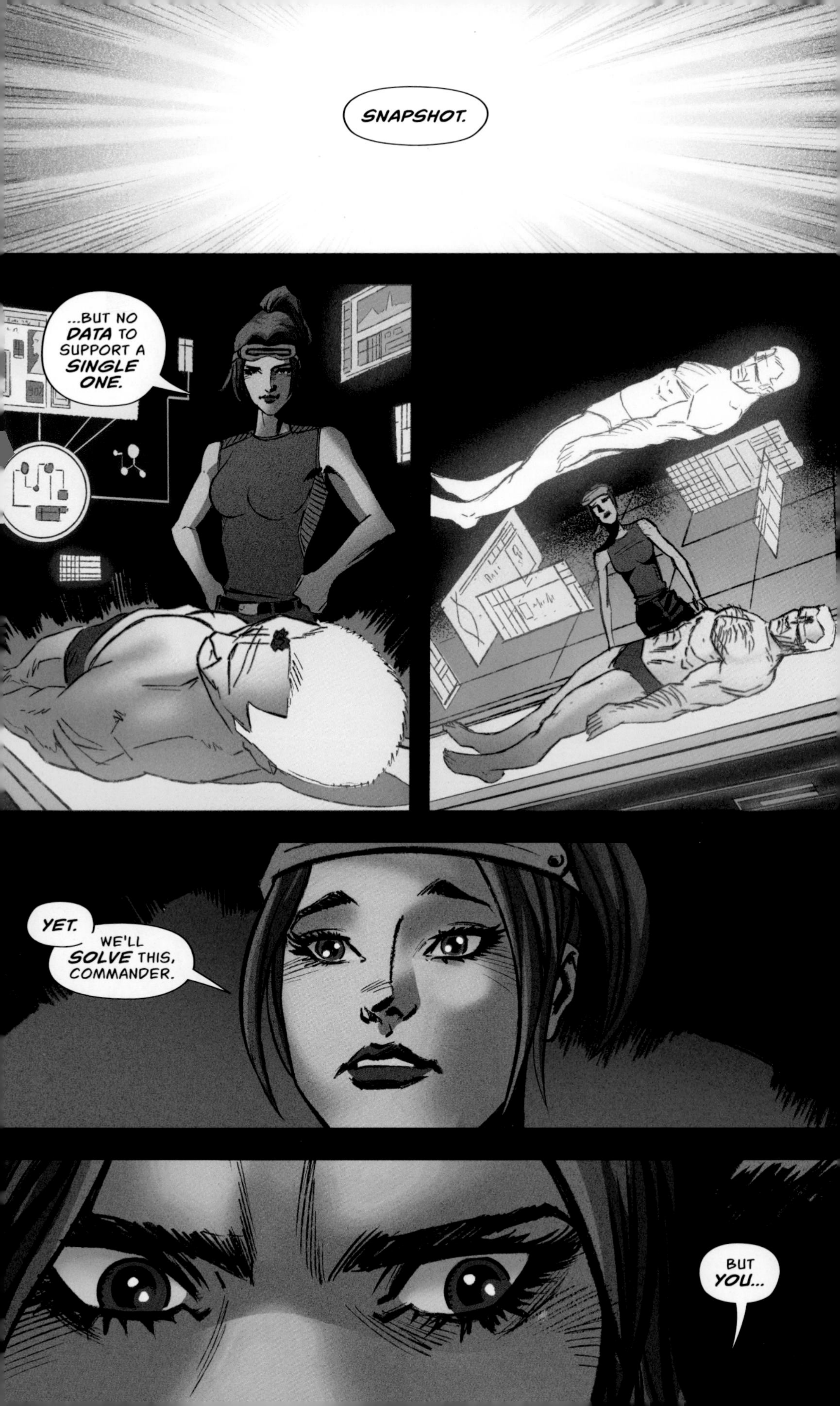
SNAPSHOT.
...BUT NO DATA TO SUPPORT A SINGLE ONE.
YET.
WE'LL SOLVE THIS, COMMANDER.
BUT YOU...

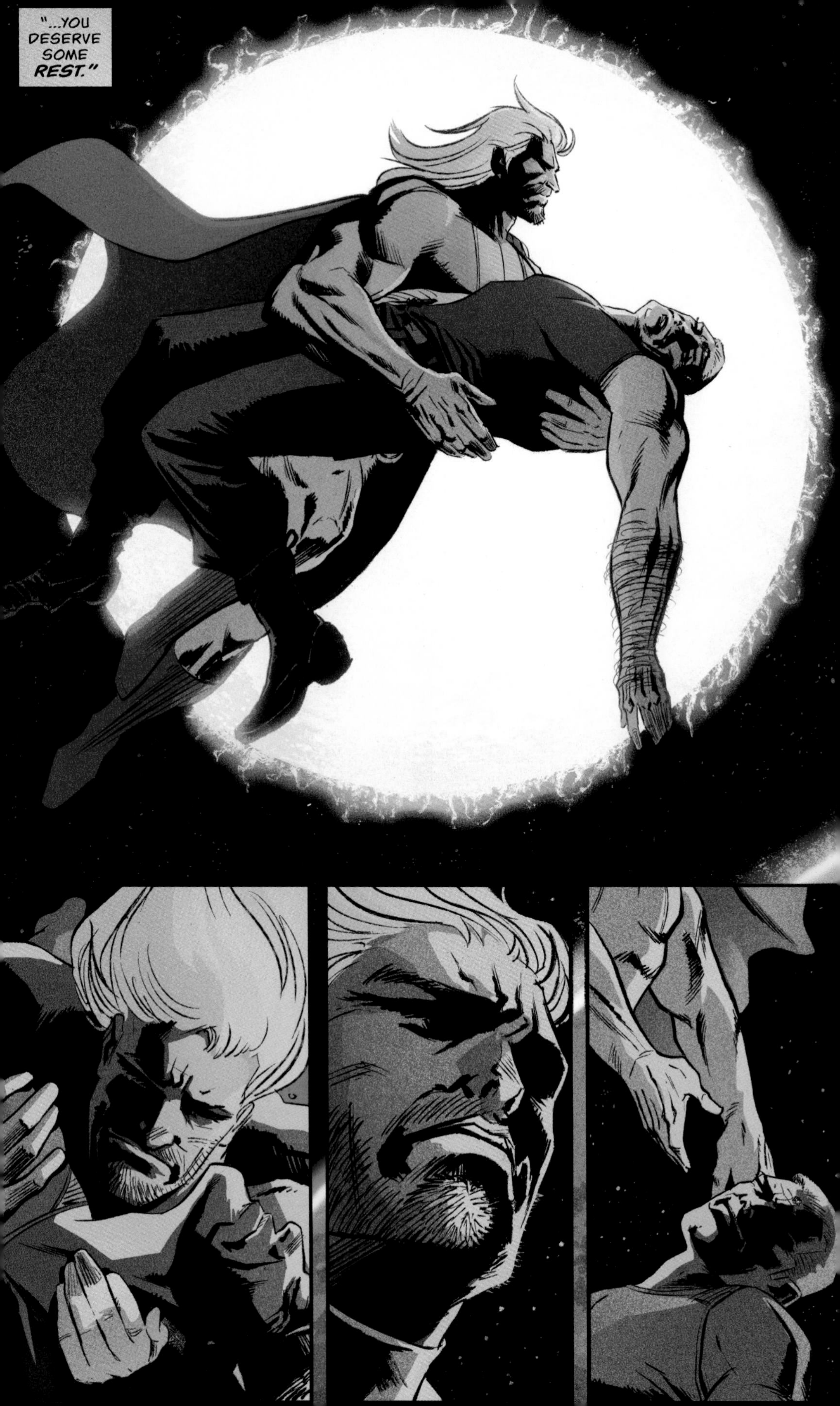
"...YOU DESERVE SOME REST."

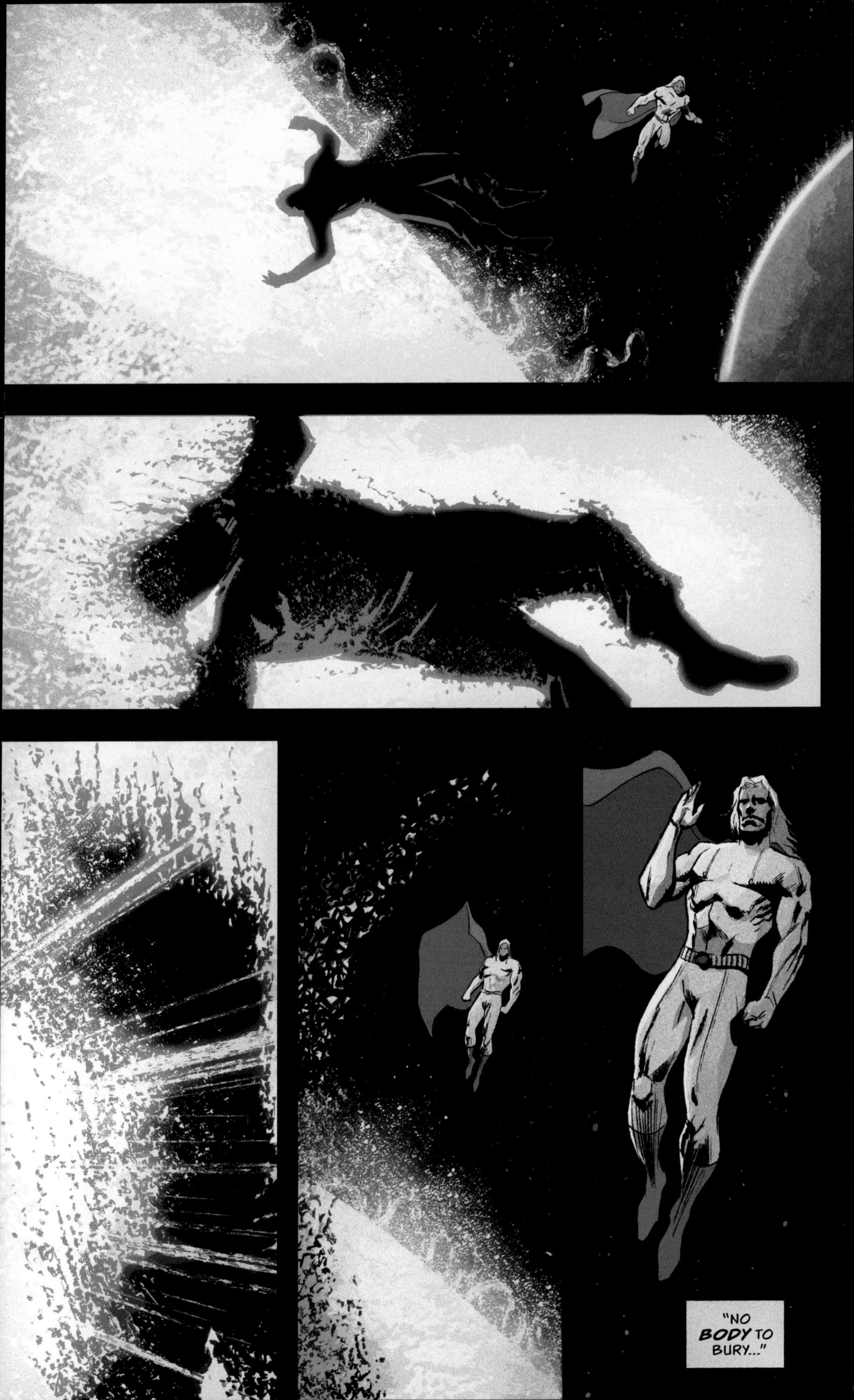
"NO BODY TO BURY..."

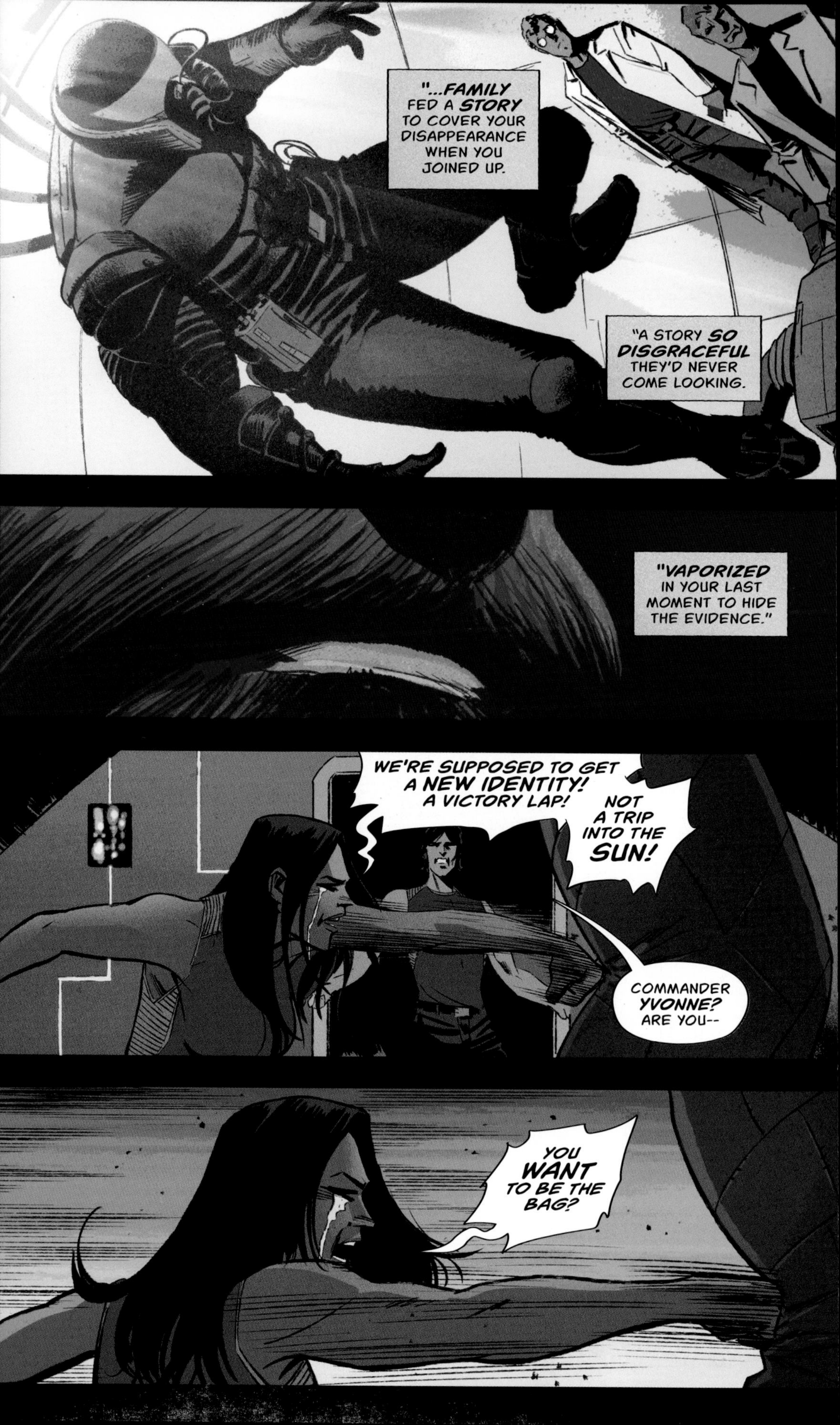
"...FAMILY FED A STORY TO COVER YOUR DISAPPEARANCE WHEN YOU JOINED UP.
"A STORY SO DISGRACEFUL THEY'D NEVER COME LOOKING.
"VAPORIZED IN YOUR LAST MOMENT TO HIDE THE EVIDENCE."
WE'RE SUPPOSED TO GET A NEW IDENTITY! A VICTORY LAP!
NOT A TRIP INTO THE SUN!
COMMANDER YVONNE? ARE YOU--
YOU WANT TO BE THE BAG?

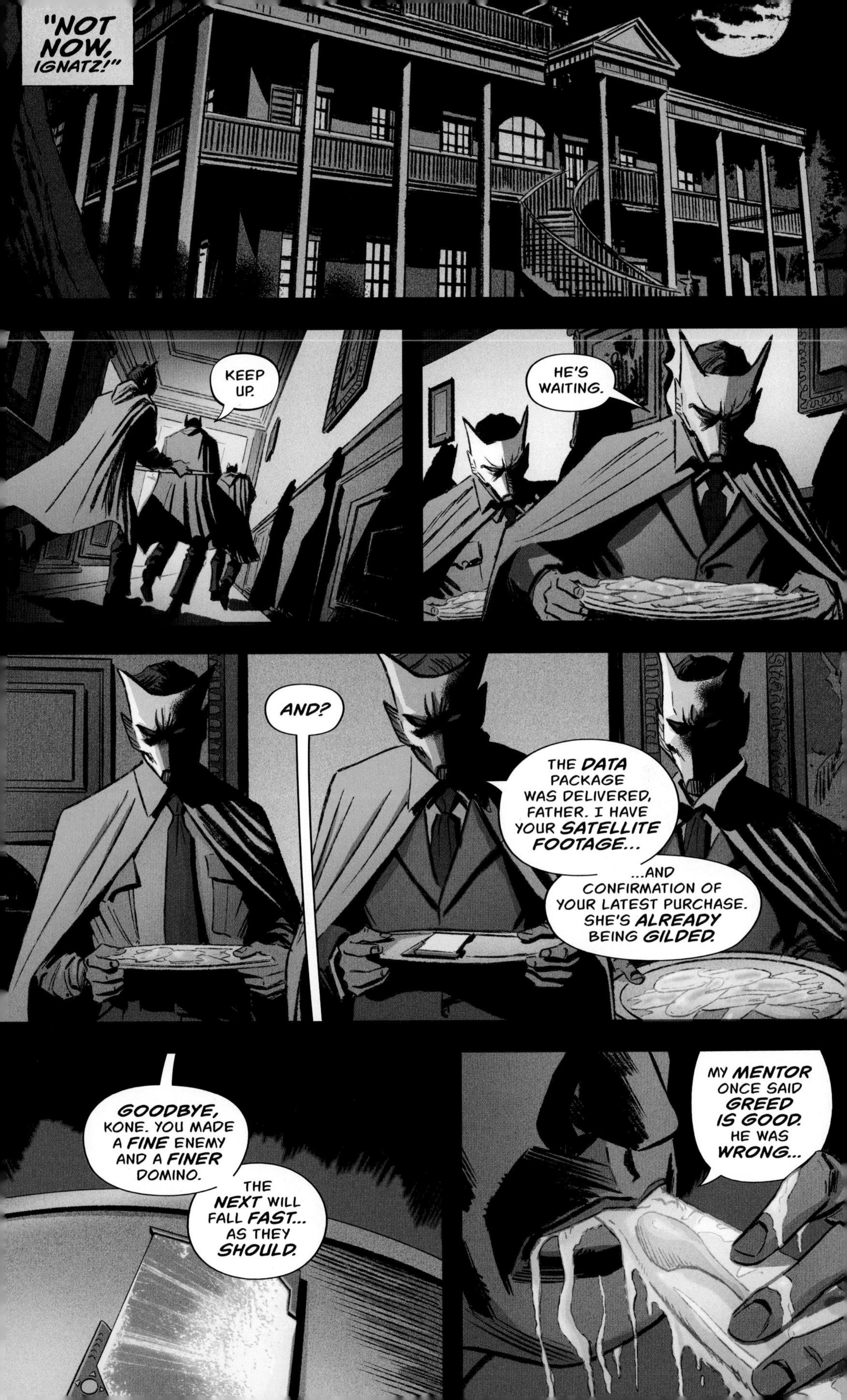
"NOT NOW, IGNATZ!"
KEEP UP.
HE'S WAITING.
AND?
THE DATA PACKAGE WAS DELIVERED, FATHER. I HAVE YOUR SATELLITE FOOTAGE...
...AND CONFIRMATION OF YOUR LATEST PURCHASE. SHE'S ALREADY BEING GILDED.
GOODBYE, KONE. YOU MADE A FINE ENEMY AND A FINER DOMINO.
THE NEXT WILL FALL FAST... AS THEY SHOULD.
MY MENTOR ONCE SAID GREED IS GOOD. HE WAS WRONG...

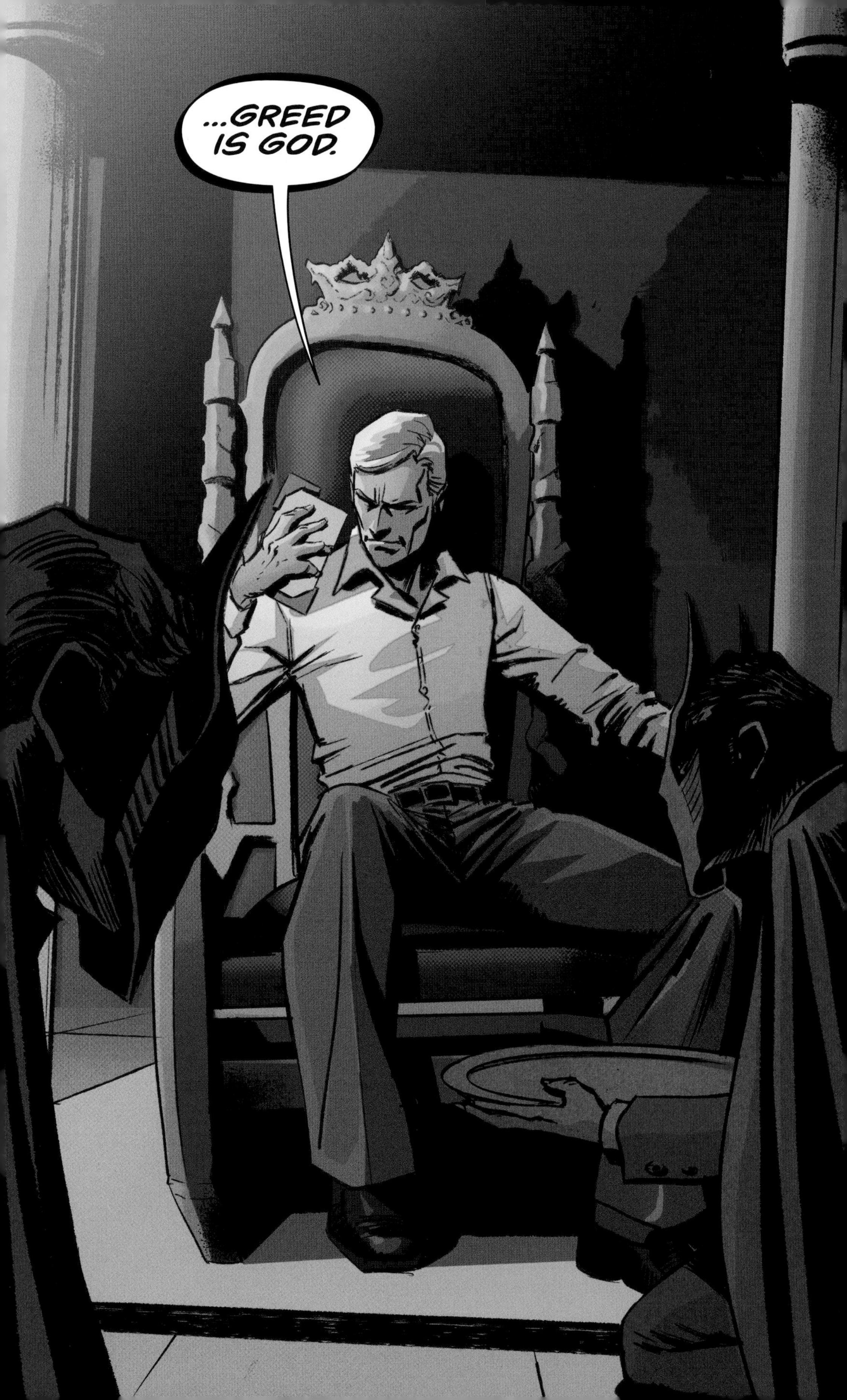
...GREED IS GOD.

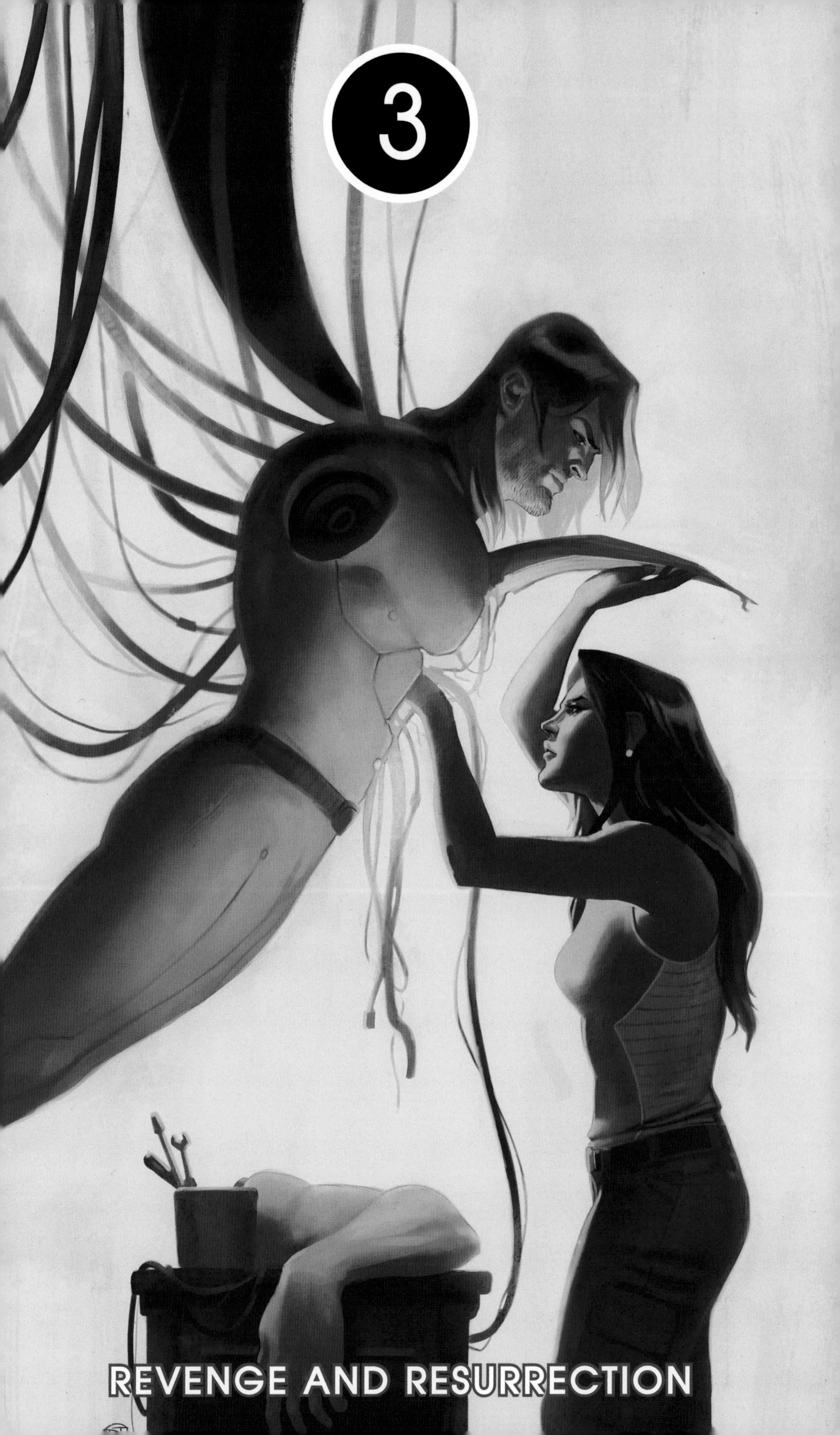
3
REVENGE AND RESURRECTION

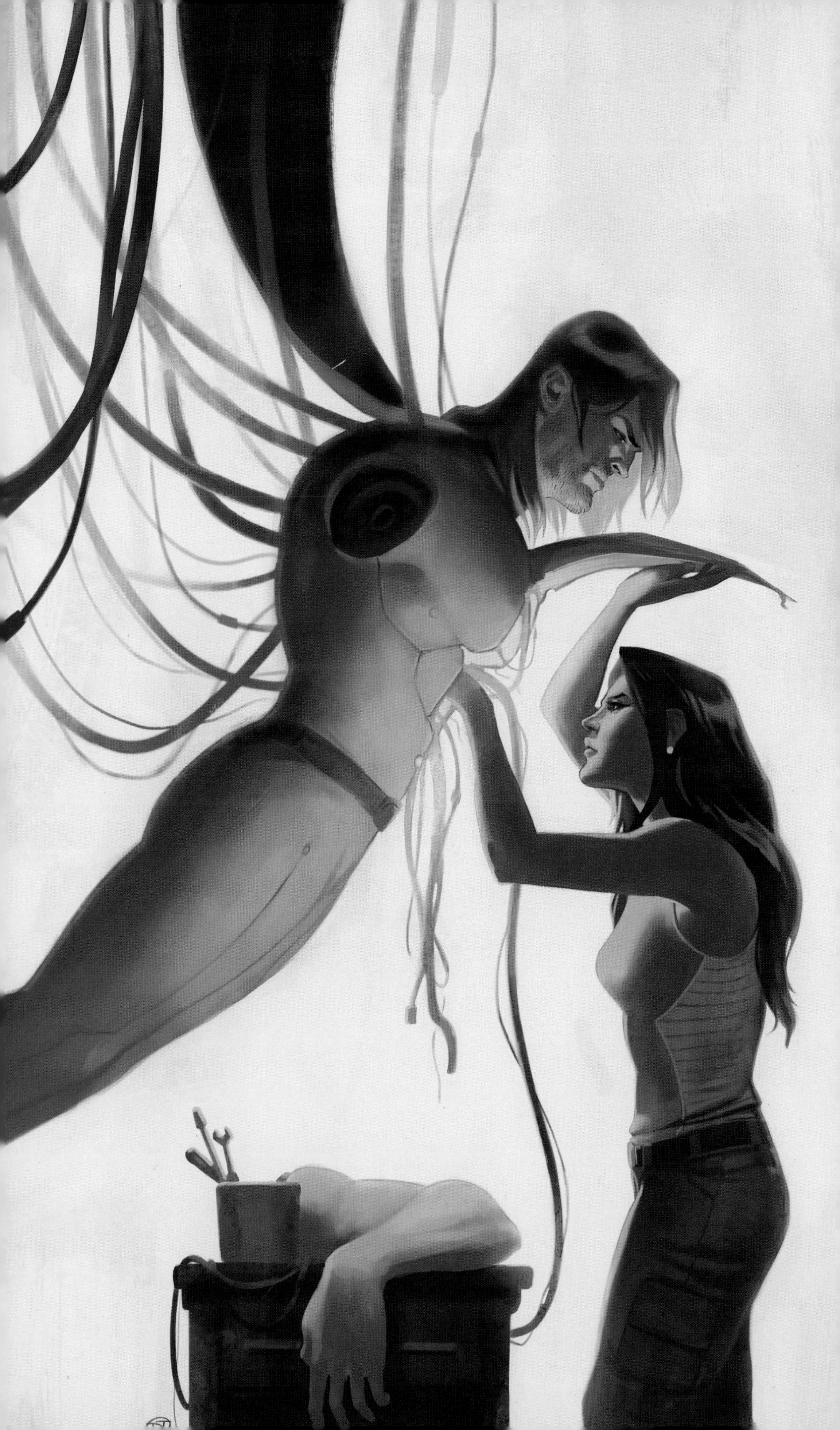

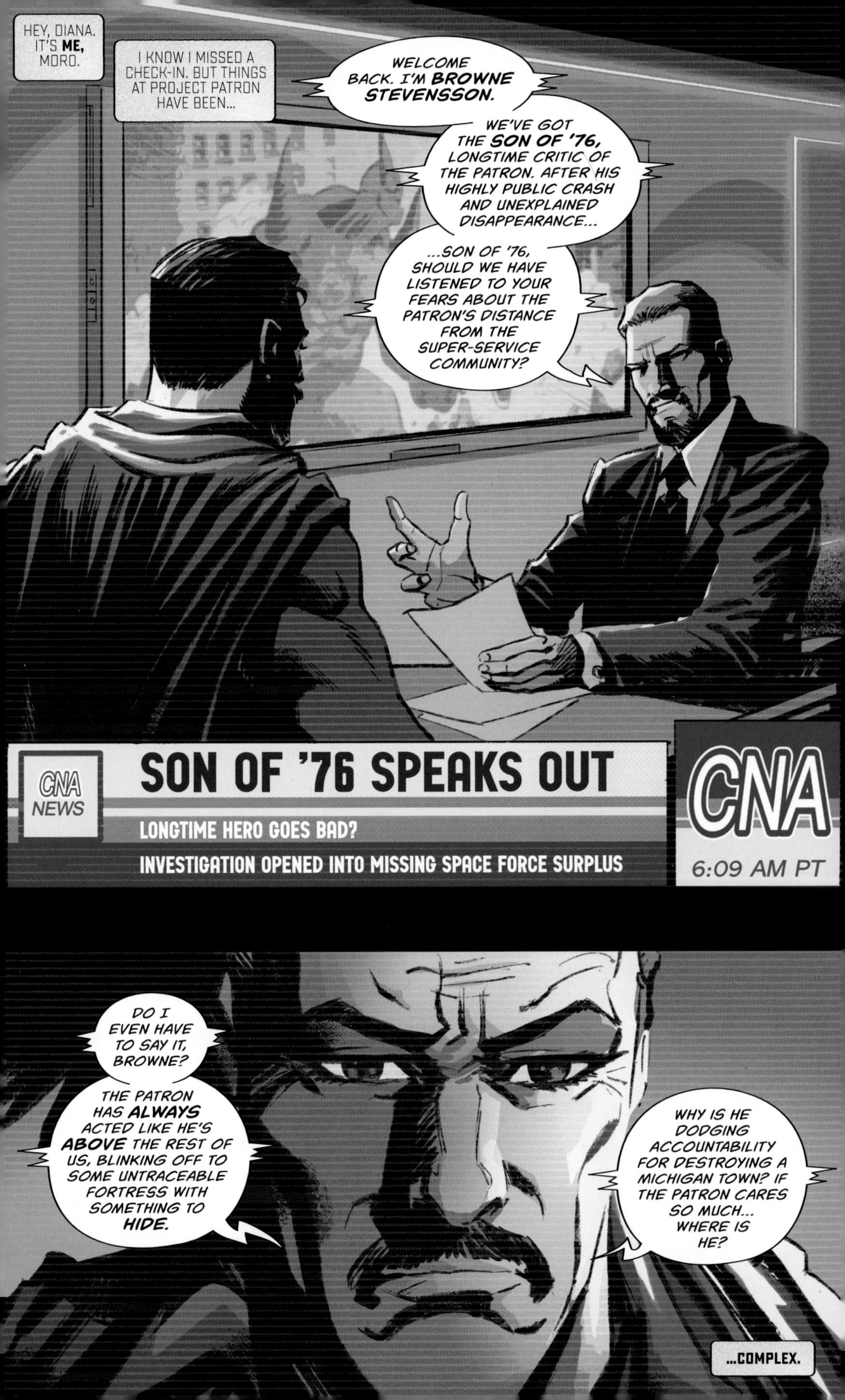
HEY, DIANA. IT'S **ME,** MORO.
I KNOW I MISSED A CHECK-IN. BUT THINGS AT PROJECT PATRON HAVE BEEN...
WELCOME BACK. I'M **BROWNE STEVENSSON.**
WE'VE GOT THE **SON OF '76,** LONGTIME CRITIC OF THE PATRON. AFTER HIS HIGHLY PUBLIC CRASH AND UNEXPLAINED DISAPPEARANCE...
...SON OF '76, SHOULD WE HAVE LISTENED TO YOUR FEARS ABOUT THE PATRON'S DISTANCE FROM THE SUPER-SERVICE COMMUNITY?
CNA NEWS
SON OF '76 SPEAKS OUT
LONGTIME HERO GOES BAD?
INVESTIGATION OPENED INTO MISSING SPACE FORCE SURPLUS
CNA
6:09 AM PT
DO I EVEN HAVE TO SAY IT, BROWNE?
THE PATRON HAS **ALWAYS** ACTED LIKE HE'S **ABOVE** THE REST OF US, BLINKING OFF TO SOME UNTRACEABLE FORTRESS WITH SOMETHING TO **HIDE.**
WHY IS HE DODGING ACCOUNTABILITY FOR DESTROYING A MICHIGAN TOWN? IF THE PATRON CARES SO MUCH... WHERE IS HE?
...COMPLEX.

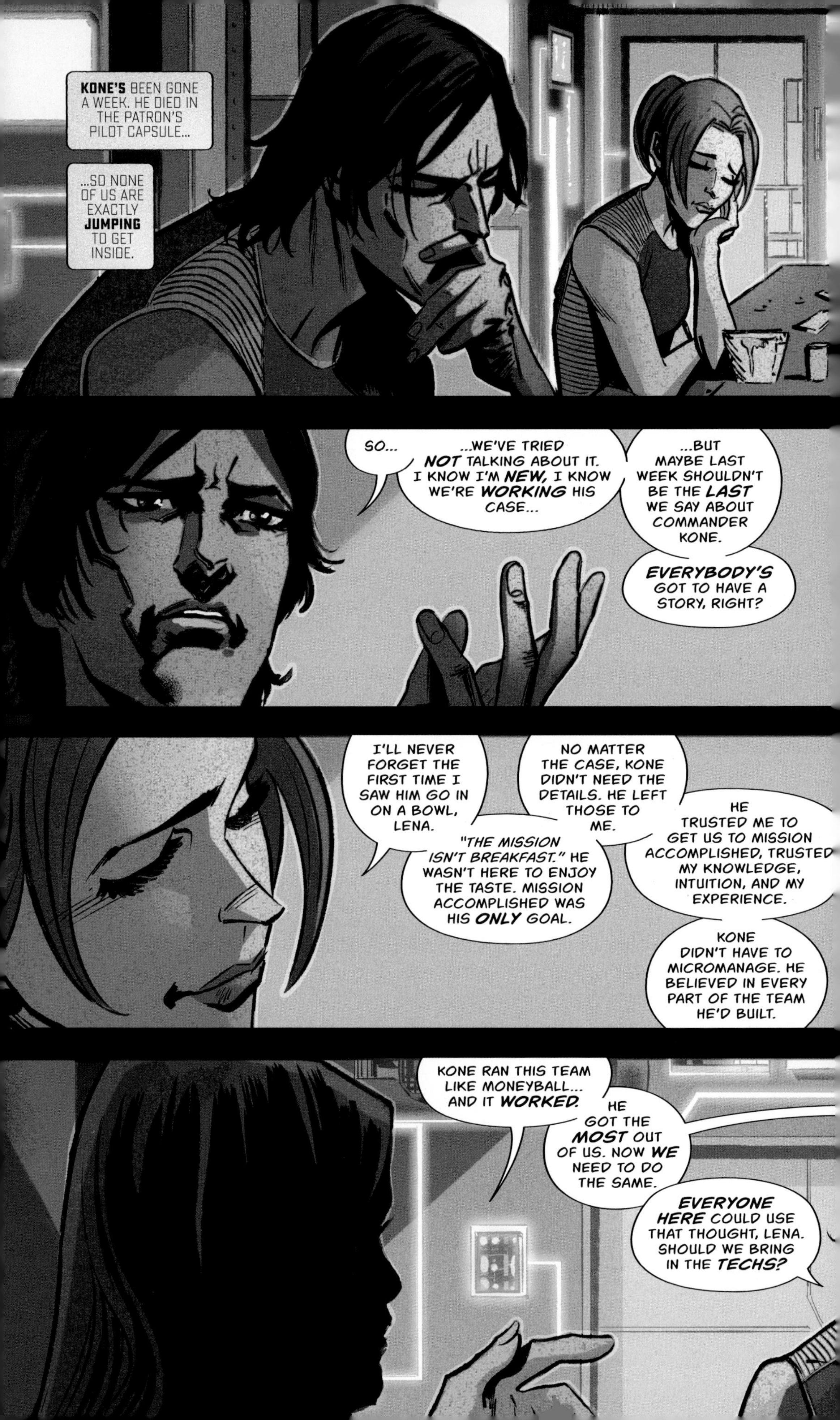
KONE'S BEEN GONE A WEEK. HE DIED IN THE PATRON'S PILOT CAPSULE...
...SO NONE OF US ARE EXACTLY JUMPING TO GET INSIDE.
SO...
...WE'VE TRIED NOT TALKING ABOUT IT. I KNOW I'M NEW, I KNOW WE'RE WORKING HIS CASE...
...BUT MAYBE LAST WEEK SHOULDN'T BE THE LAST WE SAY ABOUT COMMANDER KONE.
EVERYBODY'S GOT TO HAVE A STORY, RIGHT?
I'LL NEVER FORGET THE FIRST TIME I SAW HIM GO IN ON A BOWL, LENA.
"THE MISSION ISN'T BREAKFAST." HE WASN'T HERE TO ENJOY THE TASTE. MISSION ACCOMPLISHED WAS HIS ONLY GOAL.
NO MATTER THE CASE, KONE DIDN'T NEED THE DETAILS. HE LEFT THOSE TO ME.
HE TRUSTED ME TO GET US TO MISSION ACCOMPLISHED, TRUSTED MY KNOWLEDGE, INTUITION, AND MY EXPERIENCE.
KONE DIDN'T HAVE TO MICROMANAGE. HE BELIEVED IN EVERY PART OF THE TEAM HE'D BUILT.
KONE RAN THIS TEAM LIKE MONEYBALL... AND IT WORKED.
HE GOT THE MOST OUT OF US. NOW WE NEED TO DO THE SAME.
EVERYONE HERE COULD USE THAT THOUGHT, LENA. SHOULD WE BRING IN THE TECHS?

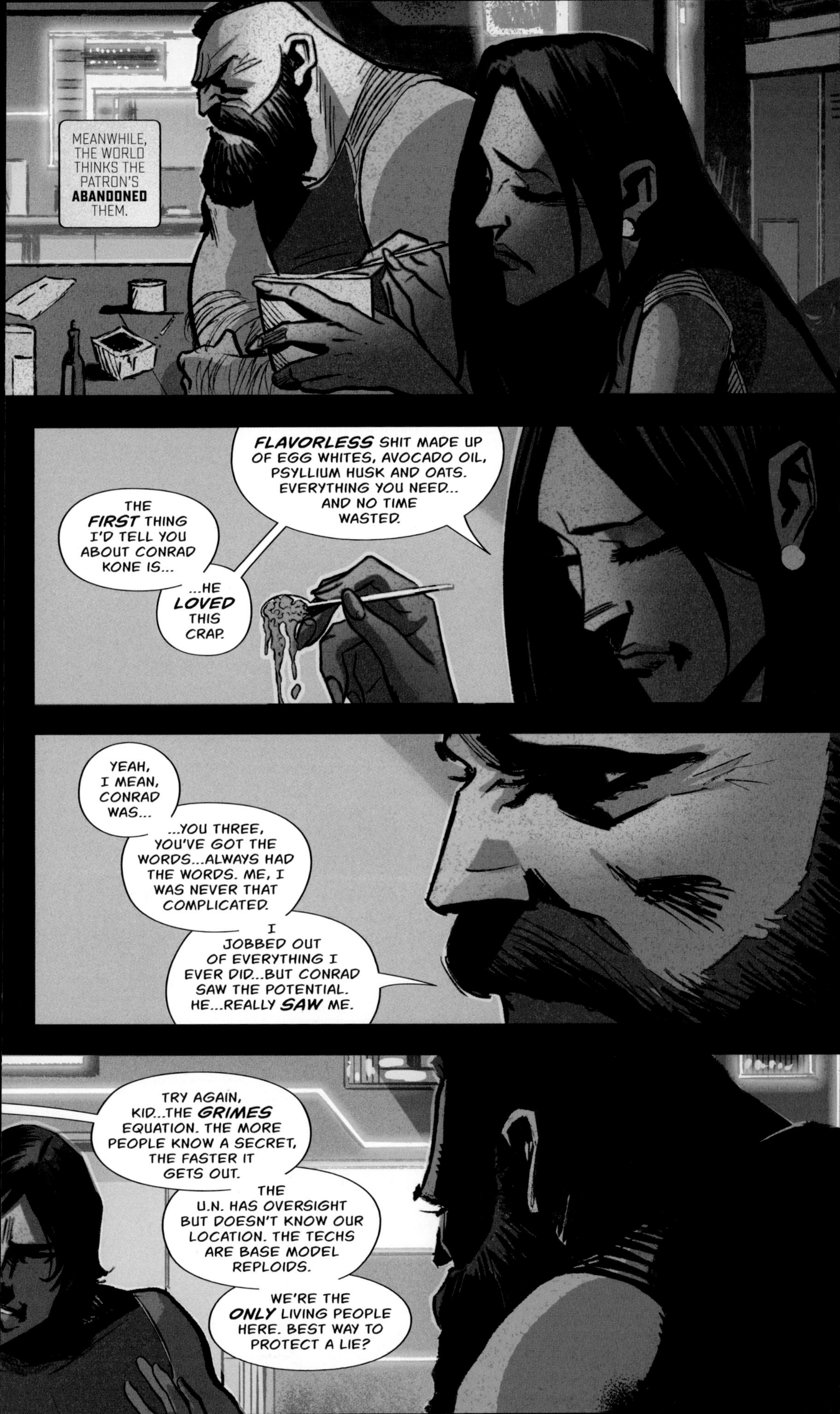

MEANWHILE, THE WORLD THINKS THE PATRON'S **ABANDONED** THEM.
THE *FIRST* THING I'D TELL YOU ABOUT CONRAD KONE IS...
...HE *LOVED* THIS CRAP.
FLAVORLESS SHIT MADE UP OF EGG WHITES, AVOCADO OIL, PSYLLIUM HUSK AND OATS. EVERYTHING YOU NEED... AND NO TIME WASTED.
YEAH, I MEAN, CONRAD WAS...
...YOU THREE, YOU'VE GOT THE WORDS...ALWAYS HAD THE WORDS. ME, I WAS NEVER THAT COMPLICATED.
I JOBBED OUT OF EVERYTHING I EVER DID...BUT CONRAD SAW THE POTENTIAL. HE...REALLY *SAW* ME.
TRY AGAIN, KID...THE *GRIMES* EQUATION. THE MORE PEOPLE KNOW A SECRET, THE FASTER IT GETS OUT.
THE U.N. HAS OVERSIGHT BUT DOESN'T KNOW OUR LOCATION. THE TECHS ARE BASE MODEL REPLOIDS.
WE'RE THE *ONLY* LIVING PEOPLE HERE. BEST WAY TO PROTECT A LIE?

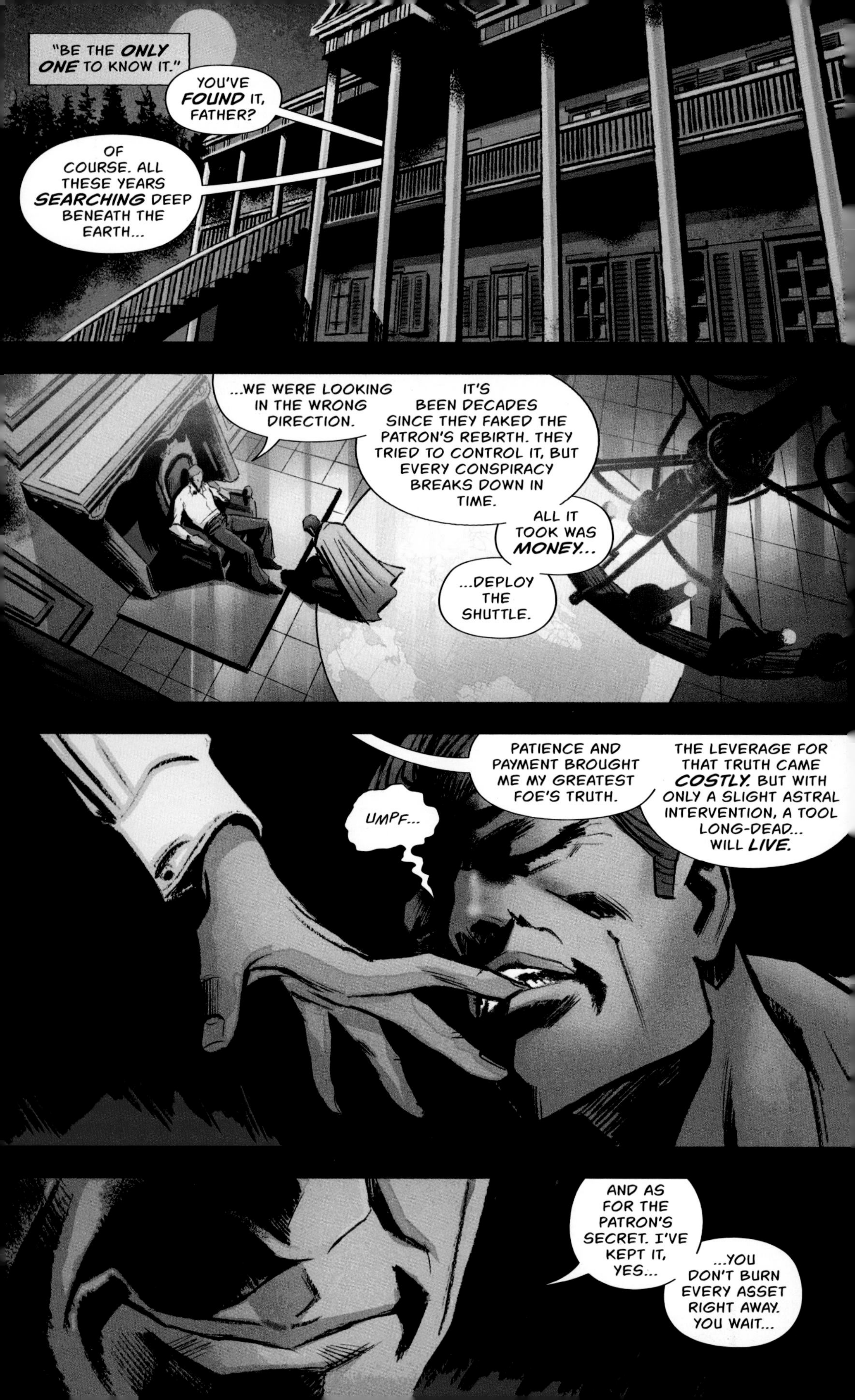
"BE THE ONLY ONE TO KNOW IT."
YOU'VE FOUND IT, FATHER?
OF COURSE. ALL THESE YEARS SEARCHING DEEP BENEATH THE EARTH...
...WE WERE LOOKING IN THE WRONG DIRECTION.
IT'S BEEN DECADES SINCE THEY FAKED THE PATRON'S REBIRTH. THEY TRIED TO CONTROL IT, BUT EVERY CONSPIRACY BREAKS DOWN IN TIME.
ALL IT TOOK WAS MONEY...
...DEPLOY THE SHUTTLE.
PATIENCE AND PAYMENT BROUGHT ME MY GREATEST FOE'S TRUTH.
THE LEVERAGE FOR THAT TRUTH CAME COSTLY. BUT WITH ONLY A SLIGHT ASTRAL INTERVENTION, A TOOL LONG-DEAD... WILL LIVE.
UMPF...
AND AS FOR THE PATRON'S SECRET. I'VE KEPT IT, YES...
...YOU DON'T BURN EVERY ASSET RIGHT AWAY. YOU WAIT...

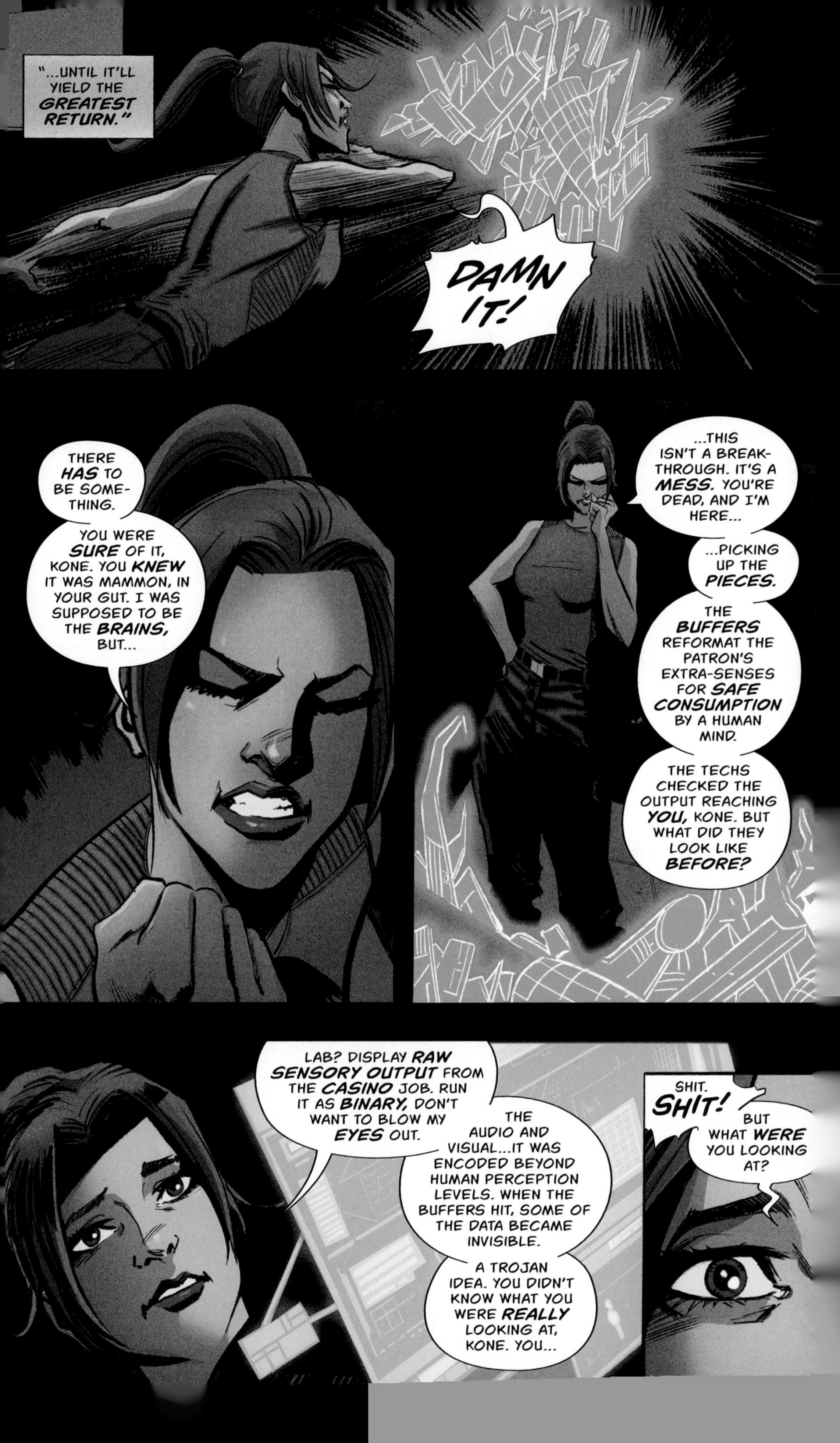
"...UNTIL IT'LL YIELD THE GREATEST RETURN."
DAMN IT!
THERE HAS TO BE SOMETHING.
YOU WERE SURE OF IT, KONE. YOU KNEW IT WAS MAMMON, IN YOUR GUT. I WAS SUPPOSED TO BE THE BRAINS, BUT...
...THIS ISN'T A BREAKTHROUGH. IT'S A MESS. YOU'RE DEAD, AND I'M HERE...
...PICKING UP THE PIECES.
THE BUFFERS REFORMAT THE PATRON'S EXTRA-SENSES FOR SAFE CONSUMPTION BY A HUMAN MIND.
THE TECHS CHECKED THE OUTPUT REACHING YOU, KONE. BUT WHAT DID THEY LOOK LIKE BEFORE?
LAB? DISPLAY RAW SENSORY OUTPUT FROM THE CASINO JOB. RUN IT AS BINARY, DON'T WANT TO BLOW MY EYES OUT.
THE AUDIO AND VISUAL...IT WAS ENCODED BEYOND HUMAN PERCEPTION LEVELS. WHEN THE BUFFERS HIT, SOME OF THE DATA BECAME INVISIBLE.
A TROJAN IDEA. YOU DIDN'T KNOW WHAT YOU WERE REALLY LOOKING AT, KONE. YOU...
SHIT. SHIT!
BUT WHAT WERE YOU LOOKING AT?

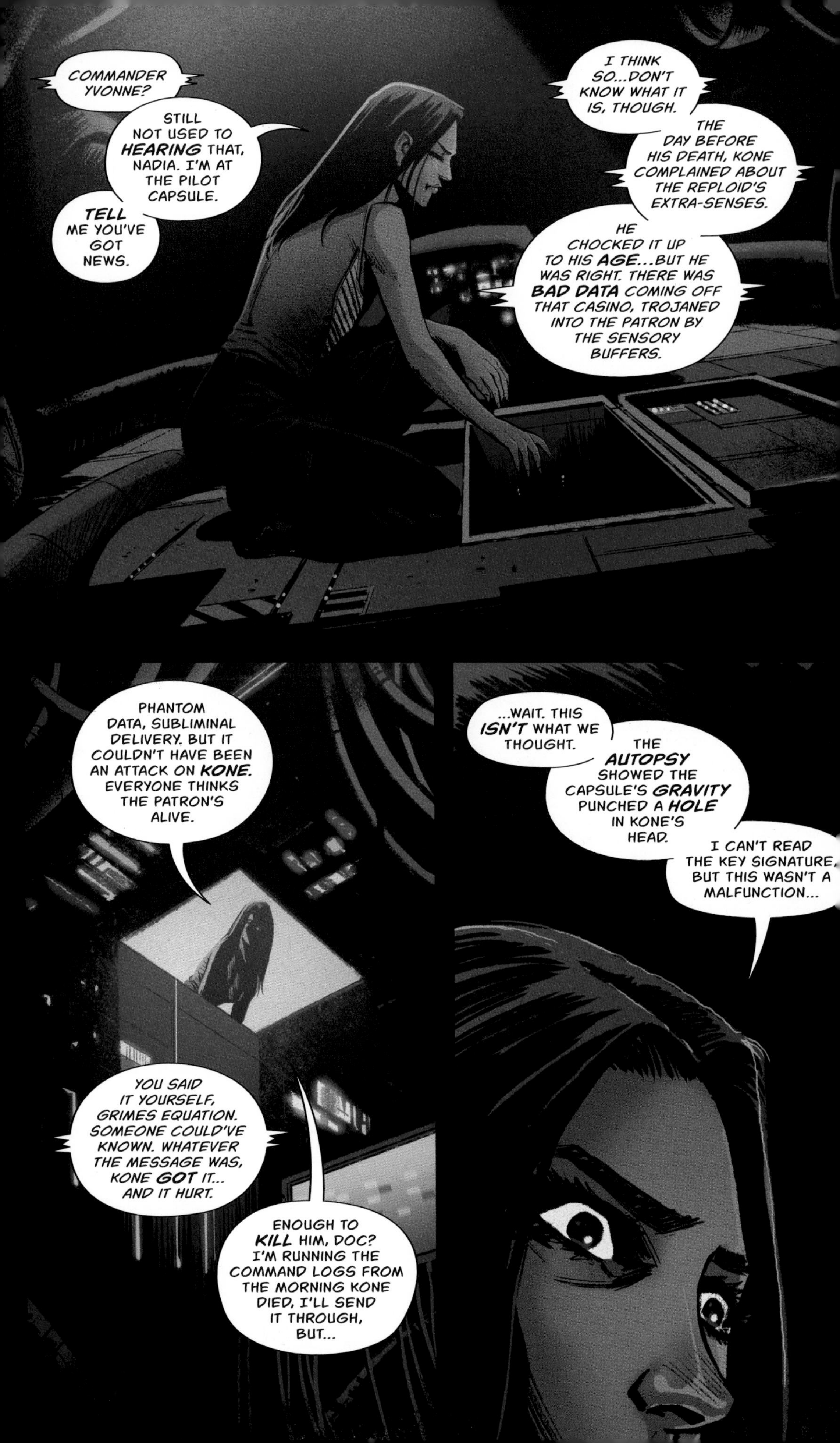
COMMANDER YVONNE?
STILL NOT USED TO HEARING THAT, NADIA. I'M AT THE PILOT CAPSULE.
TELL ME YOU'VE GOT NEWS.
I THINK SO...DON'T KNOW WHAT IT IS, THOUGH.
THE DAY BEFORE HIS DEATH, KONE COMPLAINED ABOUT THE REPLOID'S EXTRA-SENSES.
HE CHOCKED IT UP TO HIS AGE...BUT HE WAS RIGHT. THERE WAS BAD DATA COMING OFF THAT CASINO, TROJANED INTO THE PATRON BY THE SENSORY BUFFERS.
PHANTOM DATA, SUBLIMINAL DELIVERY. BUT IT COULDN'T HAVE BEEN AN ATTACK ON KONE. EVERYONE THINKS THE PATRON'S ALIVE.
YOU SAID IT YOURSELF, GRIMES EQUATION. SOMEONE COULD'VE KNOWN. WHATEVER THE MESSAGE WAS, KONE GOT IT... AND IT HURT.
ENOUGH TO KILL HIM, DOC? I'M RUNNING THE COMMAND LOGS FROM THE MORNING KONE DIED, I'LL SEND IT THROUGH, BUT...
...WAIT. THIS ISN'T WHAT WE THOUGHT.
THE AUTOPSY SHOWED THE CAPSULE'S GRAVITY PUNCHED A HOLE IN KONE'S HEAD.
I CAN'T READ THE KEY SIGNATURE, BUT THIS WASN'T A MALFUNCTION...

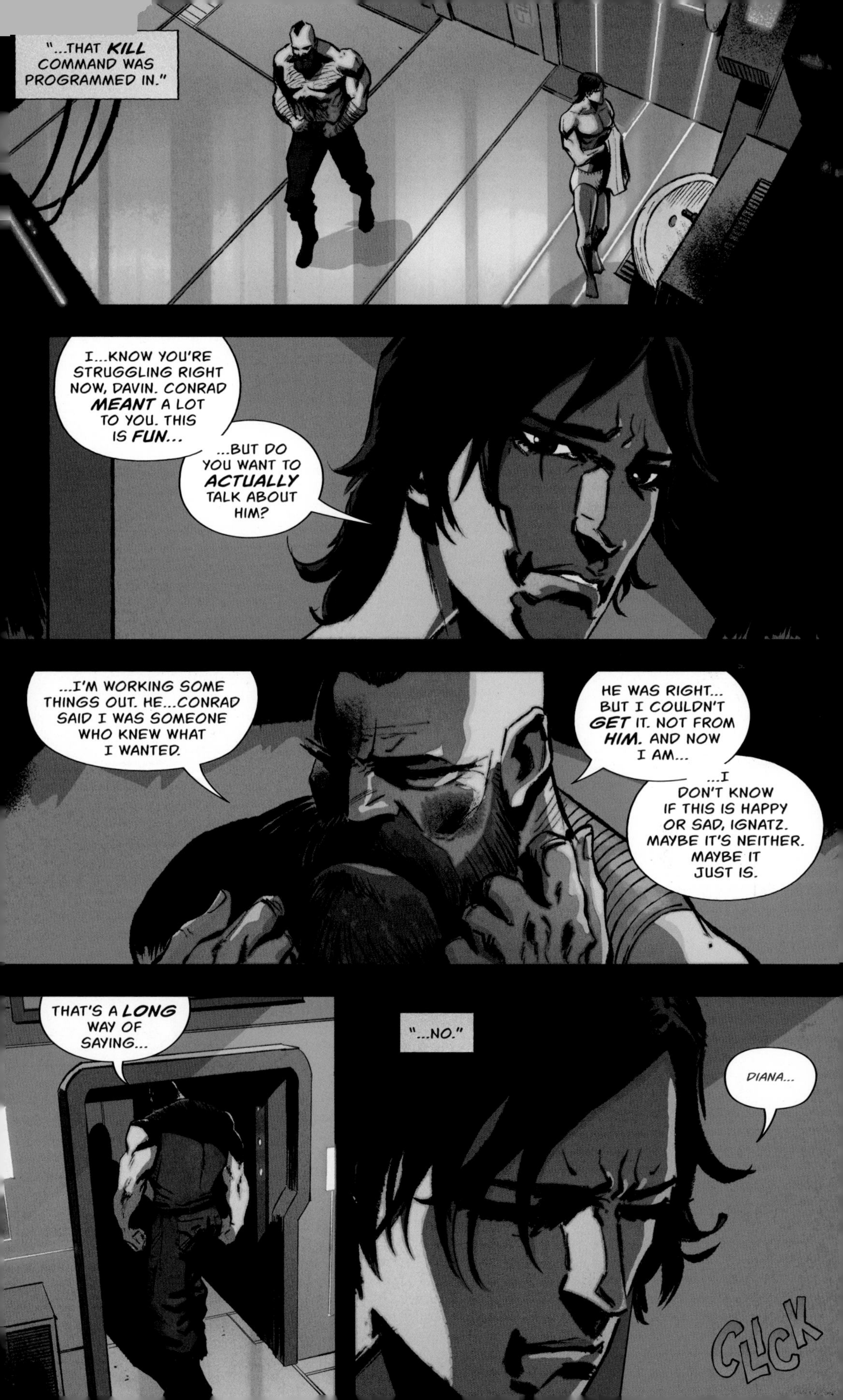
"...THAT KILL COMMAND WAS PROGRAMMED IN."
I...KNOW YOU'RE STRUGGLING RIGHT NOW, DAVIN. CONRAD MEANT A LOT TO YOU. THIS IS FUN...
...BUT DO YOU WANT TO ACTUALLY TALK ABOUT HIM?
...I'M WORKING SOME THINGS OUT. HE...CONRAD SAID I WAS SOMEONE WHO KNEW WHAT I WANTED.
HE WAS RIGHT... BUT I COULDN'T GET IT. NOT FROM HIM. AND NOW I AM...
...I DON'T KNOW IF THIS IS HAPPY OR SAD, IGNATZ. MAYBE IT'S NEITHER. MAYBE IT JUST IS.
THAT'S A LONG WAY OF SAYING...
"...NO."
DIANA...
CLICK

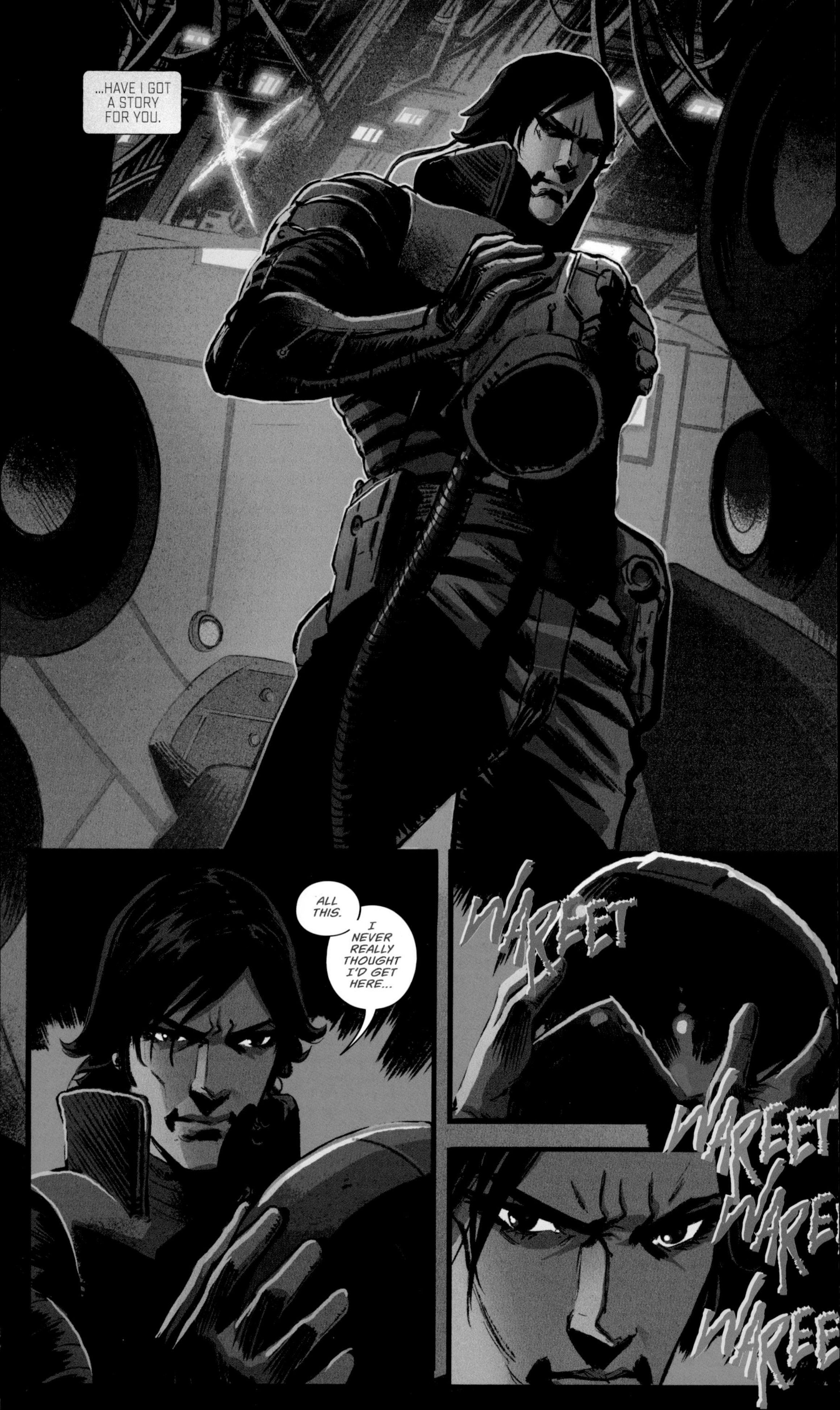

...HAVE I GOT A STORY FOR YOU.
ALL THIS.
I NEVER REALLY THOUGHT I'D GET HERE...
WAREET
WAREET

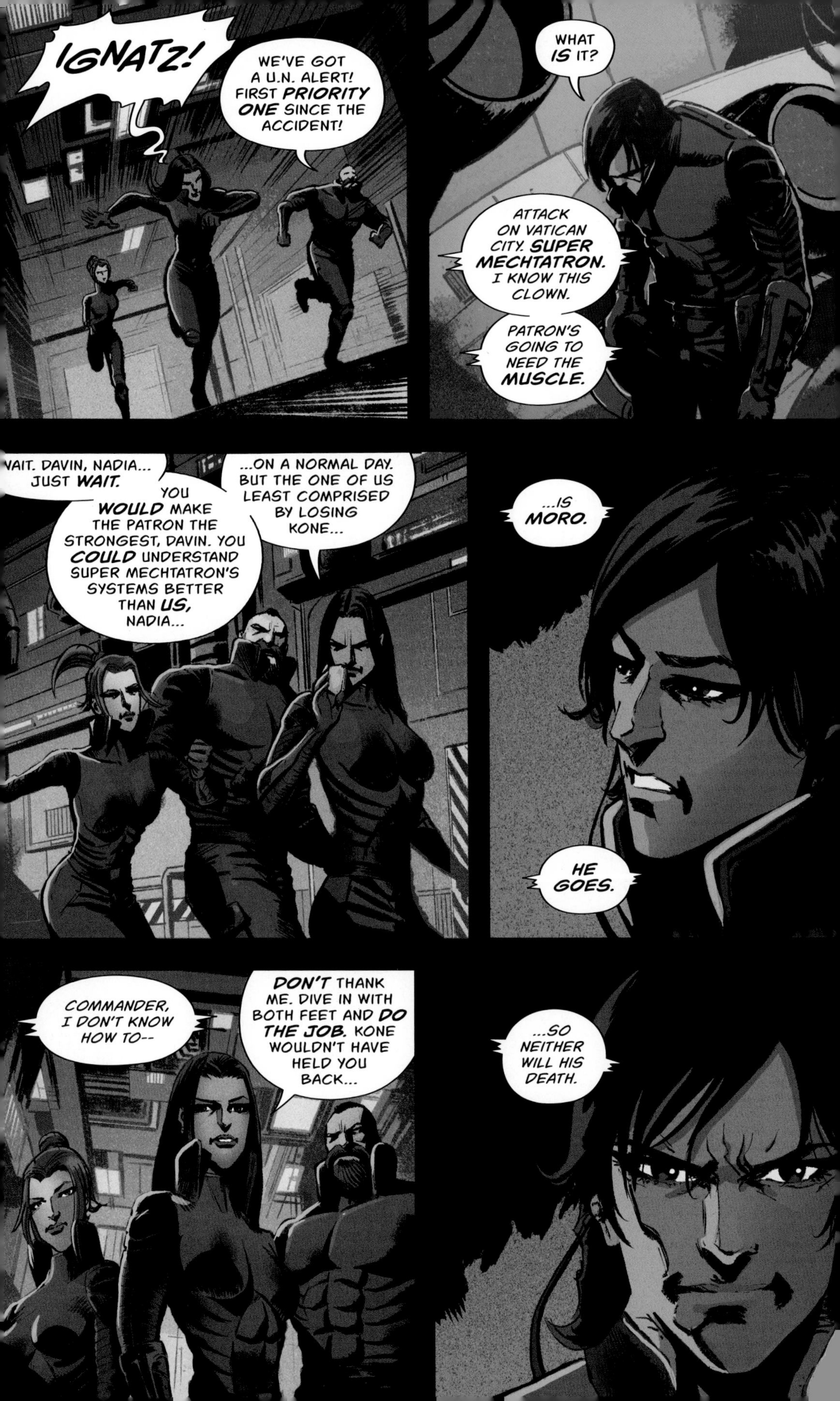
IGNATZ!
WE'VE GOT A U.N. ALERT! FIRST PRIORITY ONE SINCE THE ACCIDENT!
WHAT IS IT?
ATTACK ON VATICAN CITY. SUPER MECHTATRON. I KNOW THIS CLOWN.
PATRON'S GOING TO NEED THE MUSCLE.
VAIT. DAVIN, NADIA... JUST WAIT.
YOU WOULD MAKE THE PATRON THE STRONGEST, DAVIN. YOU COULD UNDERSTAND SUPER MECHTATRON'S SYSTEMS BETTER THAN US, NADIA...
...ON A NORMAL DAY. BUT THE ONE OF US LEAST COMPRISED BY LOSING KONE...
...IS MORO.
HE GOES.
COMMANDER, I DON'T KNOW HOW TO--
DON'T THANK ME. DIVE IN WITH BOTH FEET AND DO THE JOB. KONE WOULDN'T HAVE HELD YOU BACK...
...SO NEITHER WILL HIS DEATH.

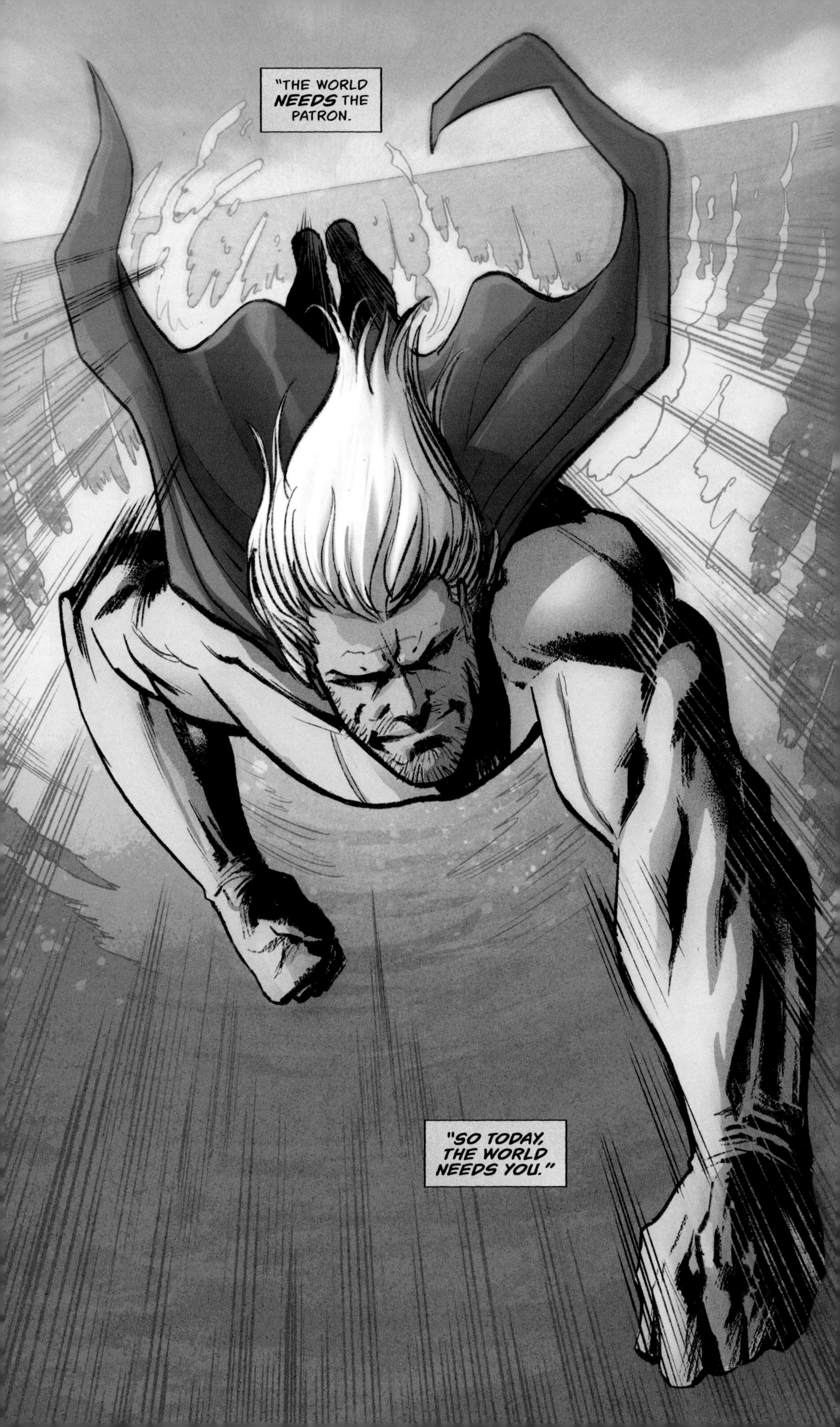
"THE WORLD NEEDS THE PATRON.
"SO TODAY, THE WORLD NEEDS YOU."

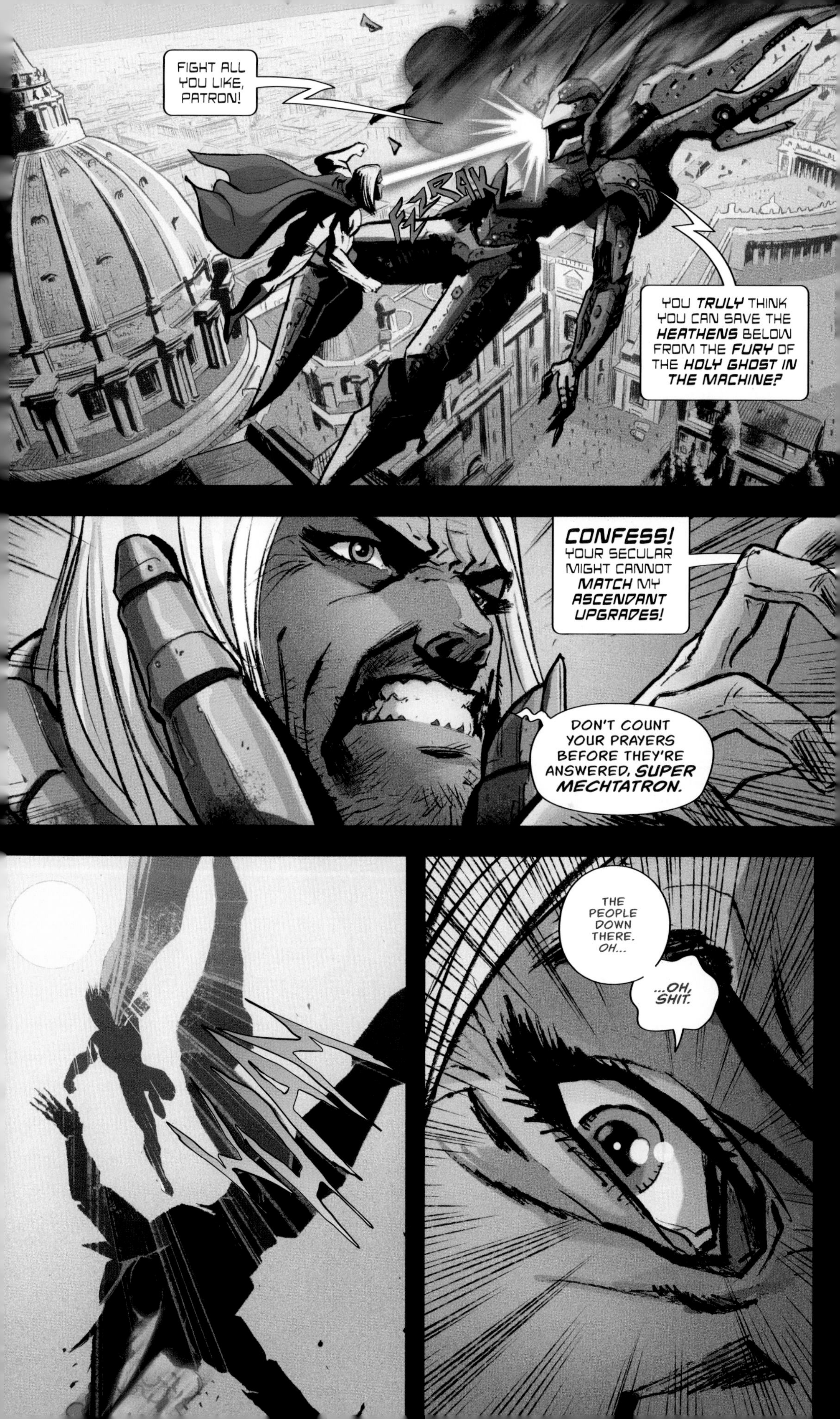
FIGHT ALL YOU LIKE, PATRON!
FZZRAK
YOU TRULY THINK YOU CAN SAVE THE HEATHENS BELOW FROM THE FURY OF THE HOLY GHOST IN THE MACHINE?
CONFESS! YOUR SECULAR MIGHT CANNOT MATCH MY ASCENDANT UPGRADES!
DON'T COUNT YOUR PRAYERS BEFORE THEY'RE ANSWERED, SUPER MECHTATRON.
THE PEOPLE DOWN THERE. OH...
...OH, SHIT.

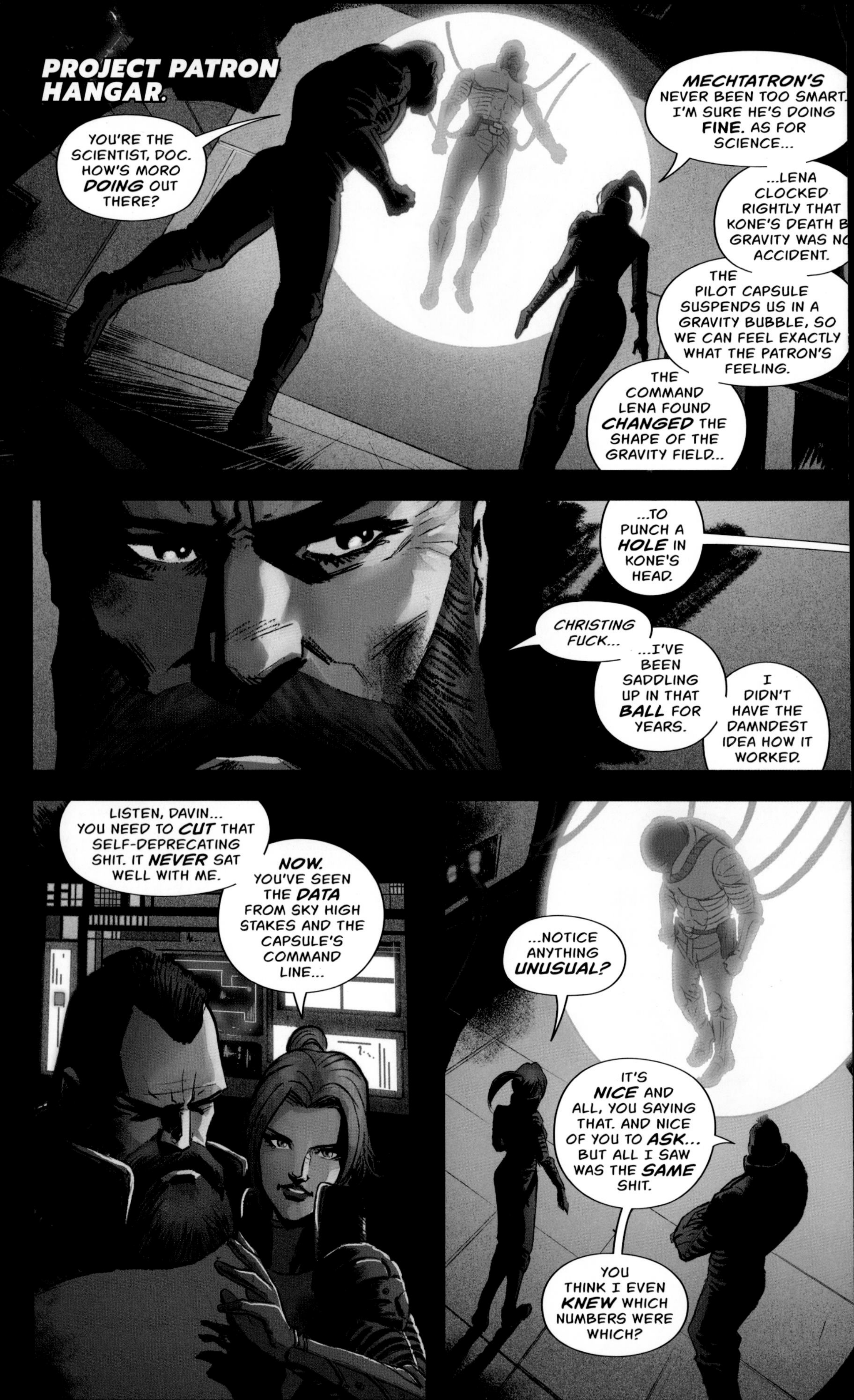
PROJECT PATRON HANGAR.
YOU'RE THE SCIENTIST, DOC. HOW'S MORO DOING OUT THERE?
MECHTATRON'S NEVER BEEN TOO SMART. I'M SURE HE'S DOING FINE. AS FOR SCIENCE...
...LENA CLOCKED RIGHTLY THAT KONE'S DEATH B GRAVITY WAS N ACCIDENT.
THE PILOT CAPSULE SUSPENDS US IN A GRAVITY BUBBLE, SO WE CAN FEEL EXACTLY WHAT THE PATRON'S FEELING.
THE COMMAND LENA FOUND CHANGED THE SHAPE OF THE GRAVITY FIELD...
...TO PUNCH A HOLE IN KONE'S HEAD.
CHRISTING FUCK...
...I'VE BEEN SADDLING UP IN THAT BALL FOR YEARS.
I DIDN'T HAVE THE DAMNDEST IDEA HOW IT WORKED.
LISTEN, DAVIN... YOU NEED TO CUT THAT SELF-DEPRECATING SHIT. IT NEVER SAT WELL WITH ME.
NOW. YOU'VE SEEN THE DATA FROM SKY HIGH STAKES AND THE CAPSULE'S COMMAND LINE...
...NOTICE ANYTHING UNUSUAL?
IT'S NICE AND ALL, YOU SAYING THAT. AND NICE OF YOU TO ASK... BUT ALL I SAW WAS THE SAME SHIT.
YOU THINK I EVEN KNEW WHICH NUMBERS WERE WHICH?

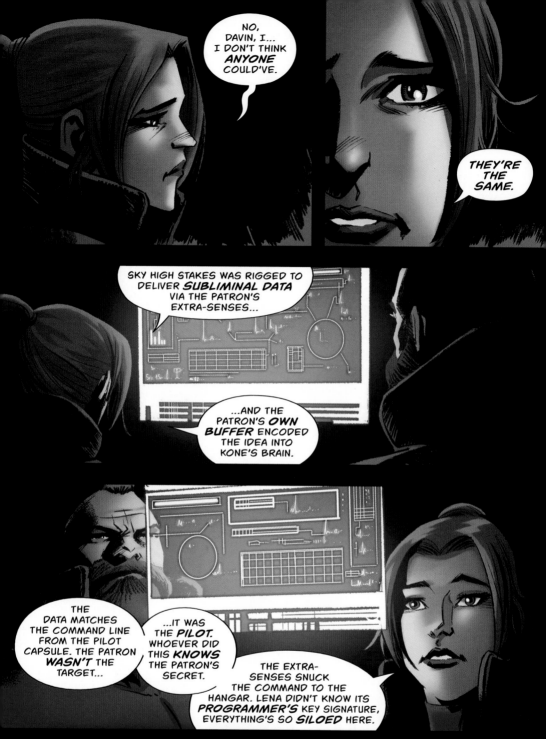

NO, DAVIN, I... I DON'T THINK *ANYONE* COULD'VE.

THEY'RE THE SAME.

SKY HIGH STAKES WAS RIGGED TO DELIVER *SUBLIMINAL DATA* VIA THE PATRON'S EXTRA-SENSES...

...AND THE PATRON'S *OWN BUFFER* ENCODED THE IDEA INTO KONE'S BRAIN.

THE DATA MATCHES THE COMMAND LINE FROM THE PILOT CAPSULE. THE PATRON *WASN'T* THE TARGET...

...IT WAS THE *PILOT.* WHOEVER DID THIS *KNOWS* THE PATRON'S SECRET.

THE EXTRA-SENSES SNUCK THE COMMAND TO THE HANGAR. LENA DIDN'T KNOW ITS *PROGRAMMER'S* KEY SIGNATURE, EVERYTHING'S SO *SILOED* HERE.

BUT I *WROTE* THE KEY SIGNATURES THAT LET US INTO THE CAPSULE'S SYSTEMS...

...IT WAS *KONE'S* KEY SIGNATURE. THIS WASN'T MURDER...

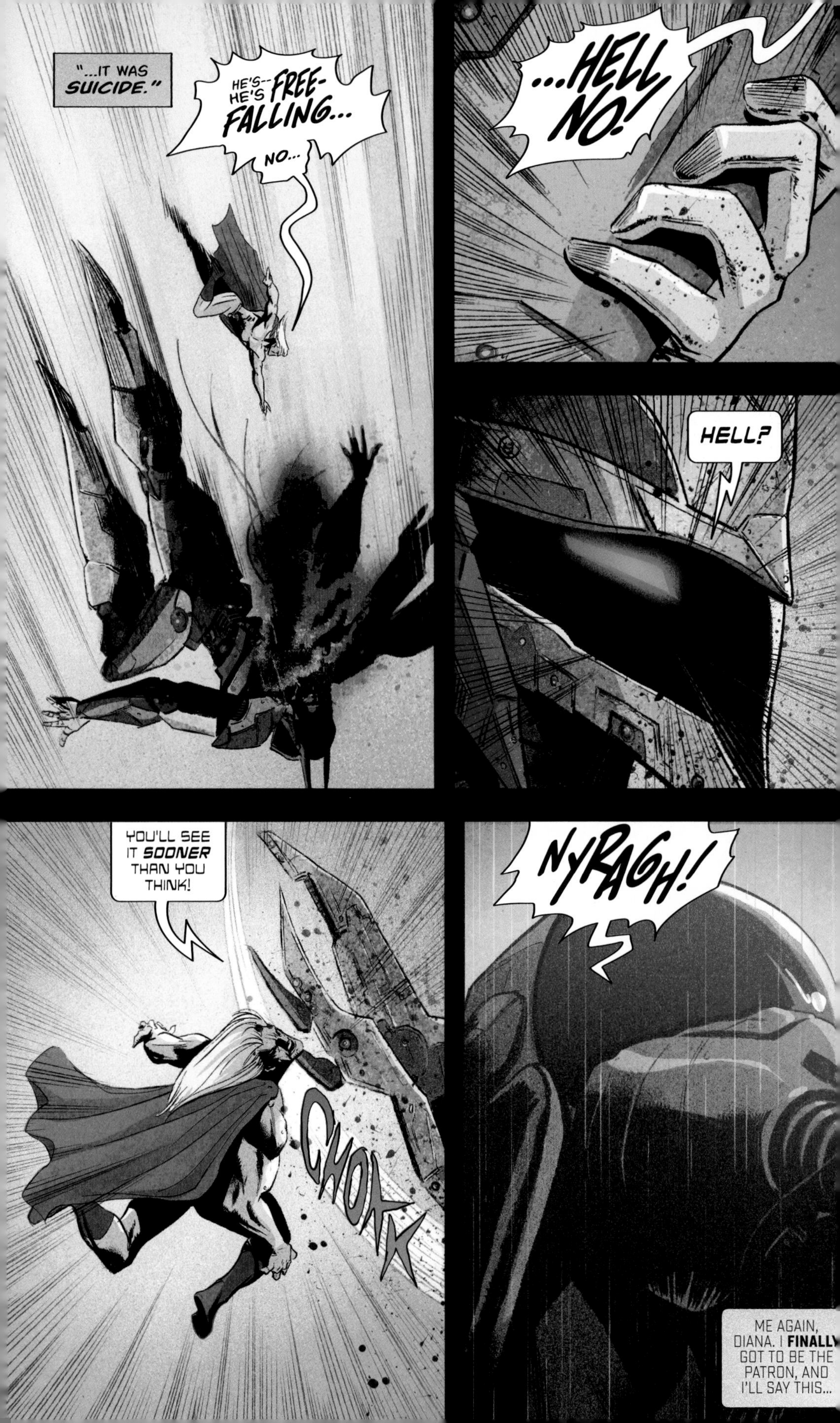
"...IT WAS SUICIDE."
HE'S-- HE'S FREE-FALLING...
NO...
...HELL NO!
HELL?
YOU'LL SEE IT SOONER THAN YOU THINK!
CHOKK
NYRAGH!
ME AGAIN, DIANA. I FINALLY GOT TO BE THE PATRON, AND I'LL SAY THIS...

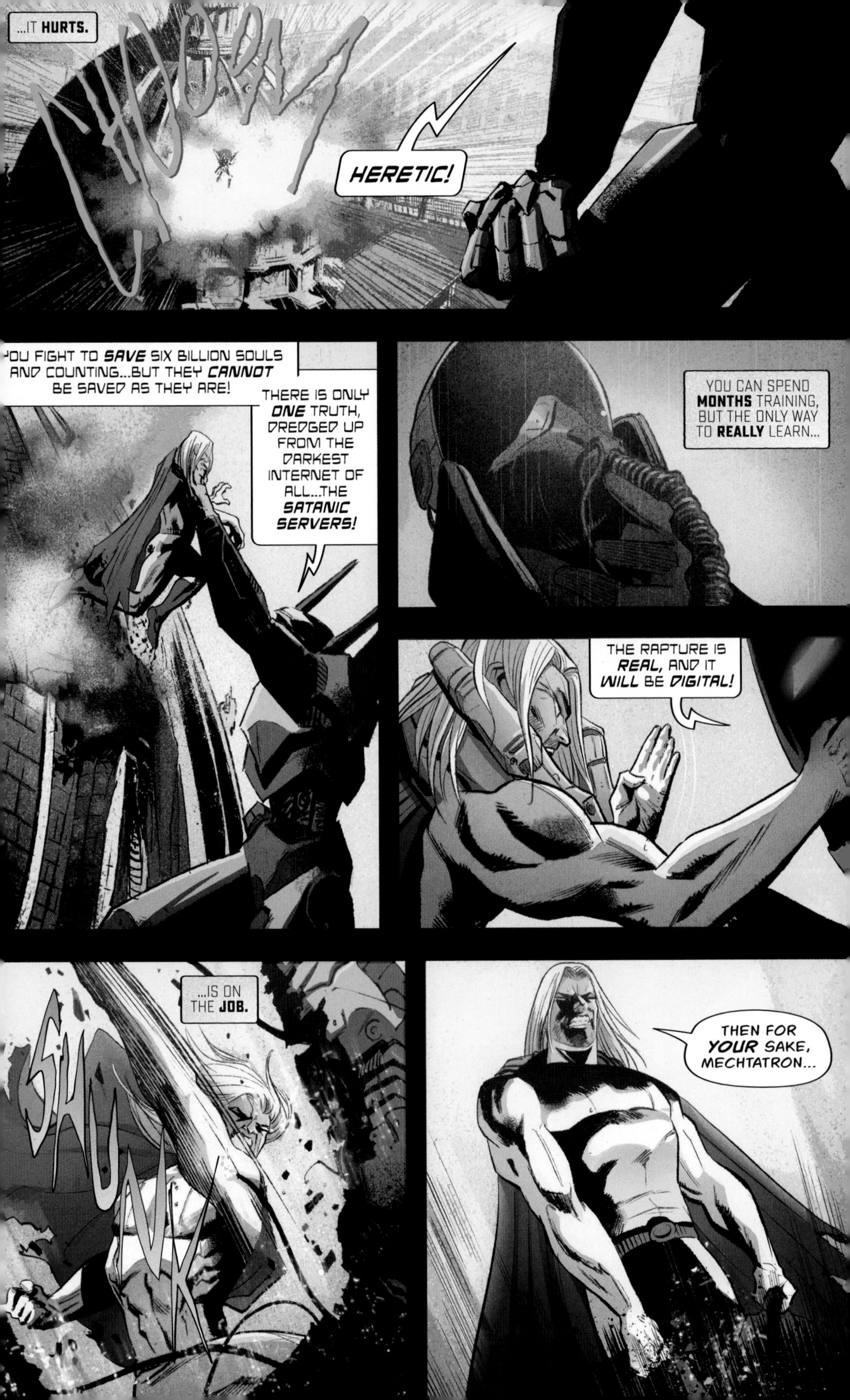
...IT HURTS.
HERETIC!
YOU FIGHT TO SAVE SIX BILLION SOULS AND COUNTING...BUT THEY CANNOT BE SAVED AS THEY ARE!
THERE IS ONLY ONE TRUTH, DREDGED UP FROM THE DARKEST INTERNET OF ALL...THE SATANIC SERVERS!
YOU CAN SPEND MONTHS TRAINING, BUT THE ONLY WAY TO REALLY LEARN...
THE RAPTURE IS REAL, AND IT WILL BE DIGITAL!
...IS ON THE JOB.
SHUNK
THEN FOR YOUR SAKE, MECHTATRON...

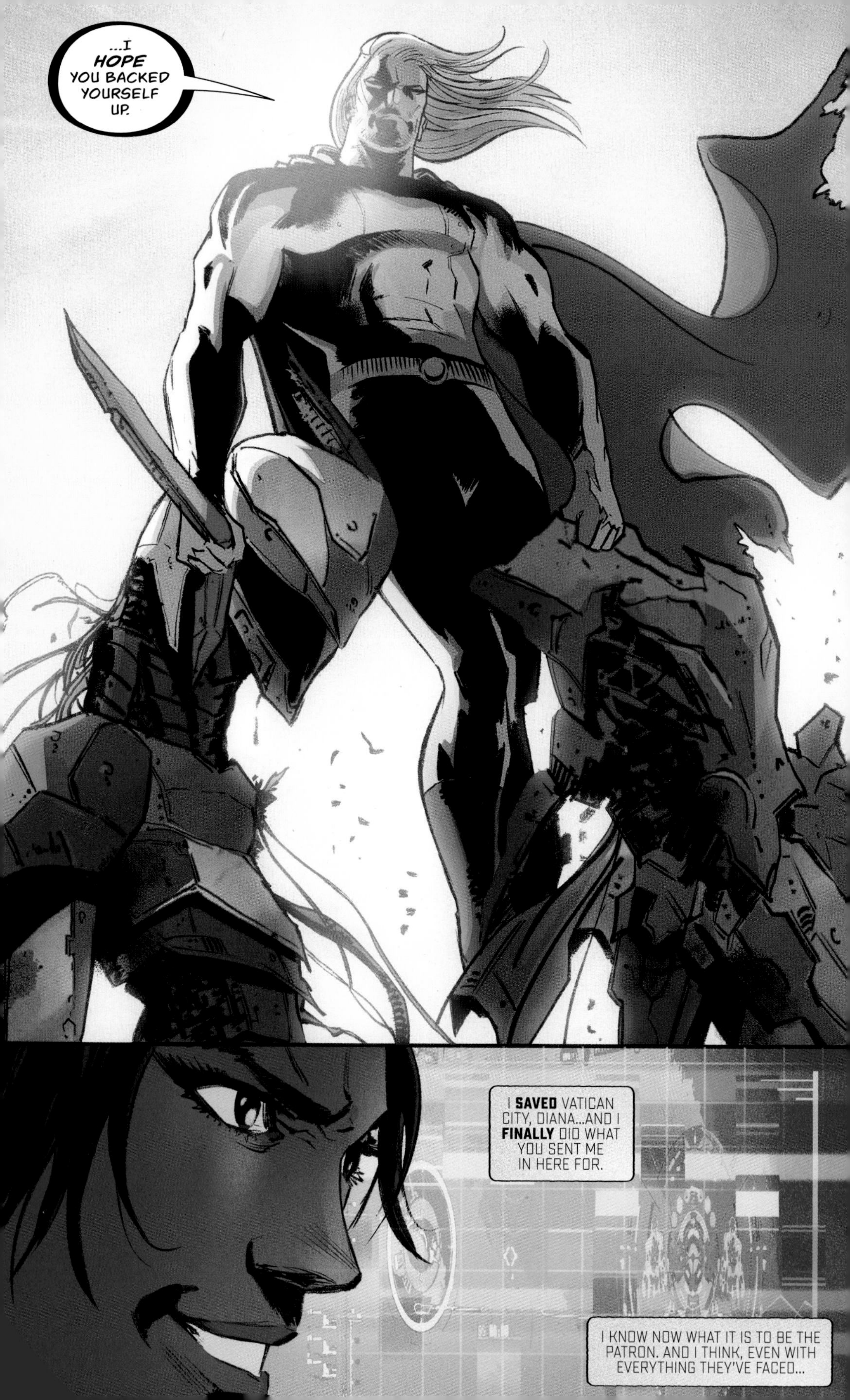
...I HOPE YOU BACKED YOURSELF UP.
I SAVED VATICAN CITY, DIANA...AND I FINALLY DID WHAT YOU SENT ME IN HERE FOR.
I KNOW NOW WHAT IT IS TO BE THE PATRON. AND I THINK, EVEN WITH EVERYTHING THEY'VE FACED...

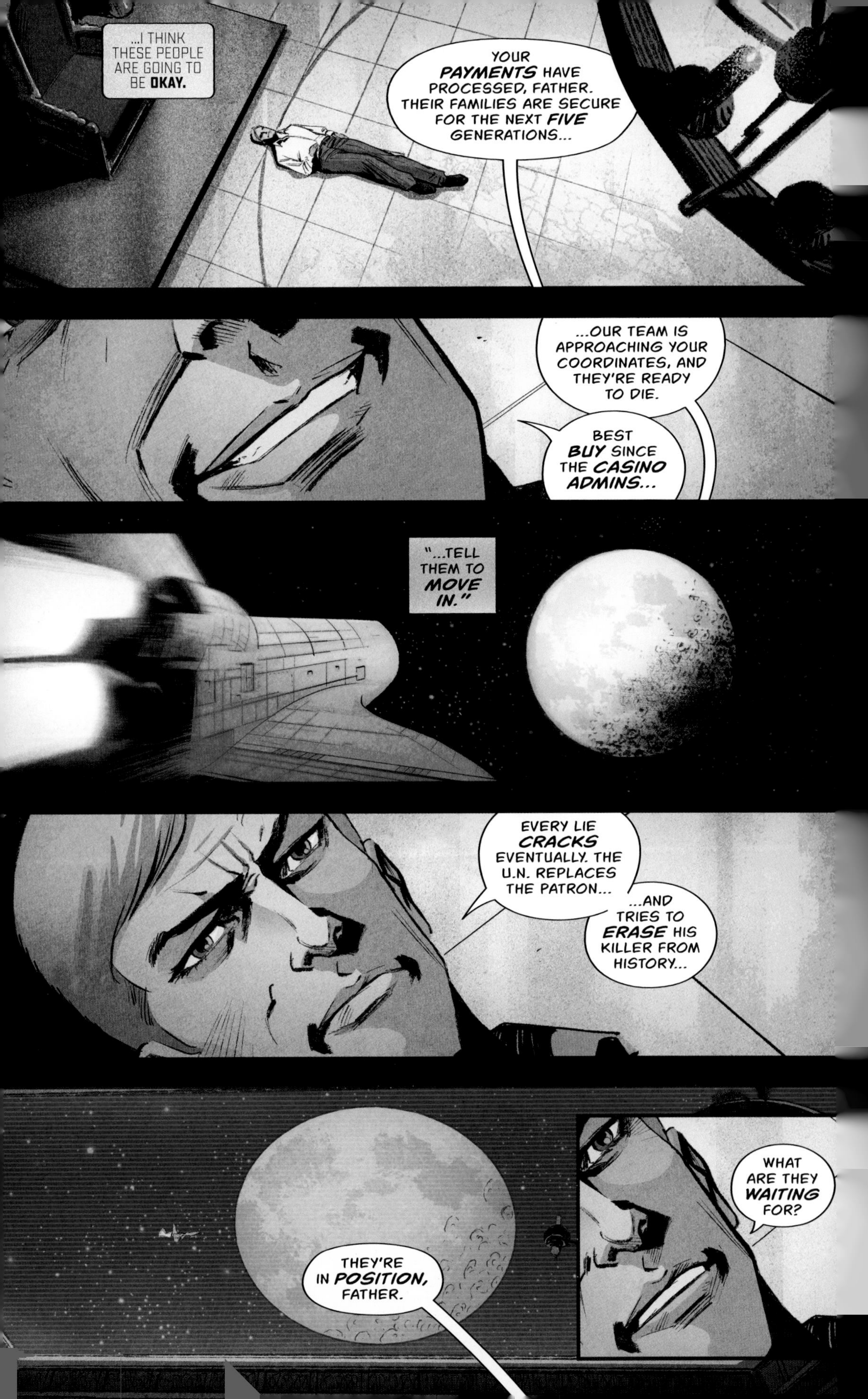
...I THINK THESE PEOPLE ARE GOING TO BE OKAY.
YOUR PAYMENTS HAVE PROCESSED, FATHER. THEIR FAMILIES ARE SECURE FOR THE NEXT FIVE GENERATIONS...
...OUR TEAM IS APPROACHING YOUR COORDINATES, AND THEY'RE READY TO DIE.
BEST BUY SINCE THE CASINO ADMINS...
"...TELL THEM TO MOVE IN."
EVERY LIE CRACKS EVENTUALLY. THE U.N. REPLACES THE PATRON...
...AND TRIES TO ERASE HIS KILLER FROM HISTORY...
WHAT ARE THEY WAITING FOR?
THEY'RE IN POSITION, FATHER.

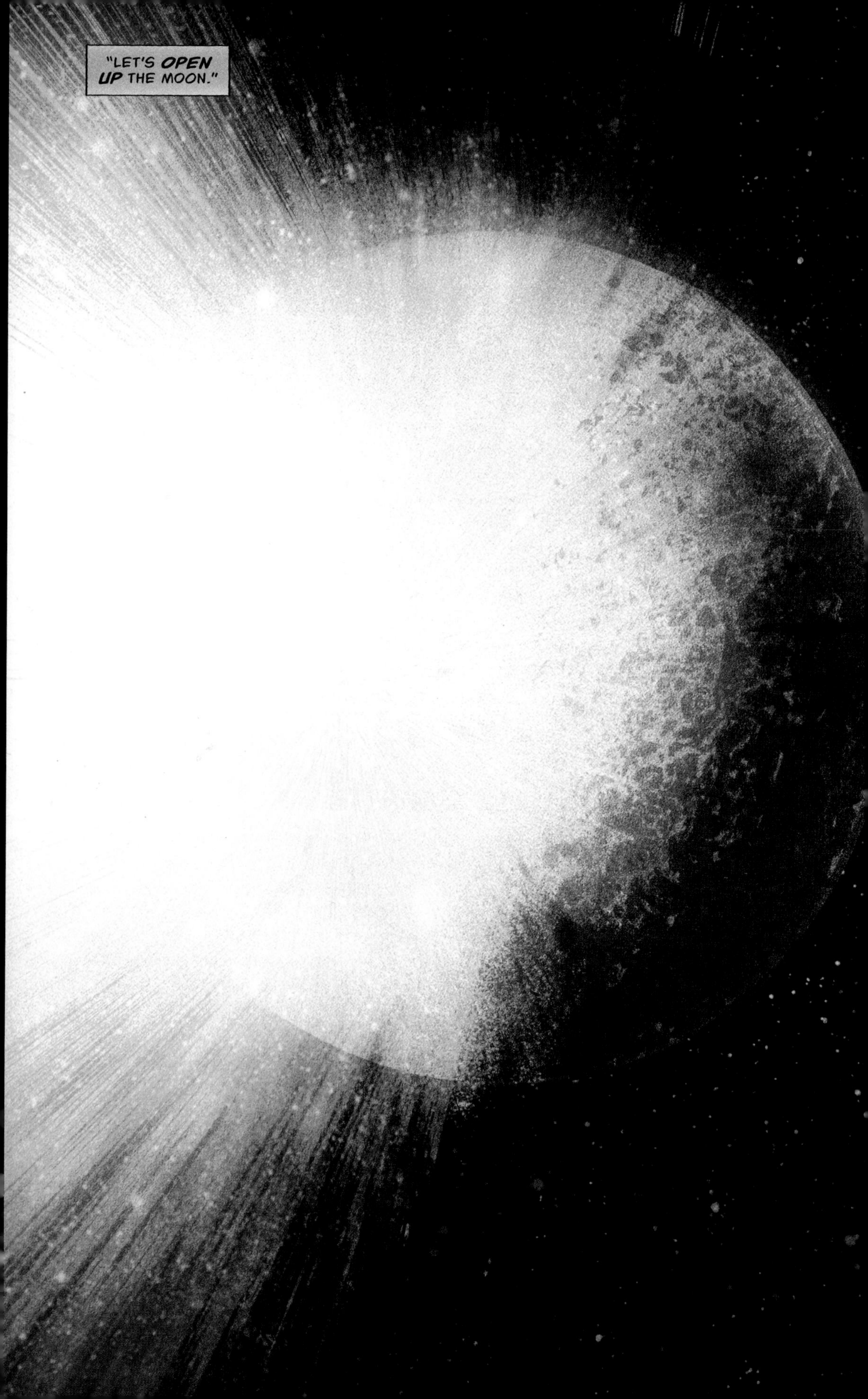
"LET'S OPEN UP THE MOON."

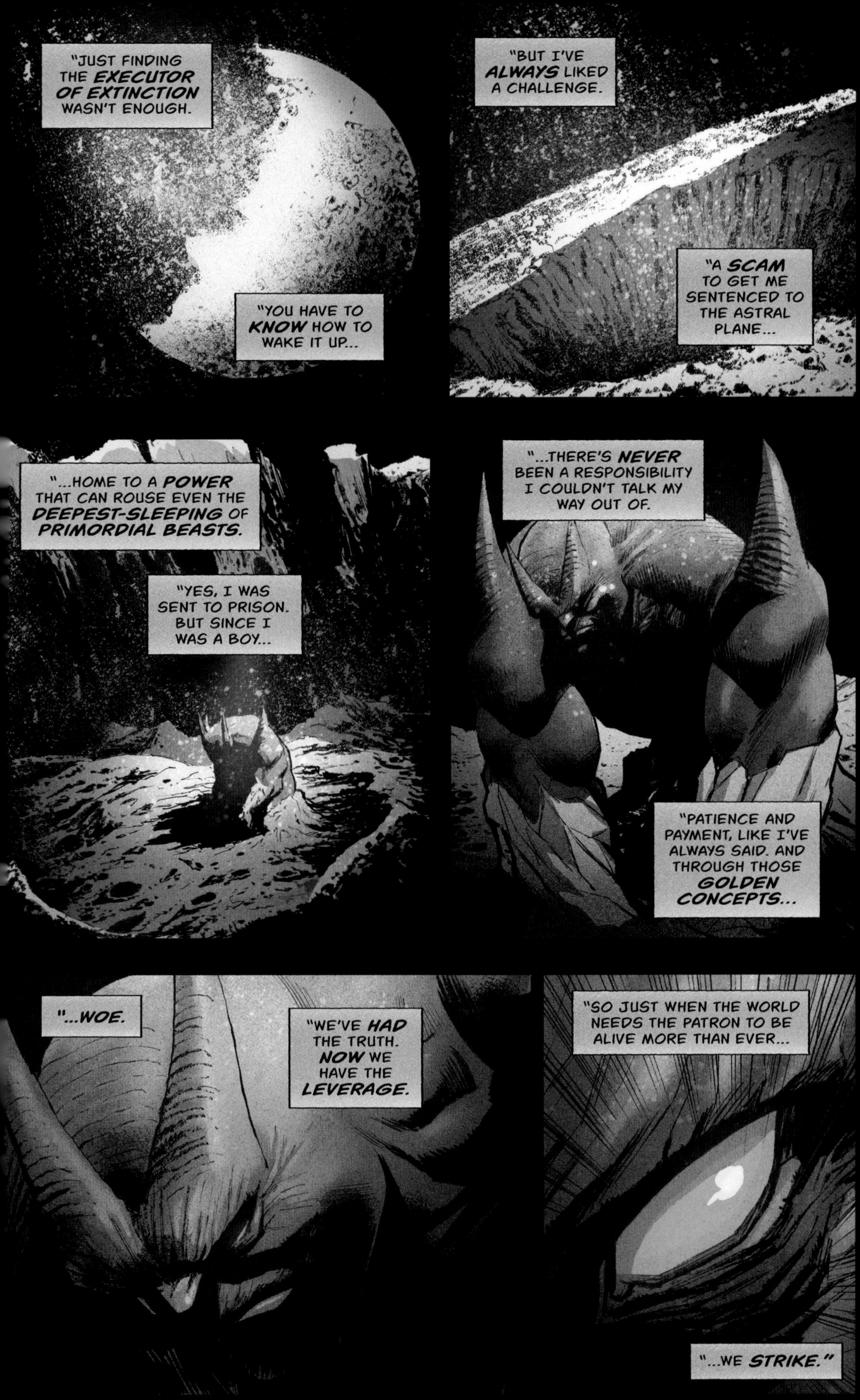
"JUST FINDING THE EXECUTOR OF EXTINCTION WASN'T ENOUGH.
"YOU HAVE TO KNOW HOW TO WAKE IT UP...
"BUT I'VE ALWAYS LIKED A CHALLENGE.
"A SCAM TO GET ME SENTENCED TO THE ASTRAL PLANE...
"...HOME TO A POWER THAT CAN ROUSE EVEN THE DEEPEST-SLEEPING OF PRIMORDIAL BEASTS.
"YES, I WAS SENT TO PRISON. BUT SINCE I WAS A BOY...
"...THERE'S NEVER BEEN A RESPONSIBILITY I COULDN'T TALK MY WAY OUT OF.
"PATIENCE AND PAYMENT, LIKE I'VE ALWAYS SAID. AND THROUGH THOSE GOLDEN CONCEPTS...
"...WOE.
"WE'VE HAD THE TRUTH. NOW WE HAVE THE LEVERAGE.
"SO JUST WHEN THE WORLD NEEDS THE PATRON TO BE ALIVE MORE THAN EVER...
"...WE STRIKE."

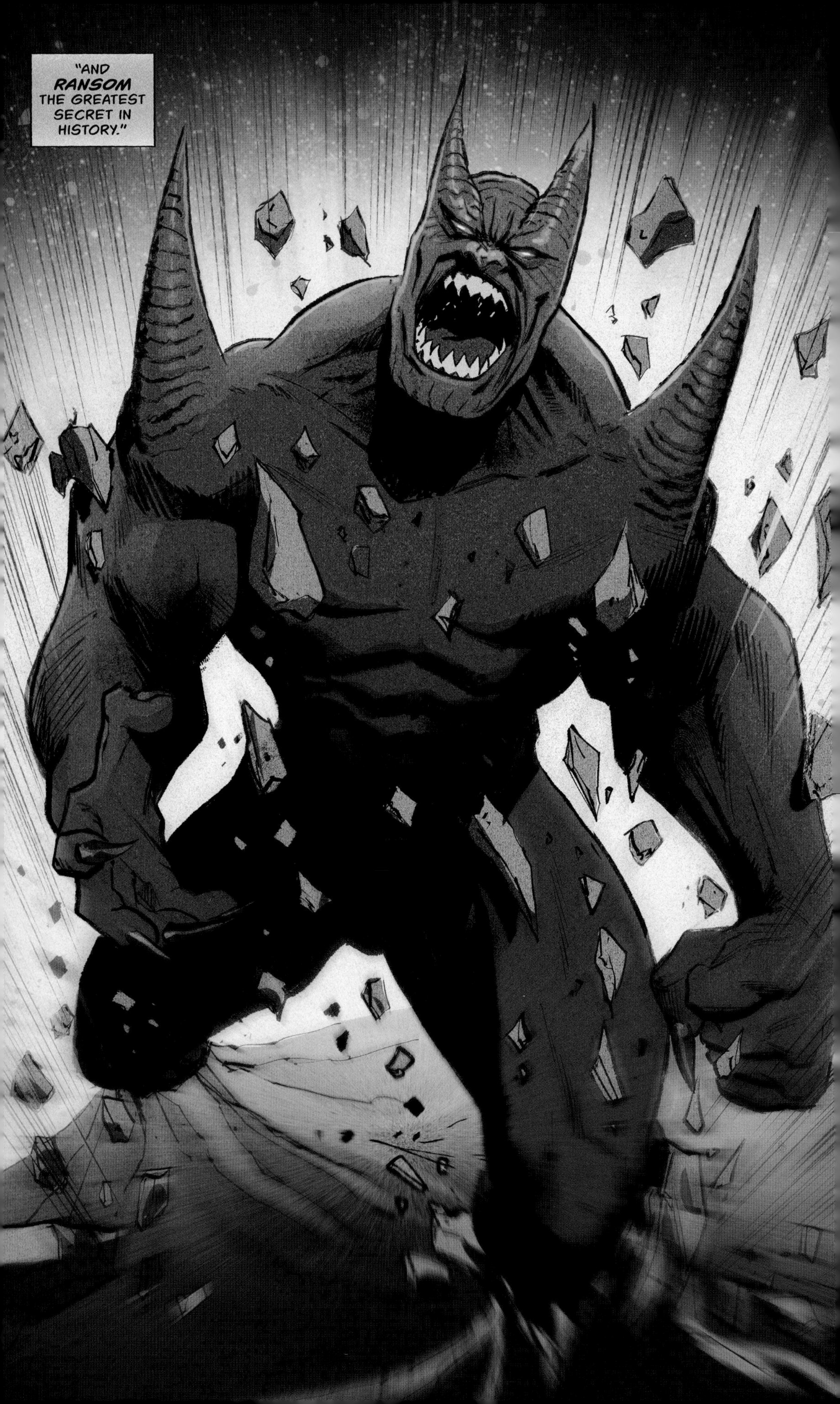
"AND RANSOM THE GREATEST SECRET IN HISTORY."

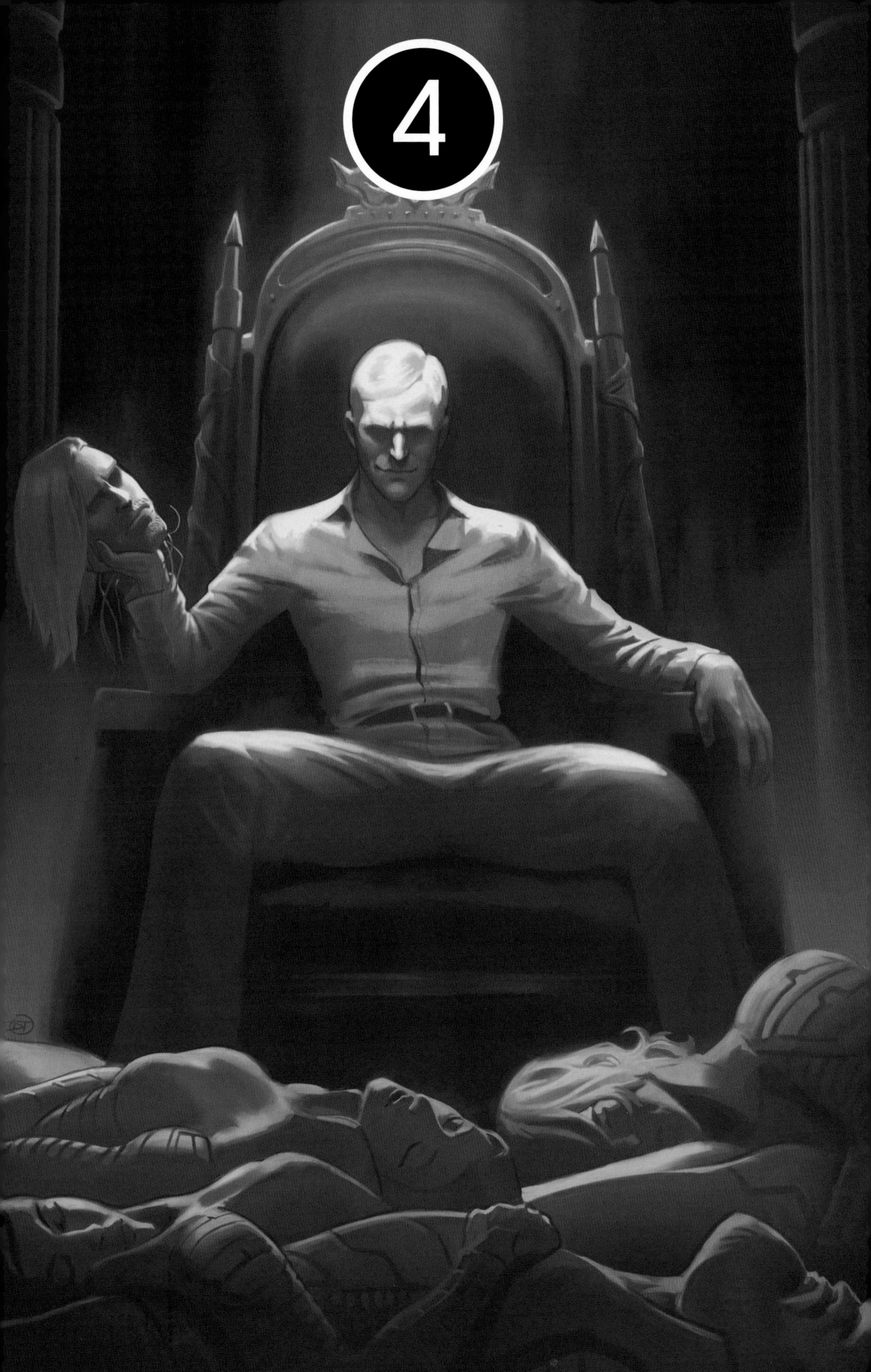
4

EXPERIMENTS AND EXTINCTION

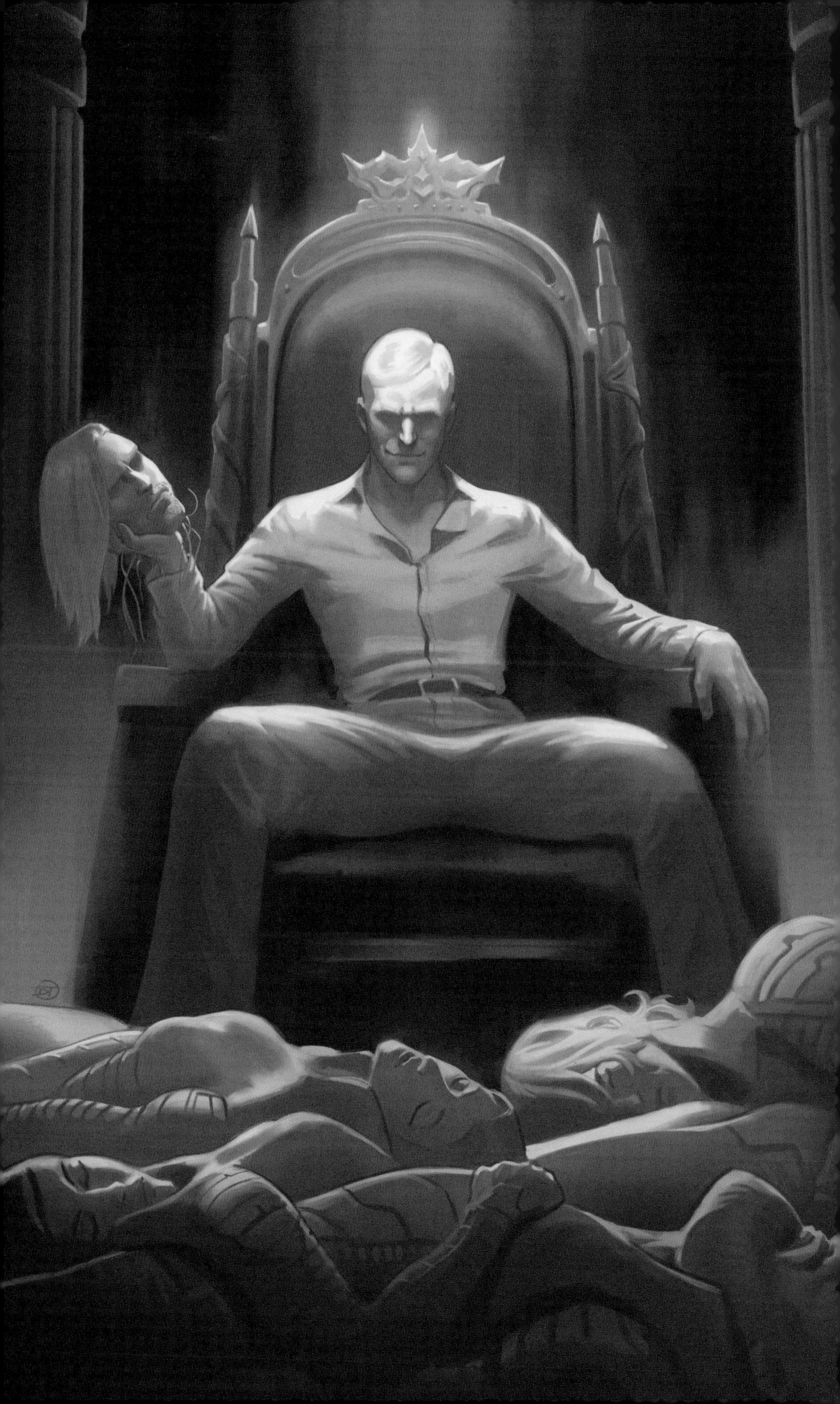

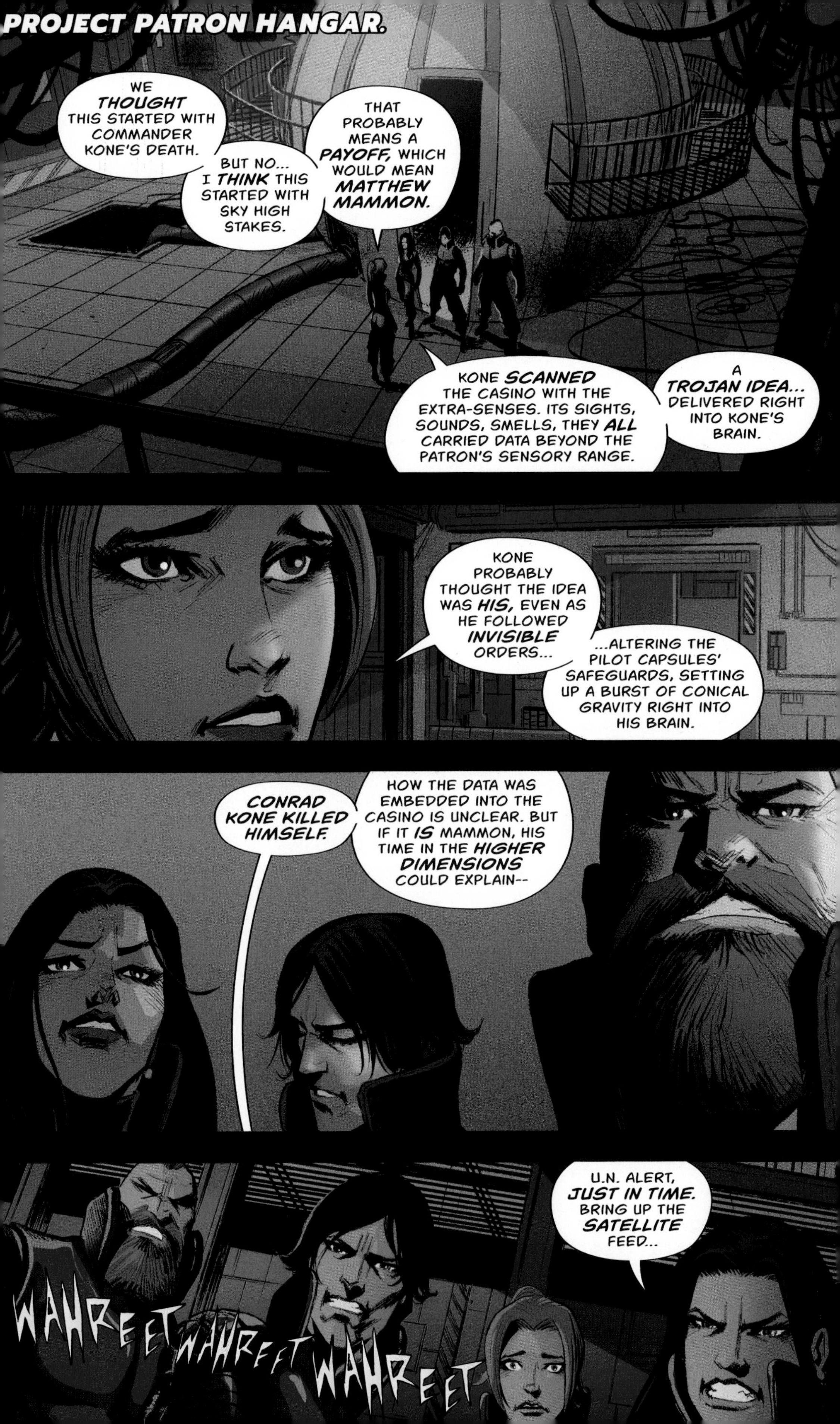
PROJECT PATRON HANGAR.
WE THOUGHT THIS STARTED WITH COMMANDER KONE'S DEATH.
BUT NO... I THINK THIS STARTED WITH SKY HIGH STAKES.
THAT PROBABLY MEANS A PAYOFF, WHICH WOULD MEAN MATTHEW MAMMON.
KONE SCANNED THE CASINO WITH THE EXTRA-SENSES. ITS SIGHTS, SOUNDS, SMELLS, THEY ALL CARRIED DATA BEYOND THE PATRON'S SENSORY RANGE.
A TROJAN IDEA... DELIVERED RIGHT INTO KONE'S BRAIN.
KONE PROBABLY THOUGHT THE IDEA WAS HIS, EVEN AS HE FOLLOWED INVISIBLE ORDERS...
...ALTERING THE PILOT CAPSULES' SAFEGUARDS, SETTING UP A BURST OF CONICAL GRAVITY RIGHT INTO HIS BRAIN.
CONRAD KONE KILLED HIMSELF.
HOW THE DATA WAS EMBEDDED INTO THE CASINO IS UNCLEAR. BUT IF IT IS MAMMON, HIS TIME IN THE HIGHER DIMENSIONS COULD EXPLAIN--
U.N. ALERT, JUST IN TIME. BRING UP THE SATELLITE FEED...
WAHREET WAHREET WAHREET

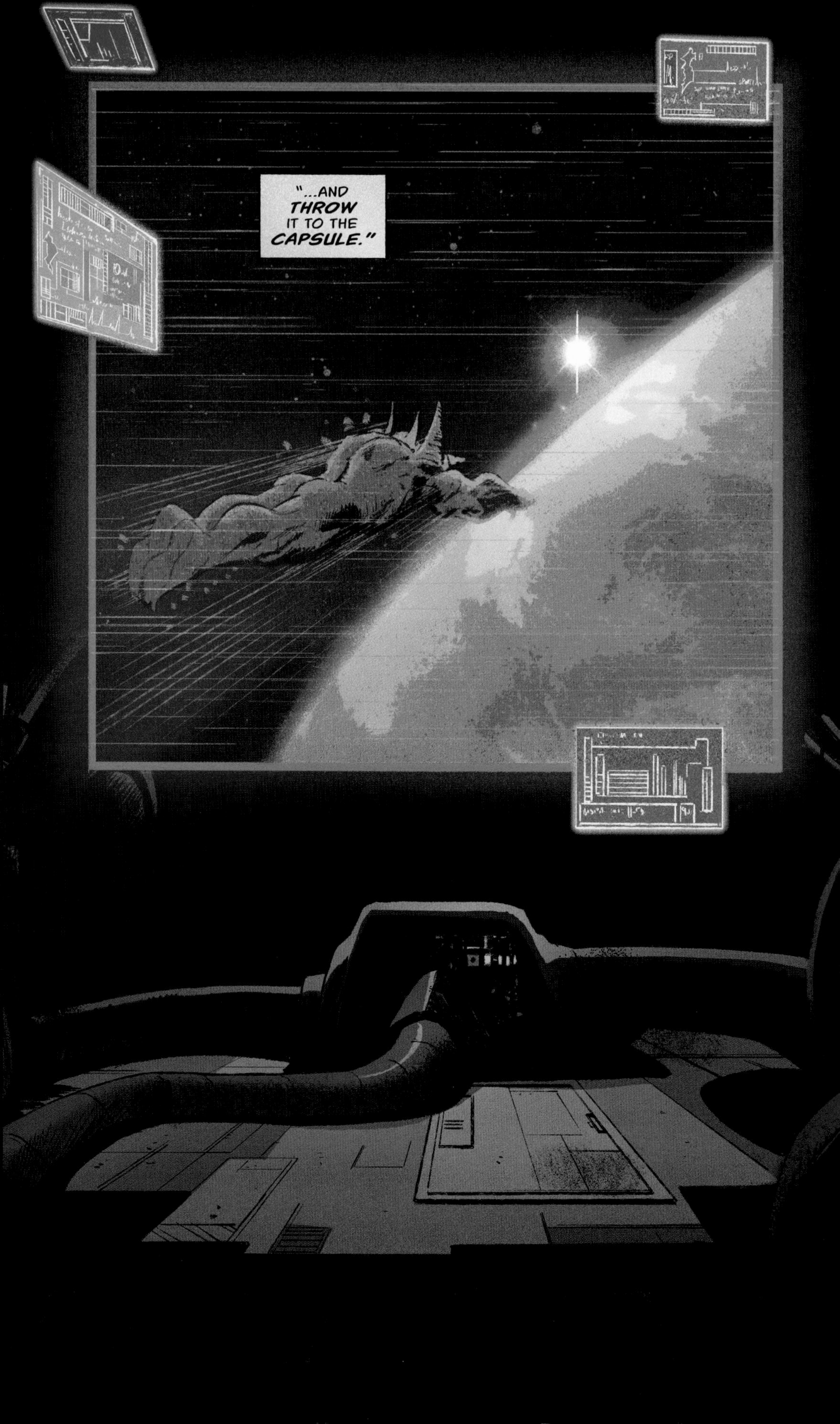
"...AND THROW IT TO THE CAPSULE."

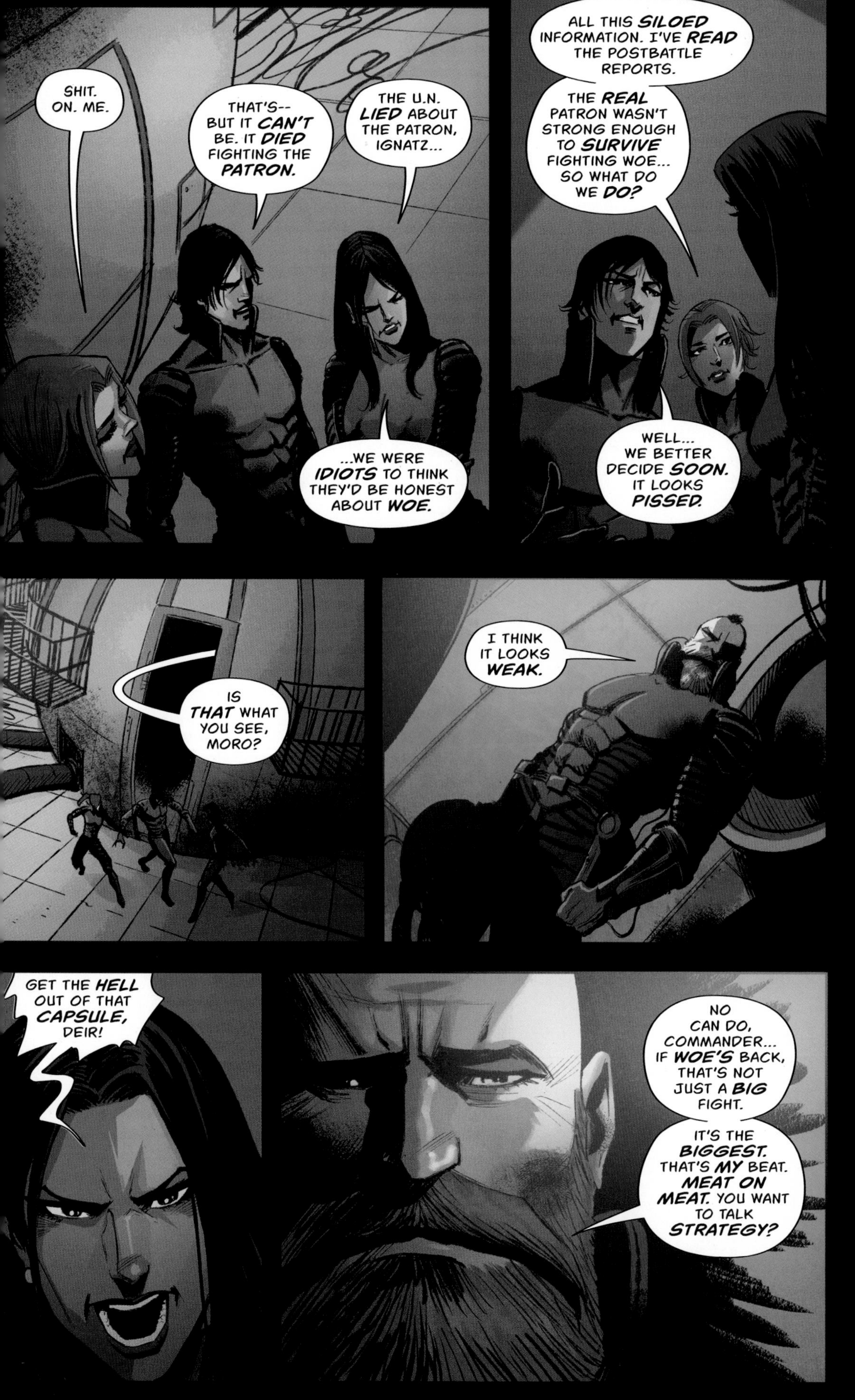
SHIT. ON. ME.
THAT'S-- BUT IT CAN'T BE. IT DIED FIGHTING THE PATRON.
THE U.N. LIED ABOUT THE PATRON, IGNATZ...
...WE WERE IDIOTS TO THINK THEY'D BE HONEST ABOUT WOE.
ALL THIS SILOED INFORMATION. I'VE READ THE POSTBATTLE REPORTS.
THE REAL PATRON WASN'T STRONG ENOUGH TO SURVIVE FIGHTING WOE... SO WHAT DO WE DO?
WELL... WE BETTER DECIDE SOON. IT LOOKS PISSED.
IS THAT WHAT YOU SEE, MORO?
I THINK IT LOOKS WEAK.
GET THE HELL OUT OF THAT CAPSULE, DEIR!
NO CAN DO, COMMANDER... IF WOE'S BACK, THAT'S NOT JUST A BIG FIGHT.
IT'S THE BIGGEST. THAT'S MY BEAT. MEAT ON MEAT. YOU WANT TO TALK STRATEGY?

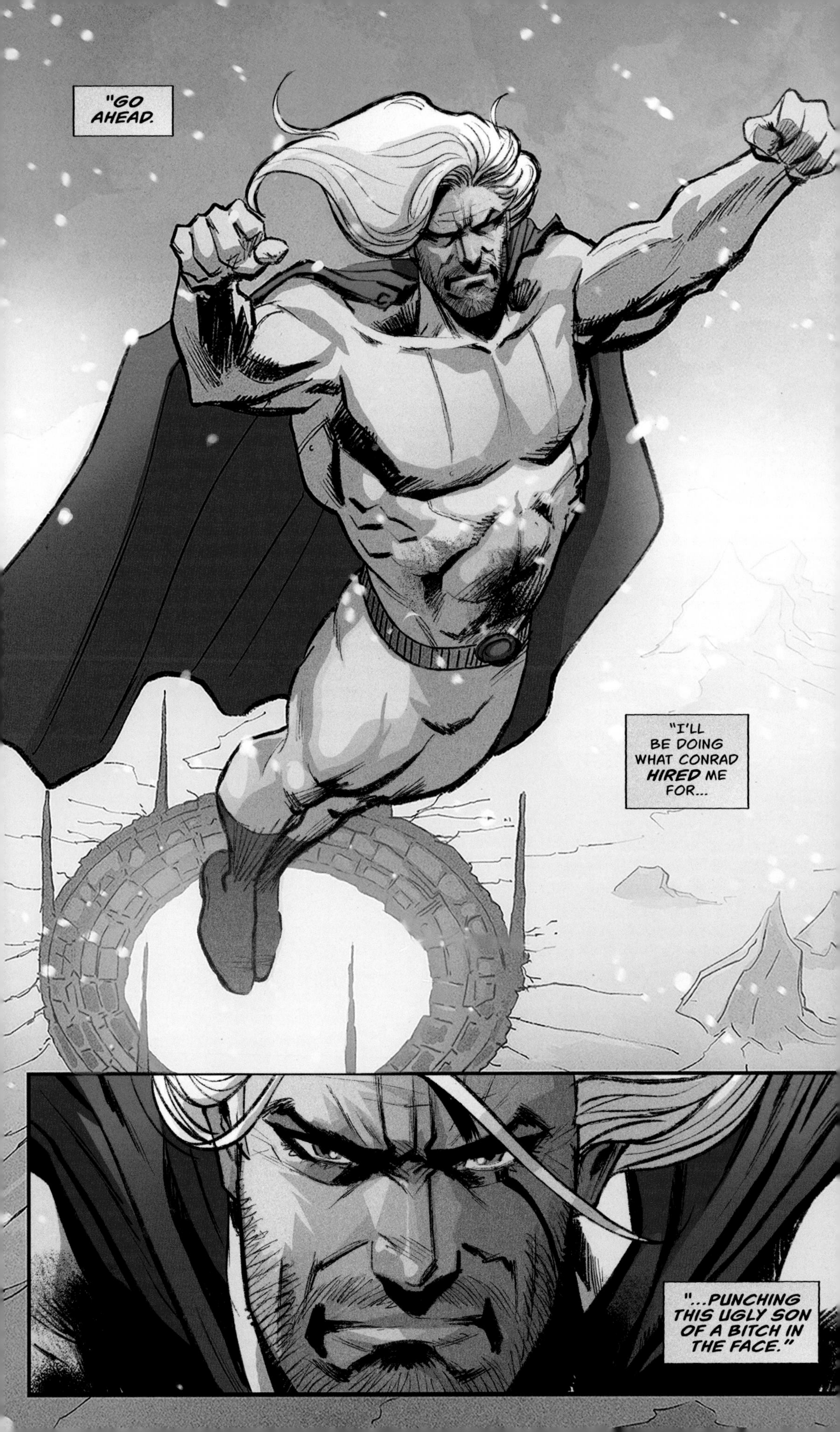
"GO AHEAD.
"I'LL BE DOING WHAT CONRAD HIRED ME FOR...
"...PUNCHING THIS UGLY SON OF A BITCH IN THE FACE."

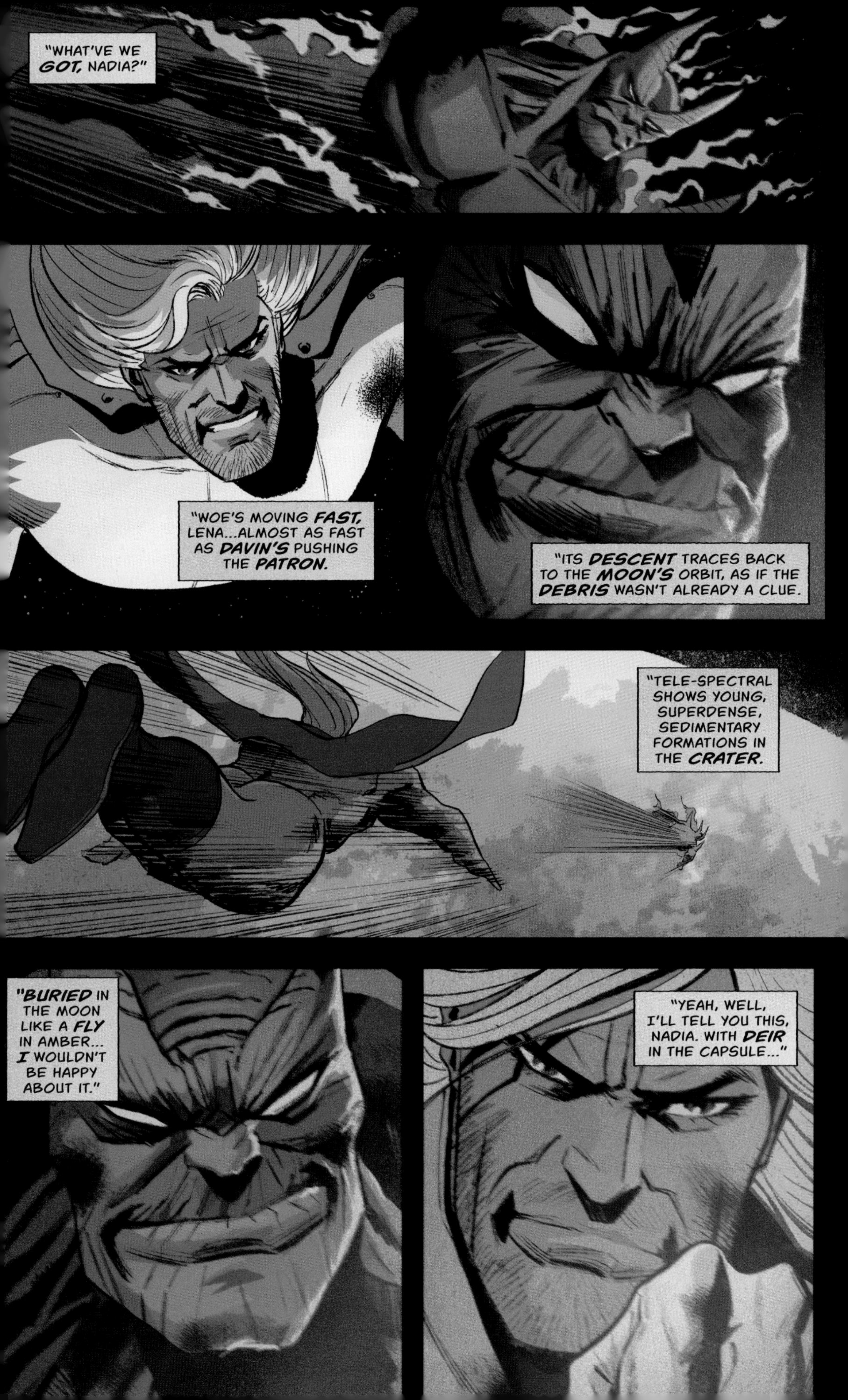
"WHAT'VE WE GOT, NADIA?"
"WOE'S MOVING FAST, LENA...ALMOST AS FAST AS DAVIN'S PUSHING THE PATRON.
"ITS DESCENT TRACES BACK TO THE MOON'S ORBIT, AS IF THE DEBRIS WASN'T ALREADY A CLUE.
"TELE-SPECTRAL SHOWS YOUNG, SUPERDENSE, SEDIMENTARY FORMATIONS IN THE CRATER.
"BURIED IN THE MOON LIKE A FLY IN AMBER... I WOULDN'T BE HAPPY ABOUT IT."
"YEAH, WELL, I'LL TELL YOU THIS, NADIA. WITH DEIR IN THE CAPSULE..."

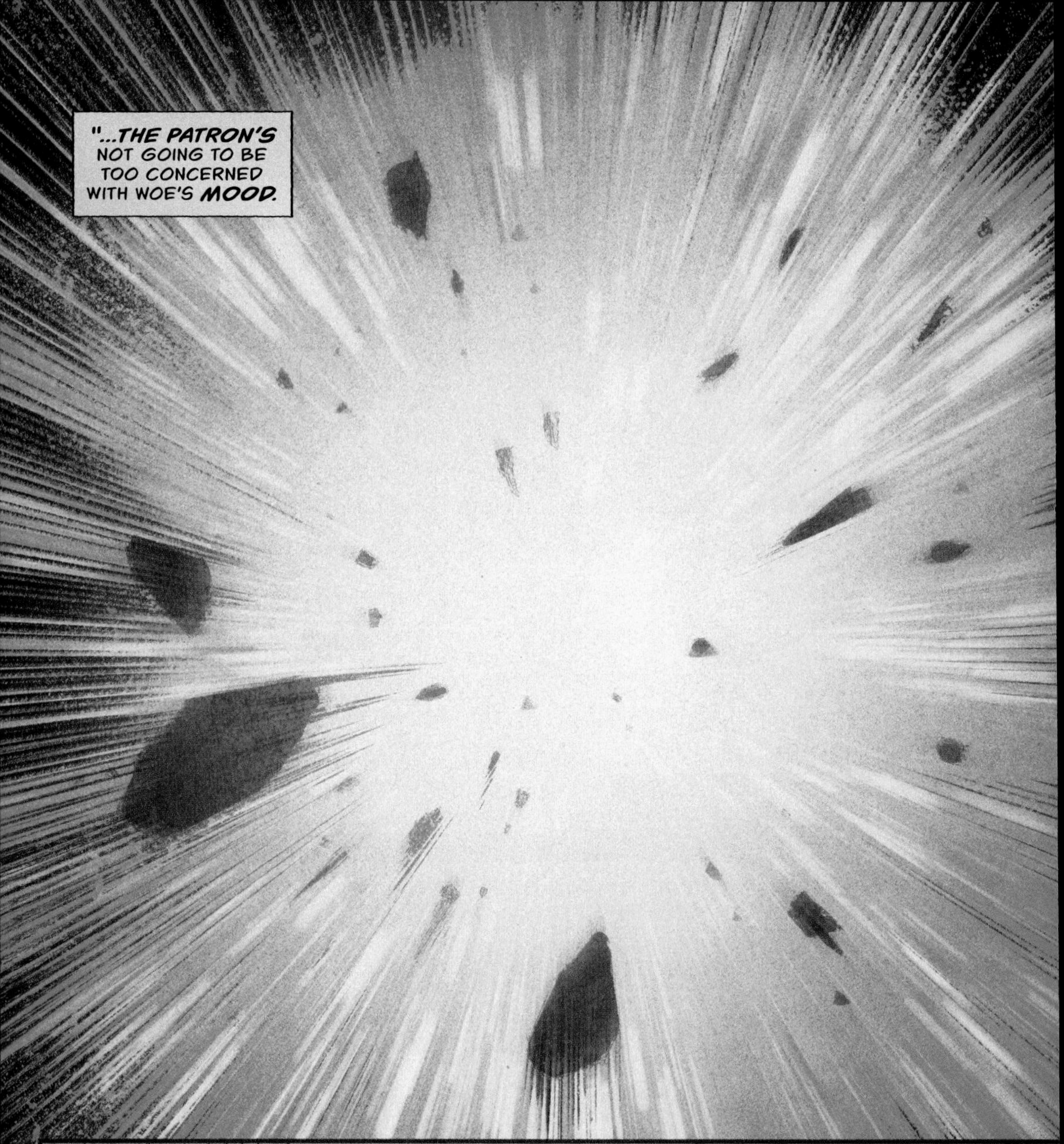
"...THE PATRON'S NOT GOING TO BE TOO CONCERNED WITH WOE'S MOOD.

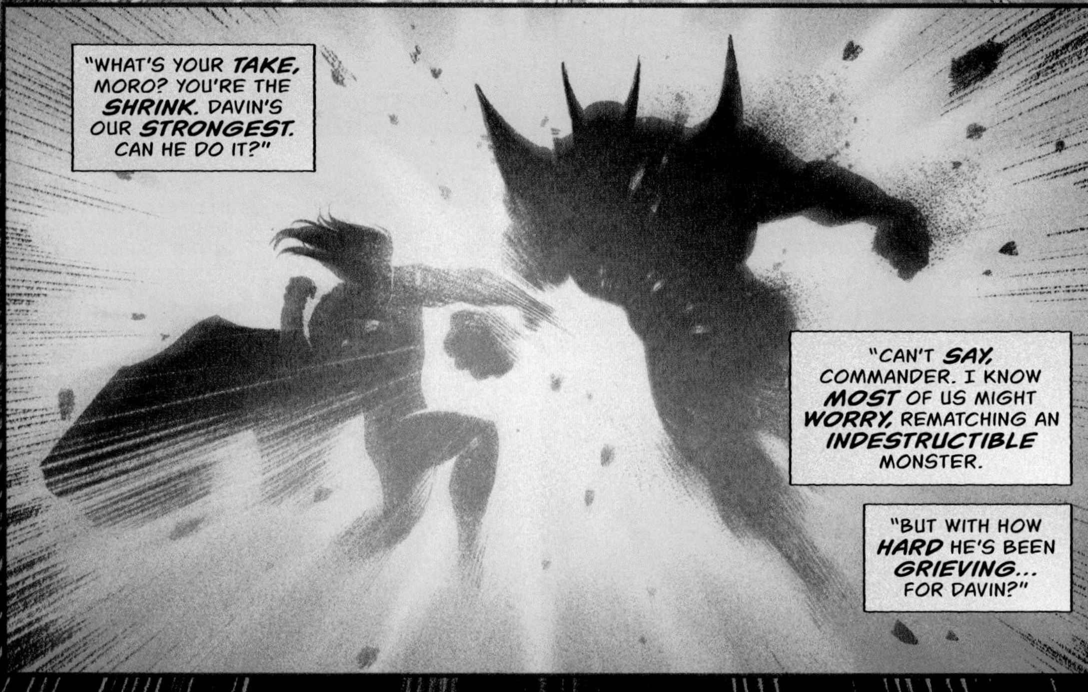
"WHAT'S YOUR TAKE, MORO? YOU'RE THE SHRINK. DAVIN'S OUR STRONGEST. CAN HE DO IT?"
"CAN'T SAY, COMMANDER. I KNOW MOST OF US MIGHT WORRY, REMATCHING AN INDESTRUCTIBLE MONSTER.
"BUT WITH HOW HARD HE'S BEEN GRIEVING... FOR DAVIN?"

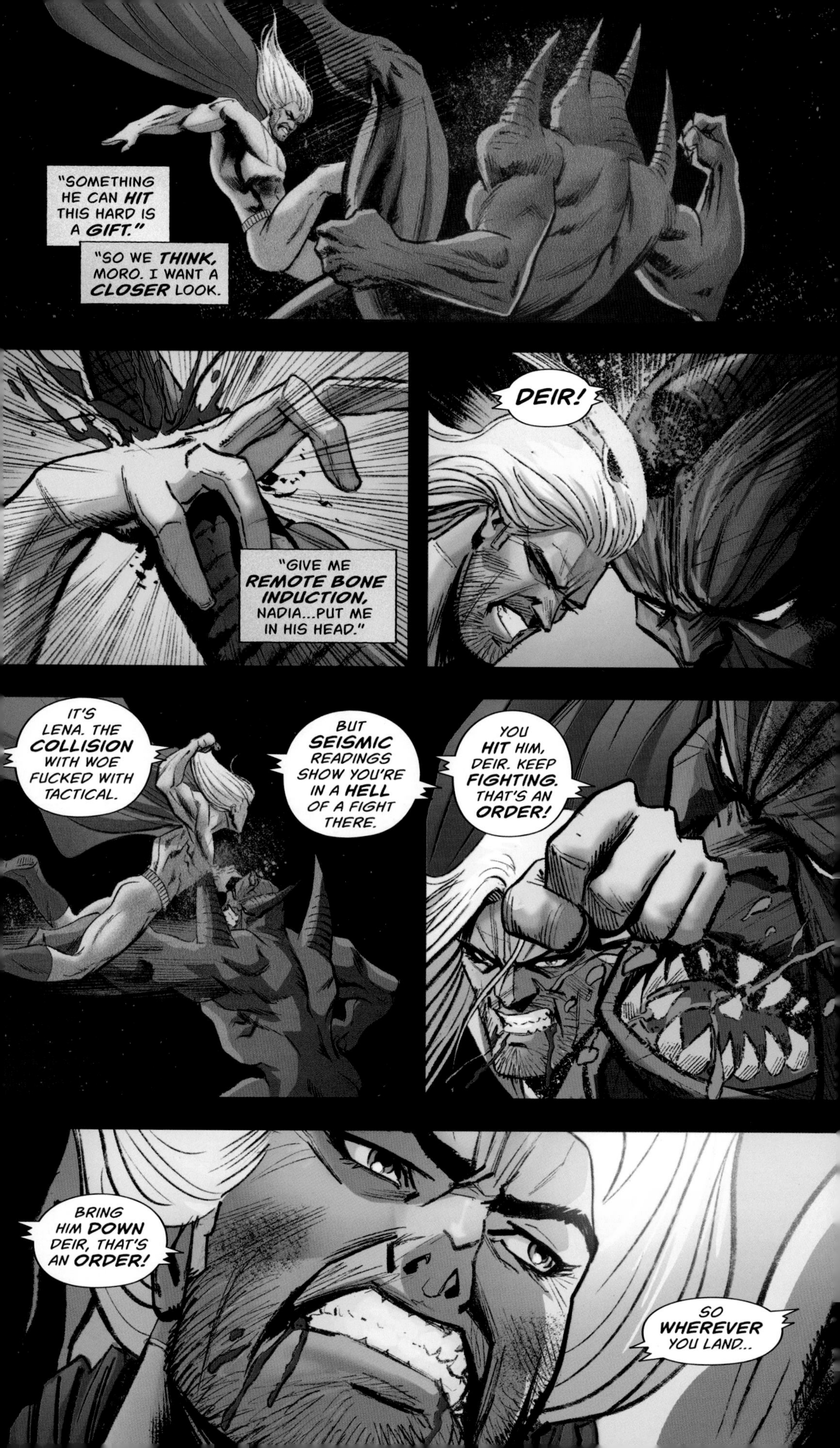
"SOMETHING HE CAN HIT THIS HARD IS A GIFT."
"SO WE THINK, MORO. I WANT A CLOSER LOOK.
"GIVE ME REMOTE BONE INDUCTION, NADIA...PUT ME IN HIS HEAD."
DEIR!
IT'S LENA. THE COLLISION WITH WOE FUCKED WITH TACTICAL.
BUT SEISMIC READINGS SHOW YOU'RE IN A HELL OF A FIGHT THERE.
YOU HIT HIM, DEIR. KEEP FIGHTING. THAT'S AN ORDER!
BRING HIM DOWN DEIR, THAT'S AN ORDER!
SO WHEREVER YOU LAND...

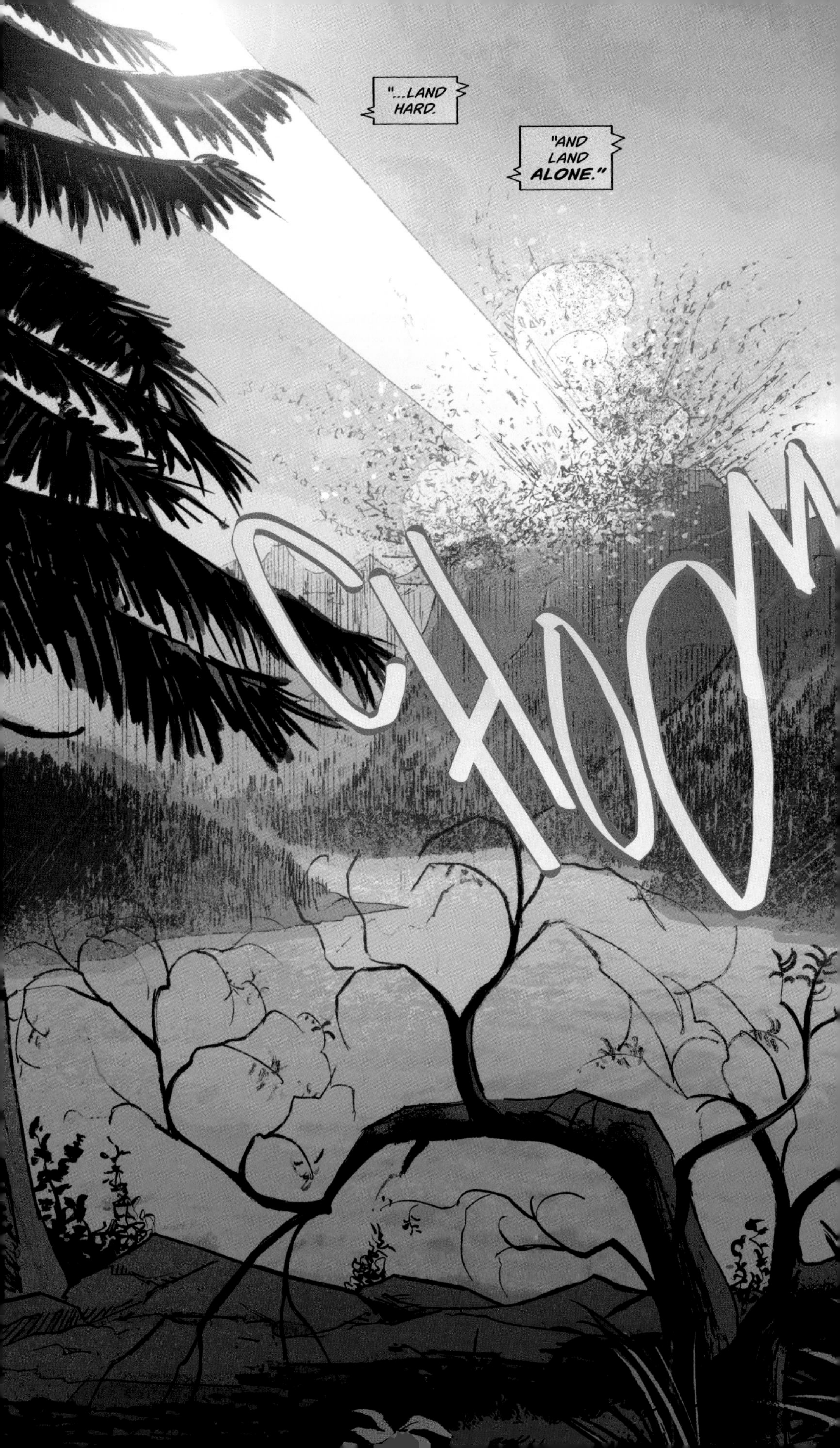
"...LAND HARD.
"AND LAND ALONE."
CHOOM

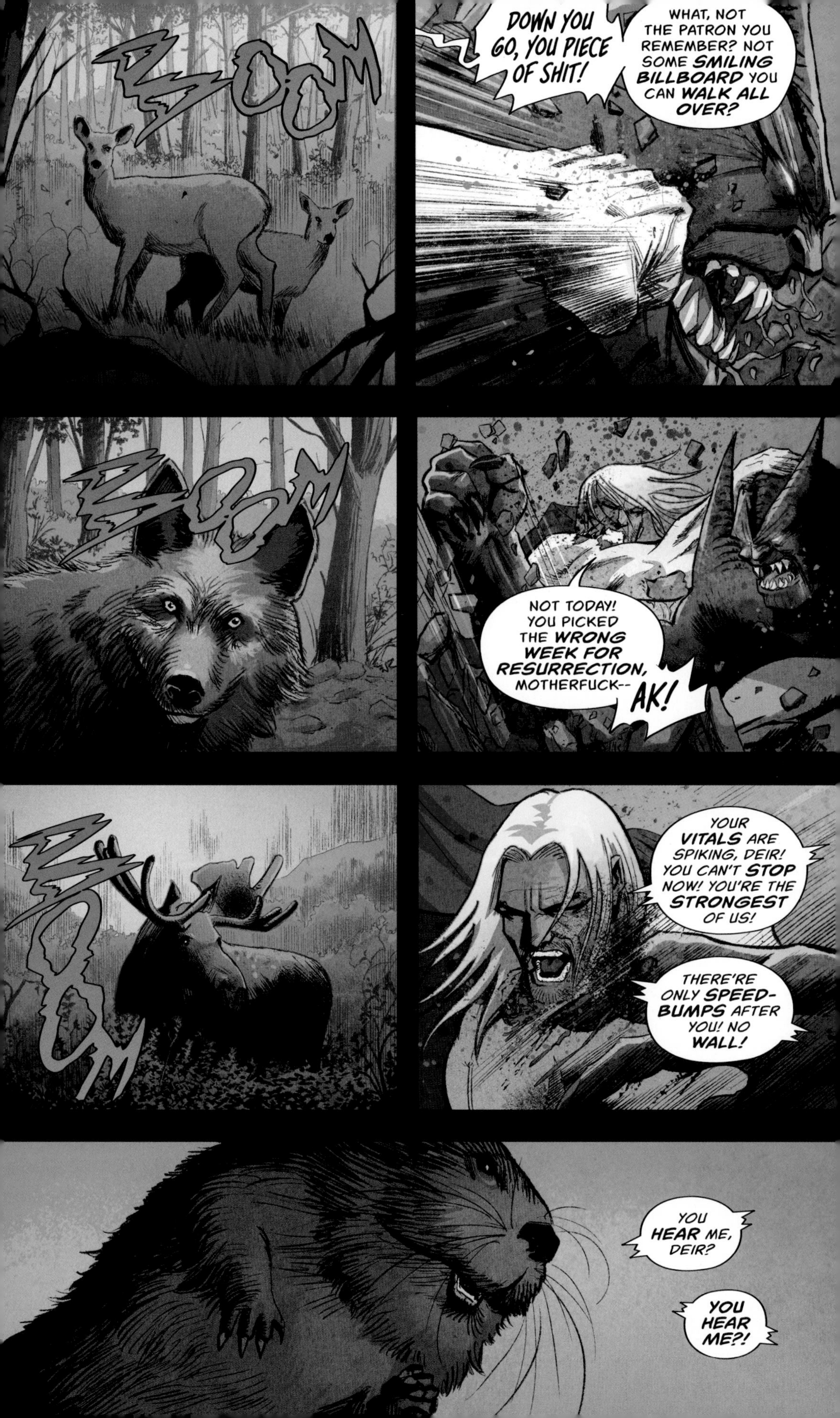
BZOOM
DOWN YOU GO, YOU PIECE OF SHIT!
WHAT, NOT THE PATRON YOU REMEMBER? NOT SOME SMILING BILLBOARD YOU CAN WALK ALL OVER?
BZOOM
NOT TODAY! YOU PICKED THE WRONG WEEK FOR RESURRECTION, MOTHERFUCK--
AK!
BZOOM
YOUR VITALS ARE SPIKING, DEIR! YOU CAN'T STOP NOW! YOU'RE THE STRONGEST OF US!
THERE'RE ONLY SPEED-BUMPS AFTER YOU! NO WALL!
YOU HEAR ME, DEIR?
YOU HEAR ME?!

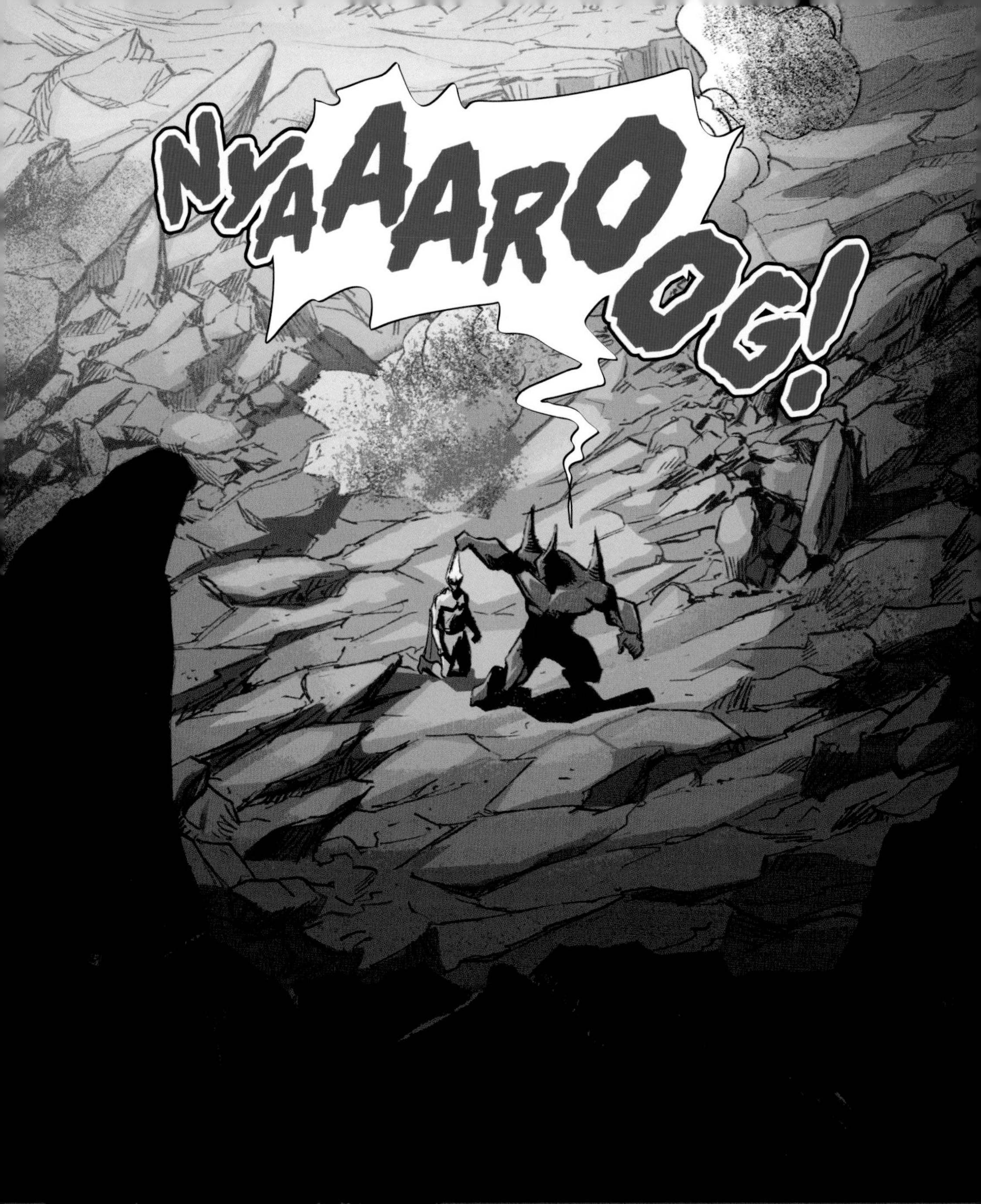
NYAAAROOOG!

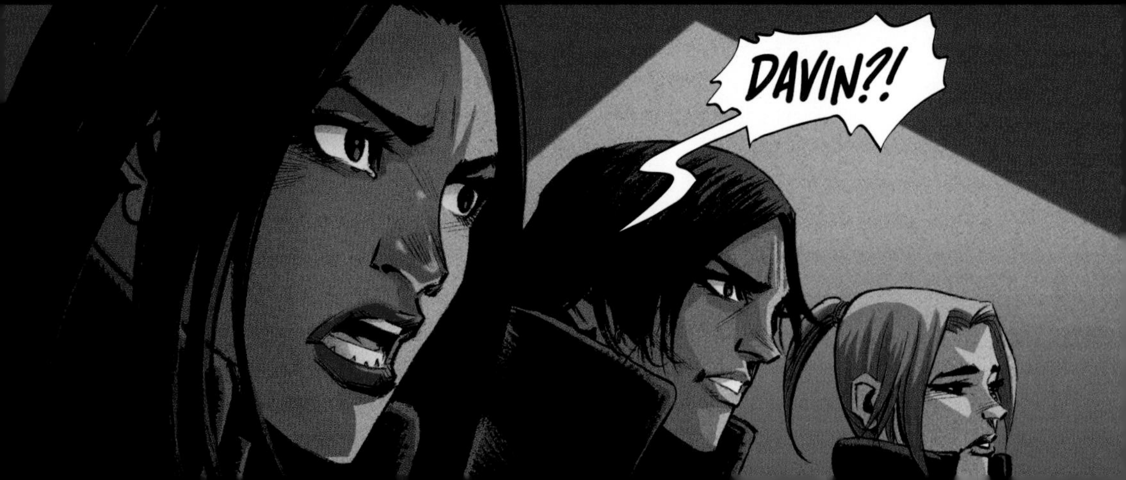
DAVIN?!

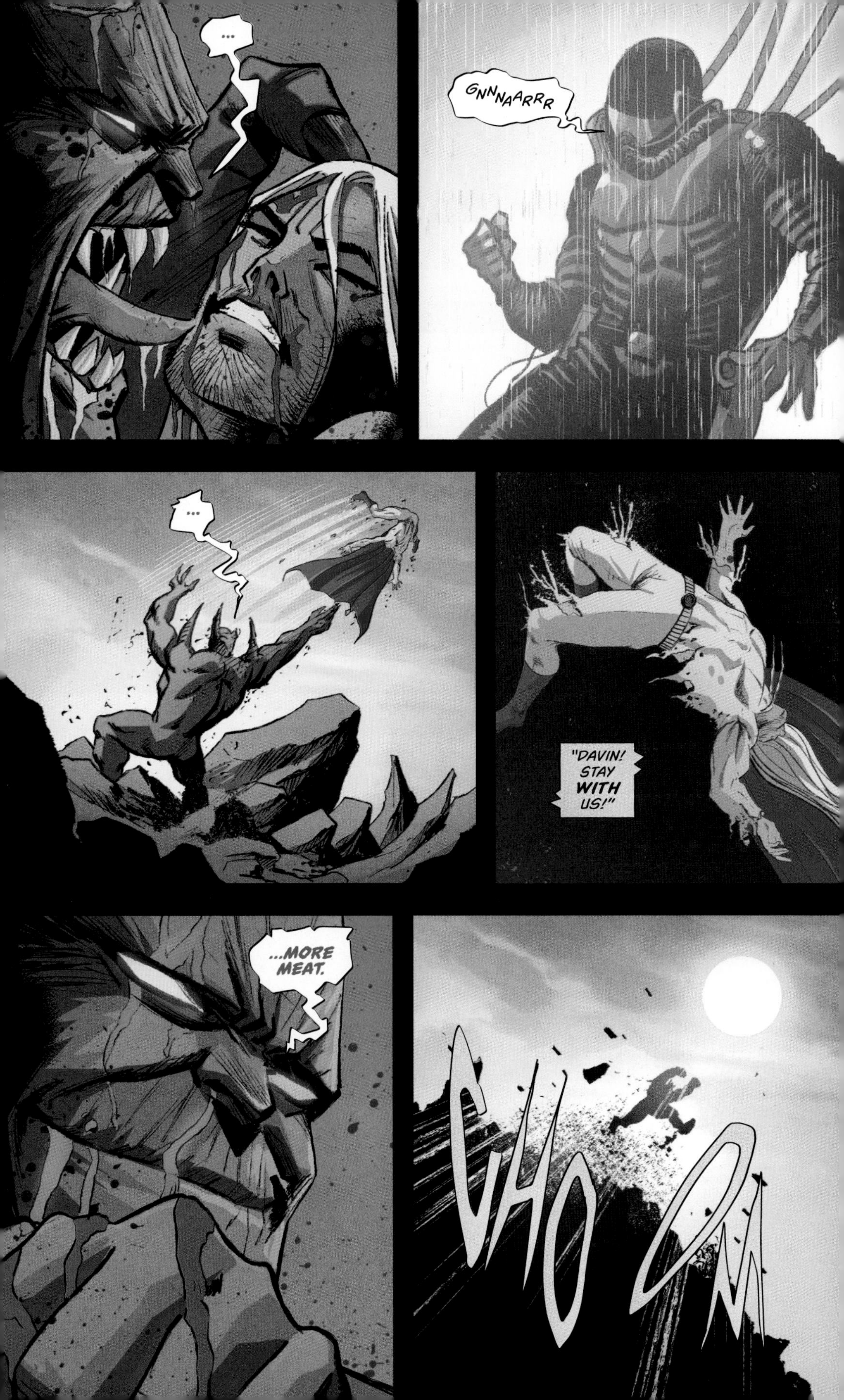
...
GNNNAARRR
...
"DAVIN! STAY WITH US!"
...MORE MEAT.
CHOOM

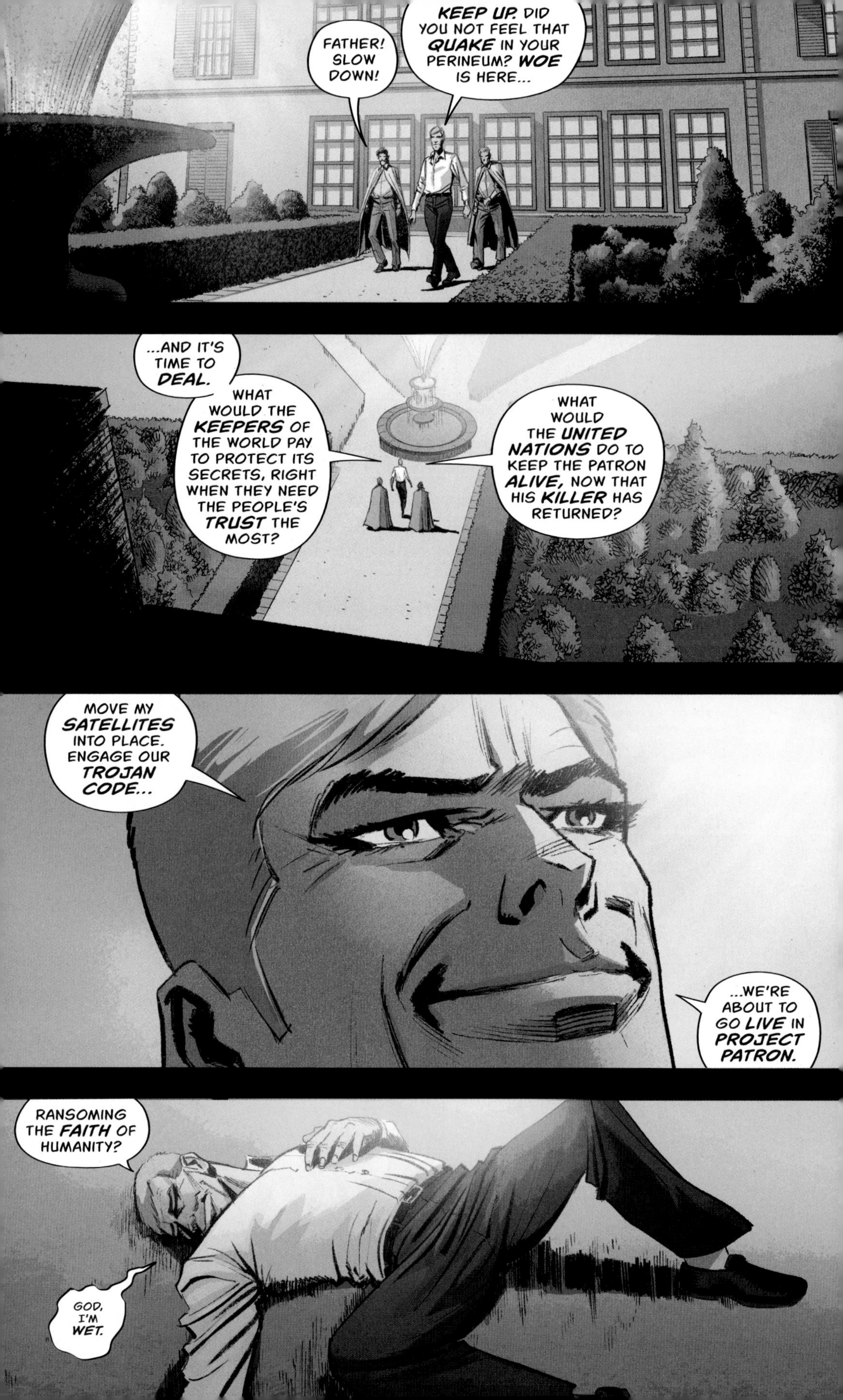
FATHER! SLOW DOWN!
KEEP UP. DID YOU NOT FEEL THAT QUAKE IN YOUR PERINEUM? WOE IS HERE...
...AND IT'S TIME TO DEAL.
WHAT WOULD THE KEEPERS OF THE WORLD PAY TO PROTECT ITS SECRETS, RIGHT WHEN THEY NEED THE PEOPLE'S TRUST THE MOST?
WHAT WOULD THE UNITED NATIONS DO TO KEEP THE PATRON ALIVE, NOW THAT HIS KILLER HAS RETURNED?
MOVE MY SATELLITES INTO PLACE. ENGAGE OUR TROJAN CODE...
...WE'RE ABOUT TO GO LIVE IN PROJECT PATRON.
RANSOMING THE FAITH OF HUMANITY?
GOD, I'M WET.

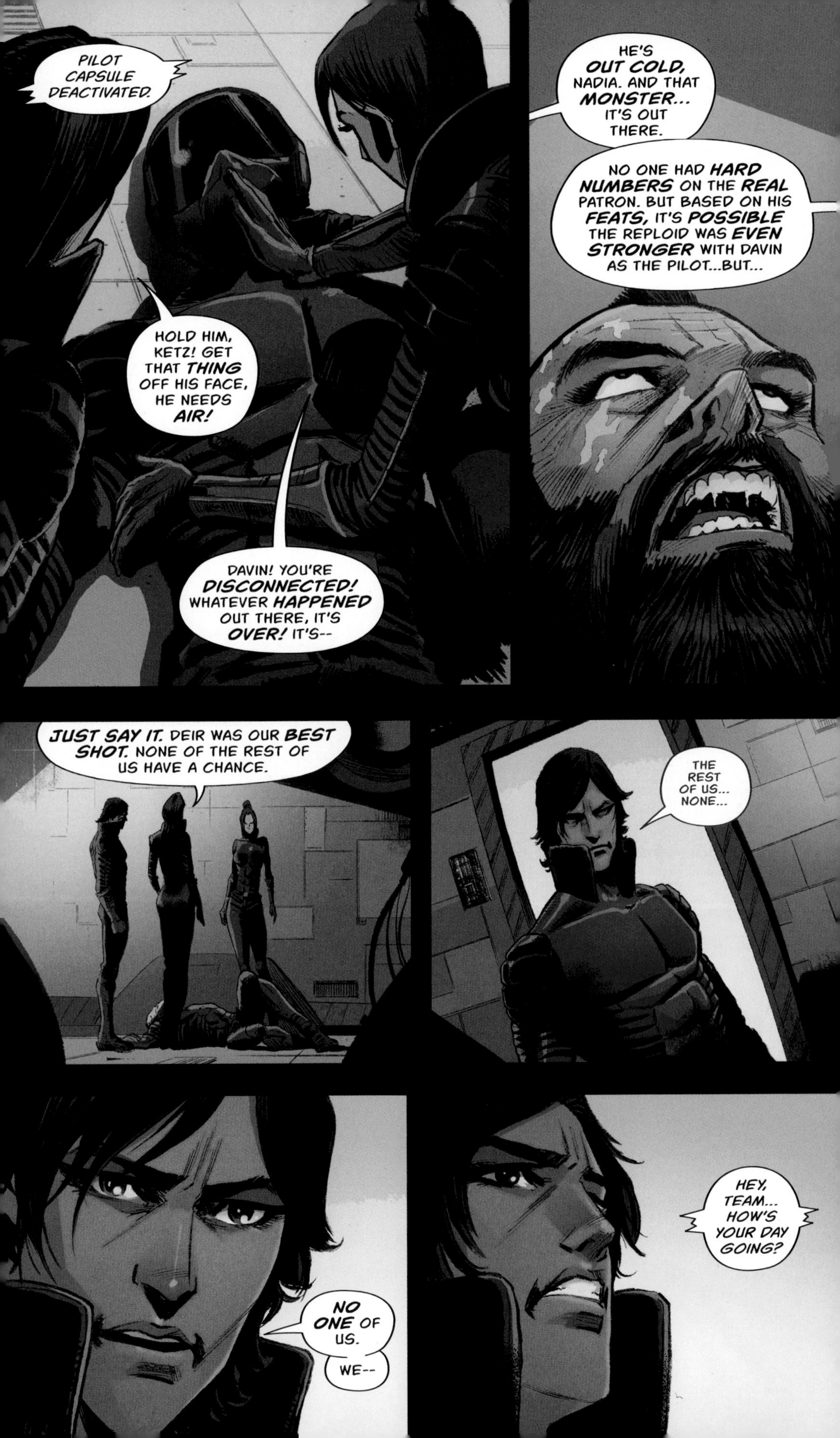
PILOT CAPSULE DEACTIVATED.
HOLD HIM, KETZ! GET THAT THING OFF HIS FACE, HE NEEDS AIR!
DAVIN! YOU'RE DISCONNECTED! WHATEVER HAPPENED OUT THERE, IT'S OVER! IT'S--
HE'S OUT COLD, NADIA. AND THAT MONSTER... IT'S OUT THERE.
NO ONE HAD HARD NUMBERS ON THE REAL PATRON. BUT BASED ON HIS FEATS, IT'S POSSIBLE THE REPLOID WAS EVEN STRONGER WITH DAVIN AS THE PILOT...BUT...
JUST SAY IT. DEIR WAS OUR BEST SHOT. NONE OF THE REST OF US HAVE A CHANCE.
THE REST OF US... NONE...
NO ONE OF US.
WE--
HEY, TEAM... HOW'S YOUR DAY GOING?

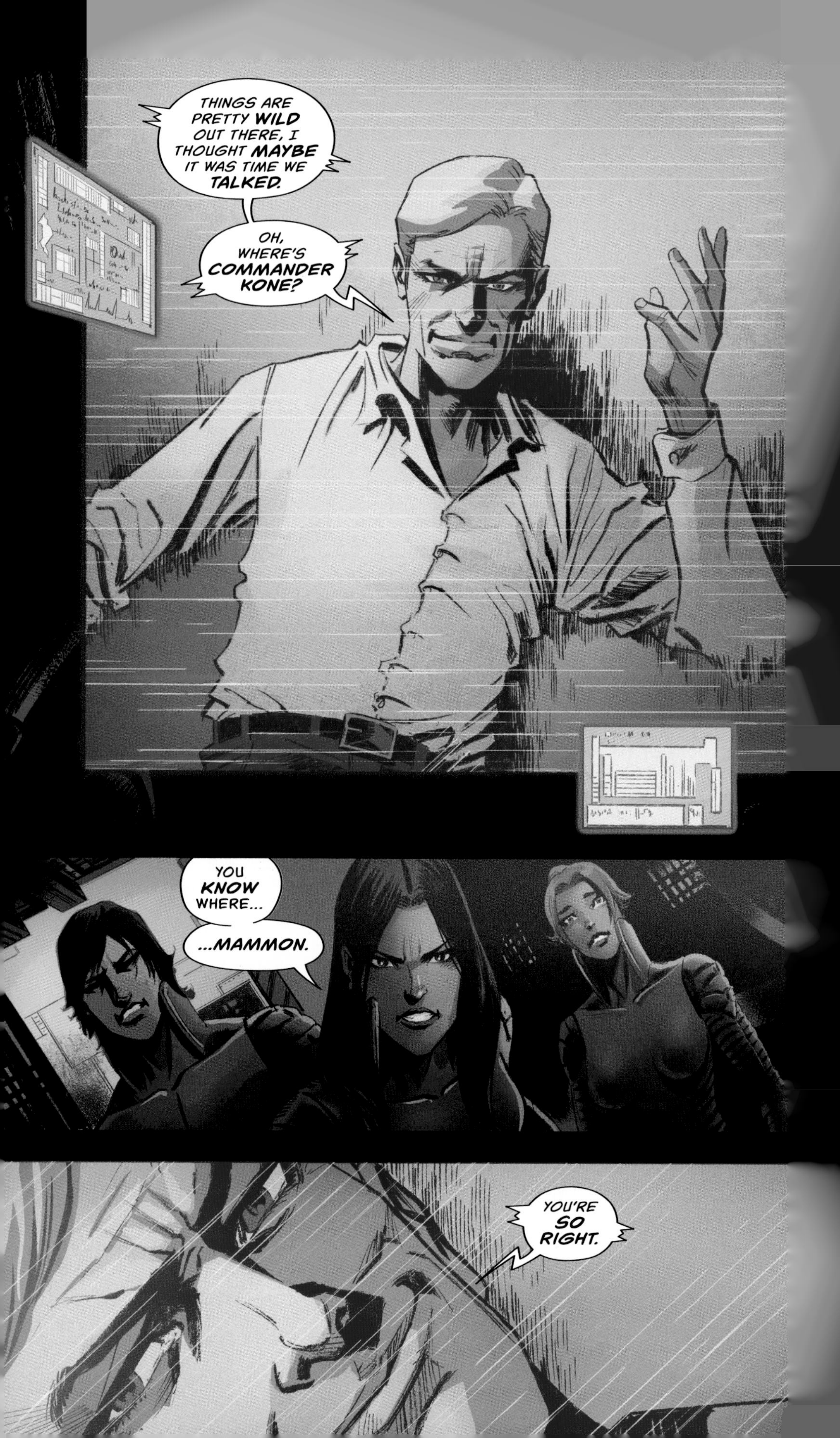
THINGS ARE PRETTY WILD OUT THERE, I THOUGHT MAYBE IT WAS TIME WE TALKED.
OH, WHERE'S COMMANDER KONE?
YOU KNOW WHERE...
...MAMMON.
YOU'RE SO RIGHT.

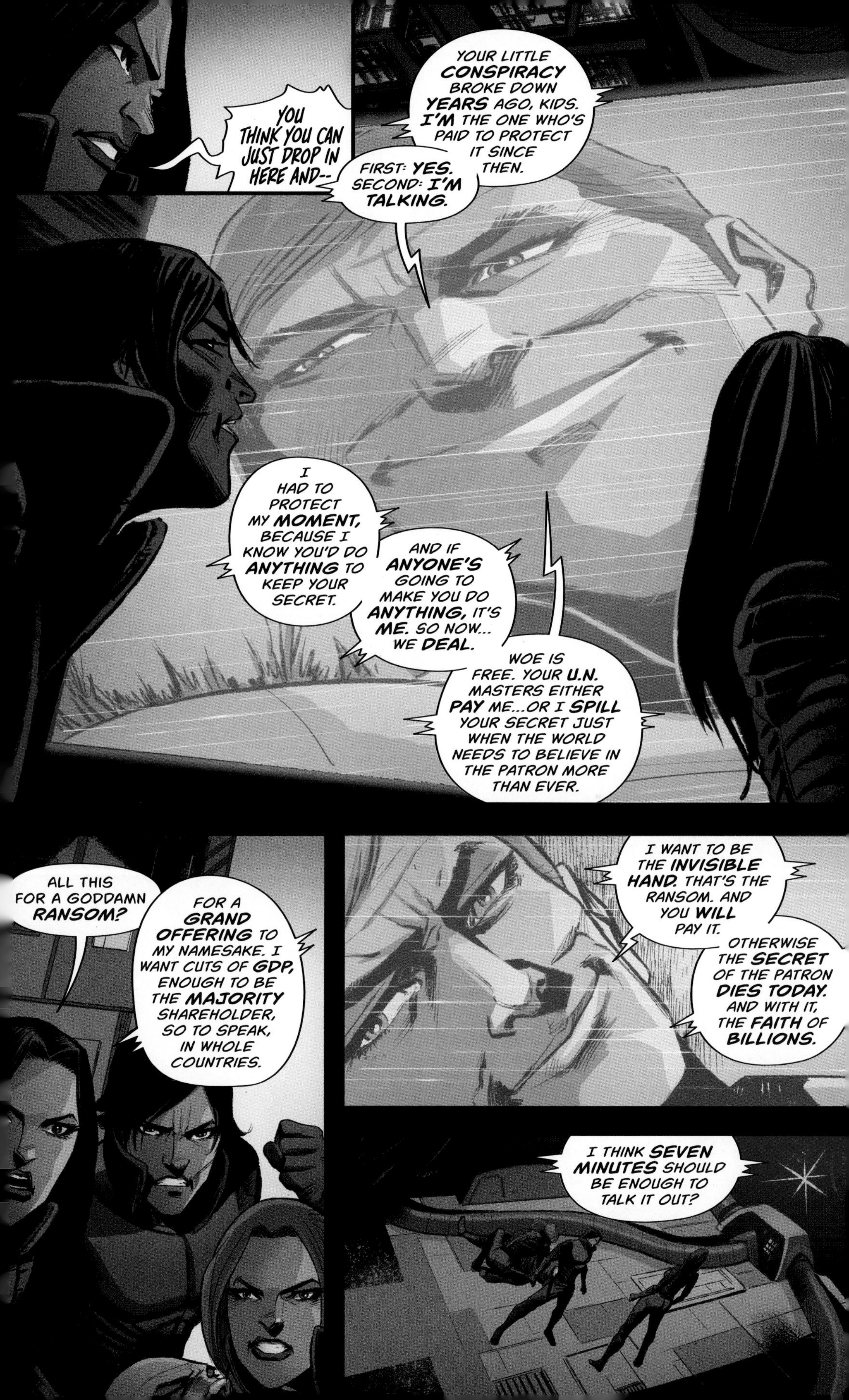
YOU THINK YOU CAN JUST DROP IN HERE AND--
YOUR LITTLE CONSPIRACY BROKE DOWN YEARS AGO, KIDS. I'M THE ONE WHO'S PAID TO PROTECT IT SINCE THEN.
FIRST: YES. SECOND: I'M TALKING.
I HAD TO PROTECT MY MOMENT, BECAUSE I KNOW YOU'D DO ANYTHING TO KEEP YOUR SECRET.
AND IF ANYONE'S GOING TO MAKE YOU DO ANYTHING, IT'S ME. SO NOW... WE DEAL.
WOE IS FREE. YOUR U.N. MASTERS EITHER PAY ME...OR I SPILL YOUR SECRET JUST WHEN THE WORLD NEEDS TO BELIEVE IN THE PATRON MORE THAN EVER.
ALL THIS FOR A GODDAMN RANSOM?
FOR A GRAND OFFERING TO MY NAMESAKE. I WANT CUTS OF GDP, ENOUGH TO BE THE MAJORITY SHAREHOLDER, SO TO SPEAK, IN WHOLE COUNTRIES.
I WANT TO BE THE INVISIBLE HAND. THAT'S THE RANSOM. AND YOU WILL PAY IT.
OTHERWISE THE SECRET OF THE PATRON DIES TODAY. AND WITH IT, THE FAITH OF BILLIONS.
I THINK SEVEN MINUTES SHOULD BE ENOUGH TO TALK IT OUT?

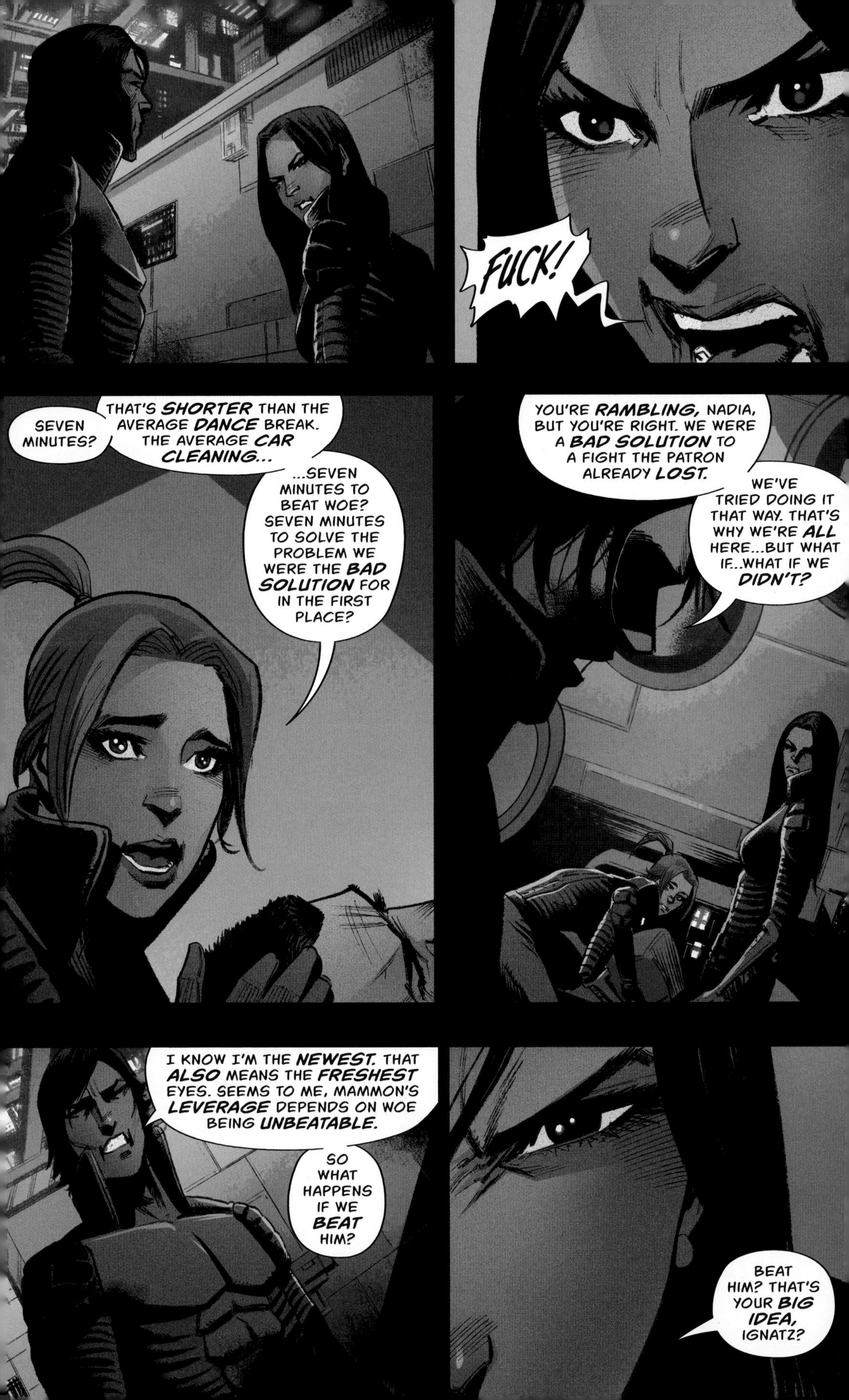
FUCK!
SEVEN MINUTES?
THAT'S SHORTER THAN THE AVERAGE DANCE BREAK. THE AVERAGE CAR CLEANING...
...SEVEN MINUTES TO BEAT WOE? SEVEN MINUTES TO SOLVE THE PROBLEM WE WERE THE BAD SOLUTION FOR IN THE FIRST PLACE?
YOU'RE RAMBLING, NADIA, BUT YOU'RE RIGHT. WE WERE A BAD SOLUTION TO A FIGHT THE PATRON ALREADY LOST.
WE'VE TRIED DOING IT THAT WAY. THAT'S WHY WE'RE ALL HERE...BUT WHAT IF...WHAT IF WE DIDN'T?
I KNOW I'M THE NEWEST. THAT ALSO MEANS THE FRESHEST EYES. SEEMS TO ME, MAMMON'S LEVERAGE DEPENDS ON WOE BEING UNBEATABLE.
SO WHAT HAPPENS IF WE BEAT HIM?
BEAT HIM? THAT'S YOUR BIG IDEA, IGNATZ?

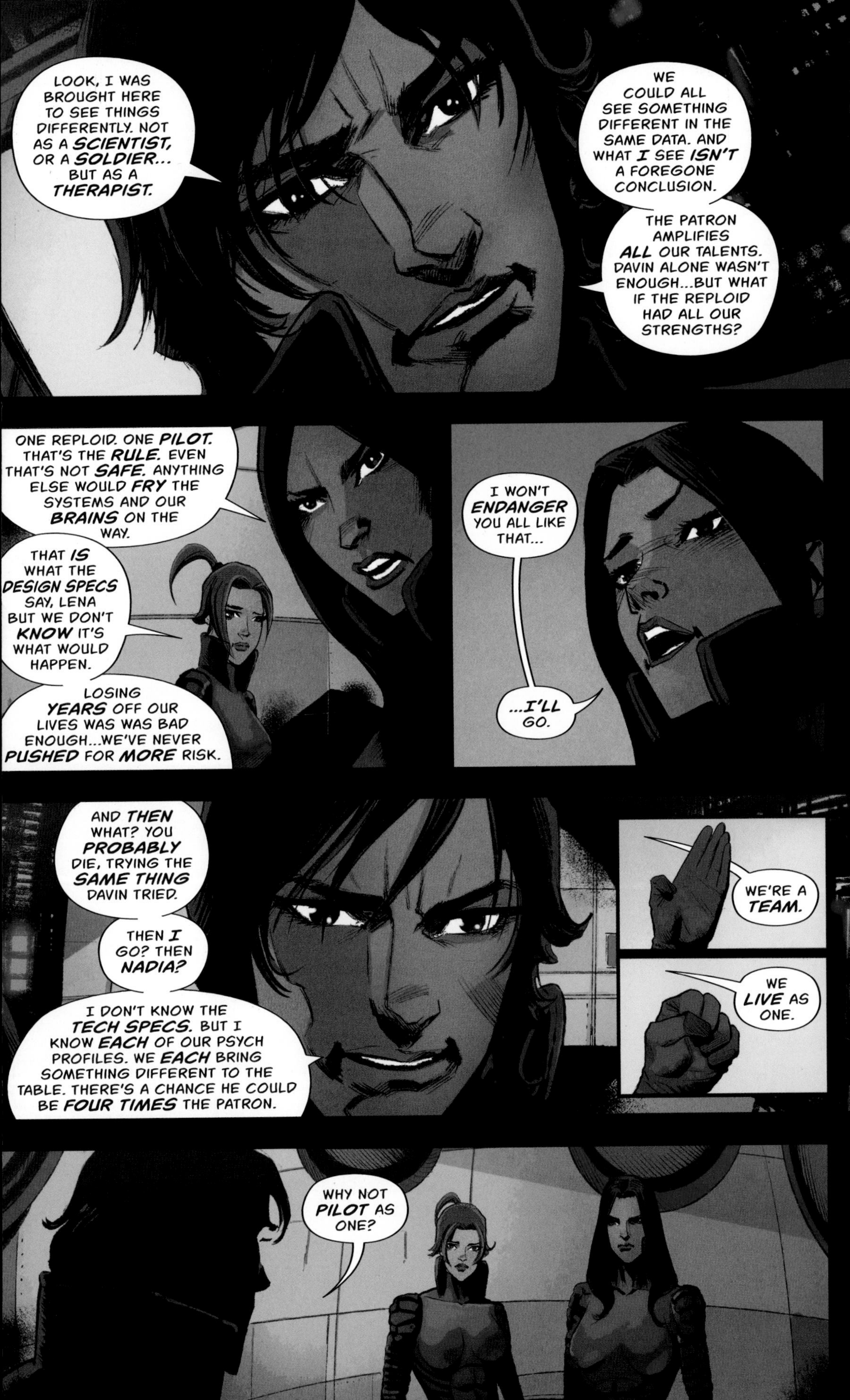
LOOK, I WAS BROUGHT HERE TO SEE THINGS DIFFERENTLY. NOT AS A SCIENTIST, OR A SOLDIER... BUT AS A THERAPIST.
WE COULD ALL SEE SOMETHING DIFFERENT IN THE SAME DATA. AND WHAT I SEE ISN'T A FOREGONE CONCLUSION.
THE PATRON AMPLIFIES ALL OUR TALENTS. DAVIN ALONE WASN'T ENOUGH...BUT WHAT IF THE REPLOID HAD ALL OUR STRENGTHS?
ONE REPLOID. ONE PILOT. THAT'S THE RULE. EVEN THAT'S NOT SAFE. ANYTHING ELSE WOULD FRY THE SYSTEMS AND OUR BRAINS ON THE WAY.
THAT IS WHAT THE DESIGN SPECS SAY, LENA BUT WE DON'T KNOW IT'S WHAT WOULD HAPPEN.
LOSING YEARS OFF OUR LIVES WAS WAS BAD ENOUGH...WE'VE NEVER PUSHED FOR MORE RISK.
I WON'T ENDANGER YOU ALL LIKE THAT...
...I'LL GO.
AND THEN WHAT? YOU PROBABLY DIE, TRYING THE SAME THING DAVIN TRIED.
THEN I GO? THEN NADIA?
I DON'T KNOW THE TECH SPECS. BUT I KNOW EACH OF OUR PSYCH PROFILES. WE EACH BRING SOMETHING DIFFERENT TO THE TABLE. THERE'S A CHANCE HE COULD BE FOUR TIMES THE PATRON.
WE'RE A TEAM.
WE LIVE AS ONE.
WHY NOT PILOT AS ONE?

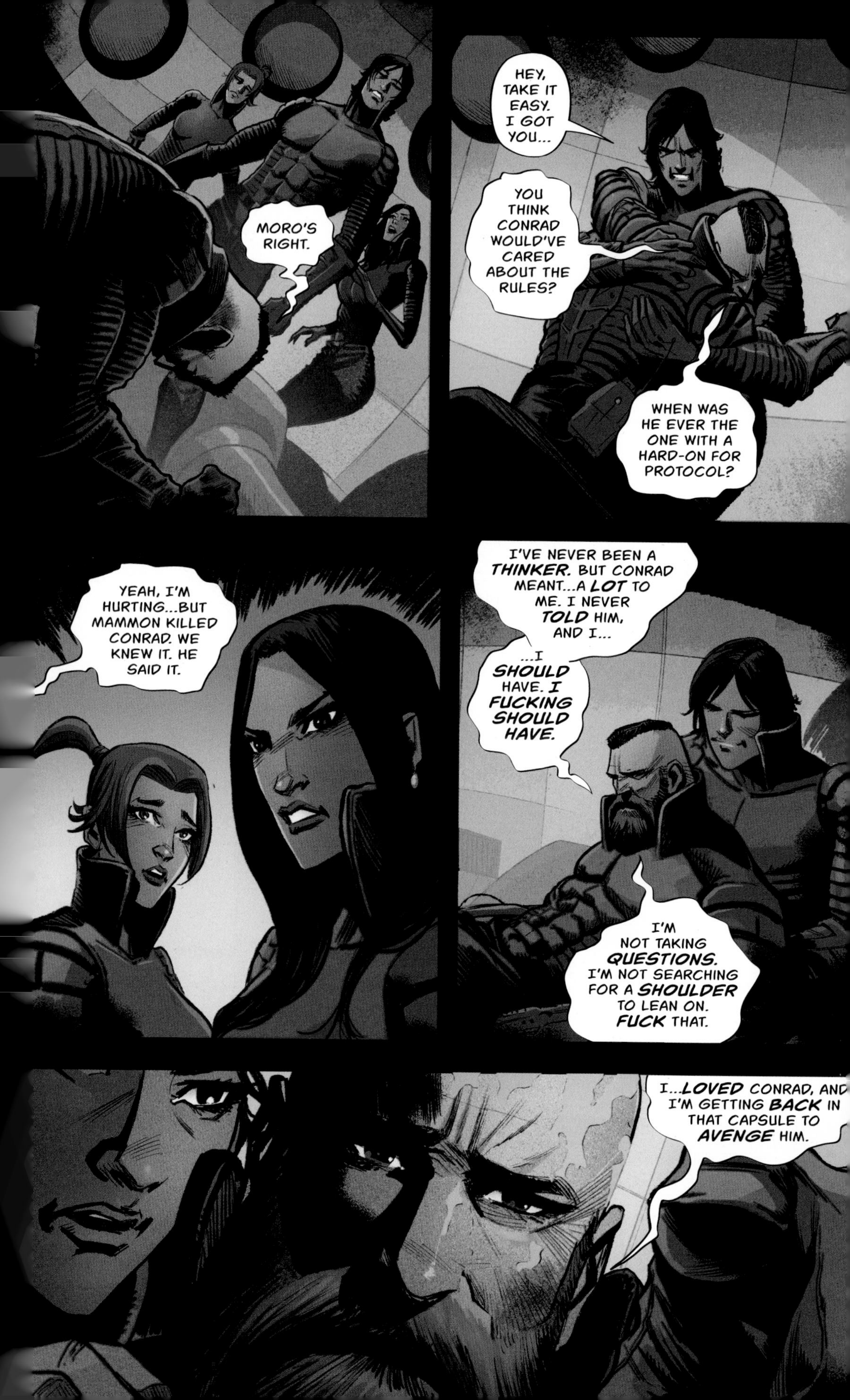
MORO'S RIGHT.
HEY, TAKE IT EASY. I GOT YOU...
YOU THINK CONRAD WOULD'VE CARED ABOUT THE RULES?
WHEN WAS HE EVER THE ONE WITH A HARD-ON FOR PROTOCOL?
YEAH, I'M HURTING...BUT MAMMON KILLED CONRAD. WE KNEW IT. HE SAID IT.
I'VE NEVER BEEN A THINKER. BUT CONRAD MEANT...A LOT TO ME. I NEVER TOLD HIM, AND I...
...I SHOULD HAVE. I FUCKING SHOULD HAVE.
I'M NOT TAKING QUESTIONS. I'M NOT SEARCHING FOR A SHOULDER TO LEAN ON. FUCK THAT.
I...LOVED CONRAD, AND I'M GETTING BACK IN THAT CAPSULE TO AVENGE HIM.

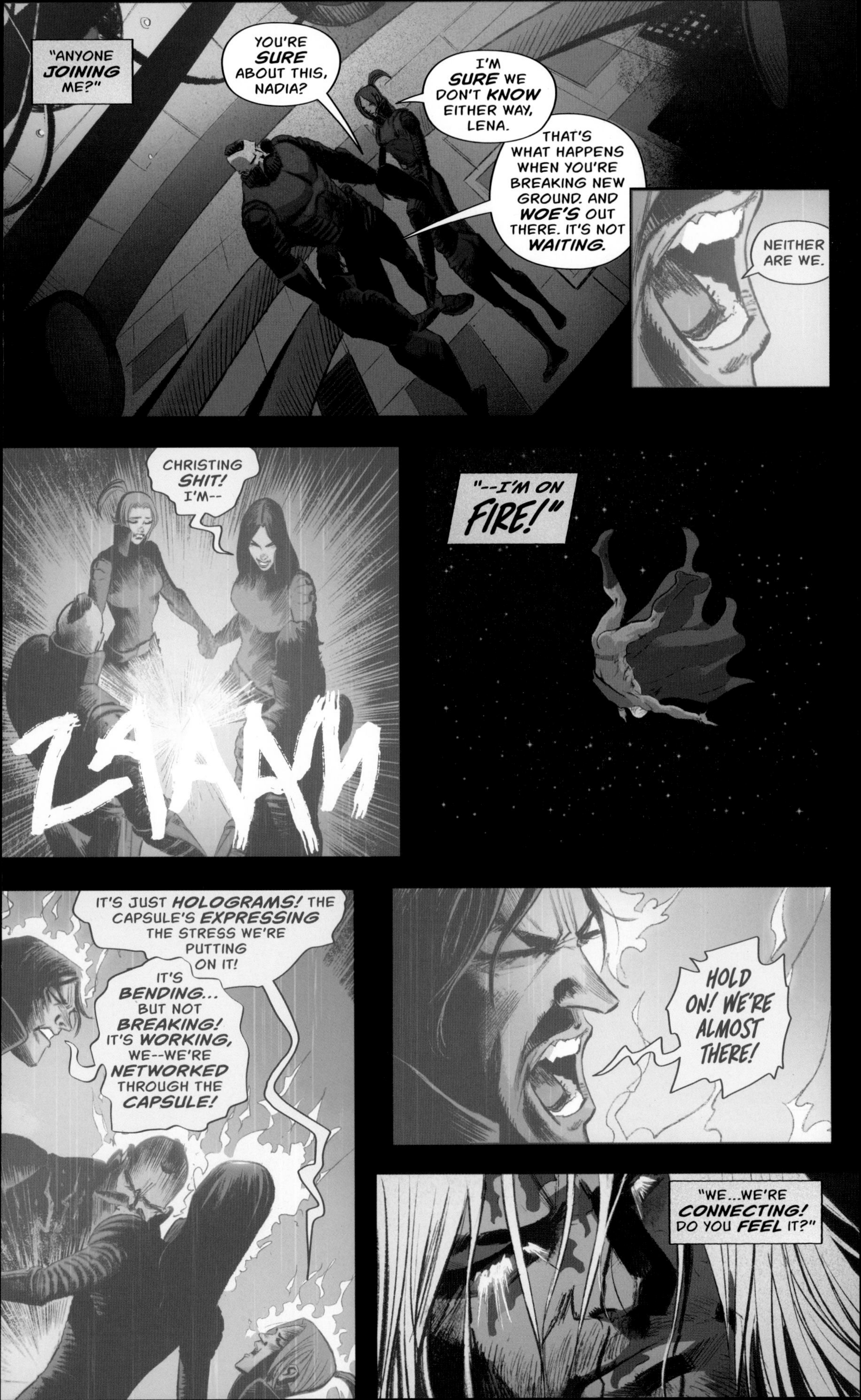
"ANYONE JOINING ME?"
YOU'RE SURE ABOUT THIS, NADIA?
I'M SURE WE DON'T KNOW EITHER WAY, LENA.
THAT'S WHAT HAPPENS WHEN YOU'RE BREAKING NEW GROUND. AND WOE'S OUT THERE. IT'S NOT WAITING.
NEITHER ARE WE.
CHRISTING SHIT! I'M--
ZAAAM
"--I'M ON FIRE!"
IT'S JUST HOLOGRAMS! THE CAPSULE'S EXPRESSING THE STRESS WE'RE PUTTING ON IT!
IT'S BENDING... BUT NOT BREAKING! IT'S WORKING, WE--WE'RE NETWORKED THROUGH THE CAPSULE!
HOLD ON! WE'RE ALMOST THERE!
"WE...WE'RE CONNECTING! DO YOU FEEL IT?"

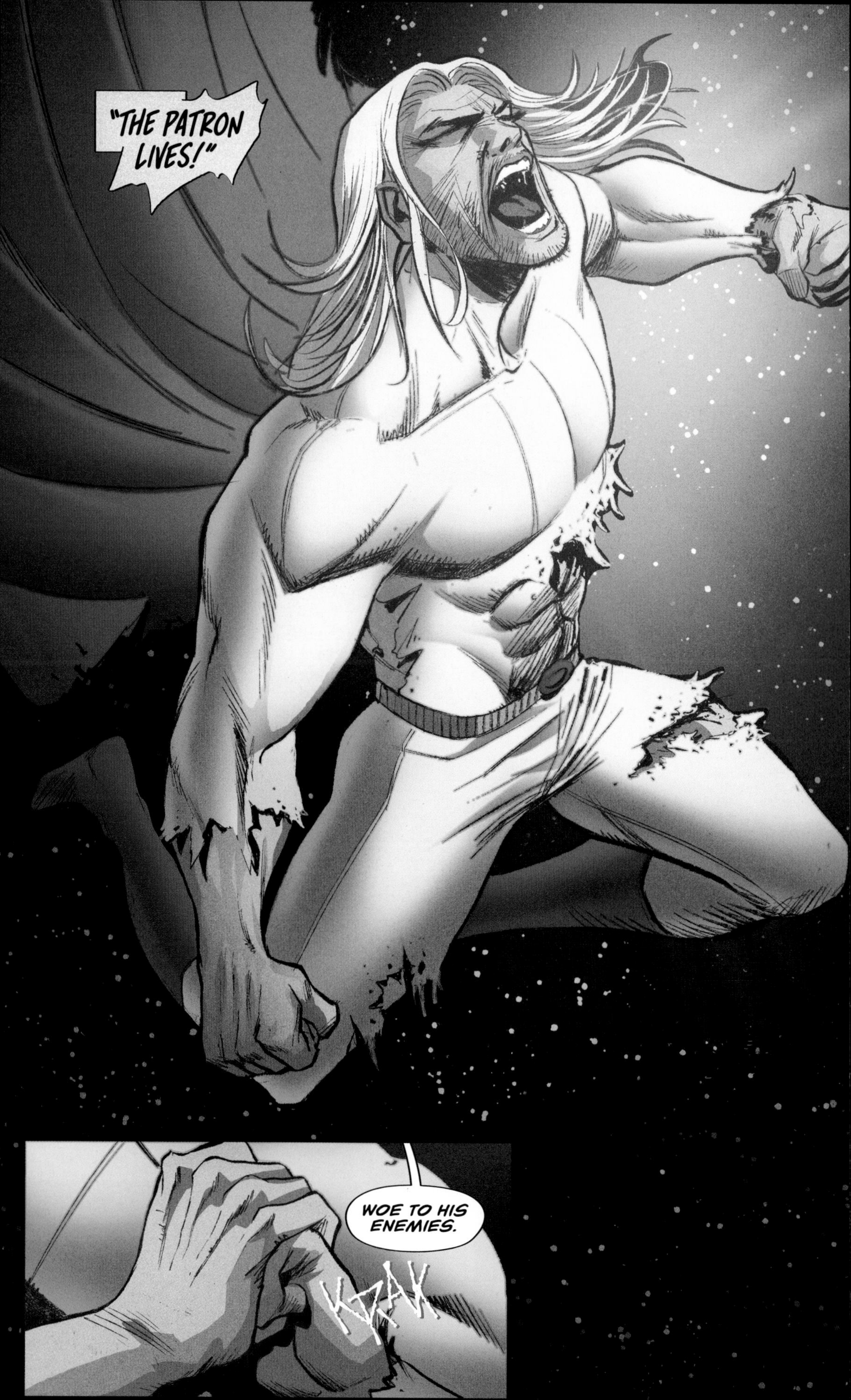
"THE PATRON LIVES!"
WOE TO HIS ENEMIES.
KRAK

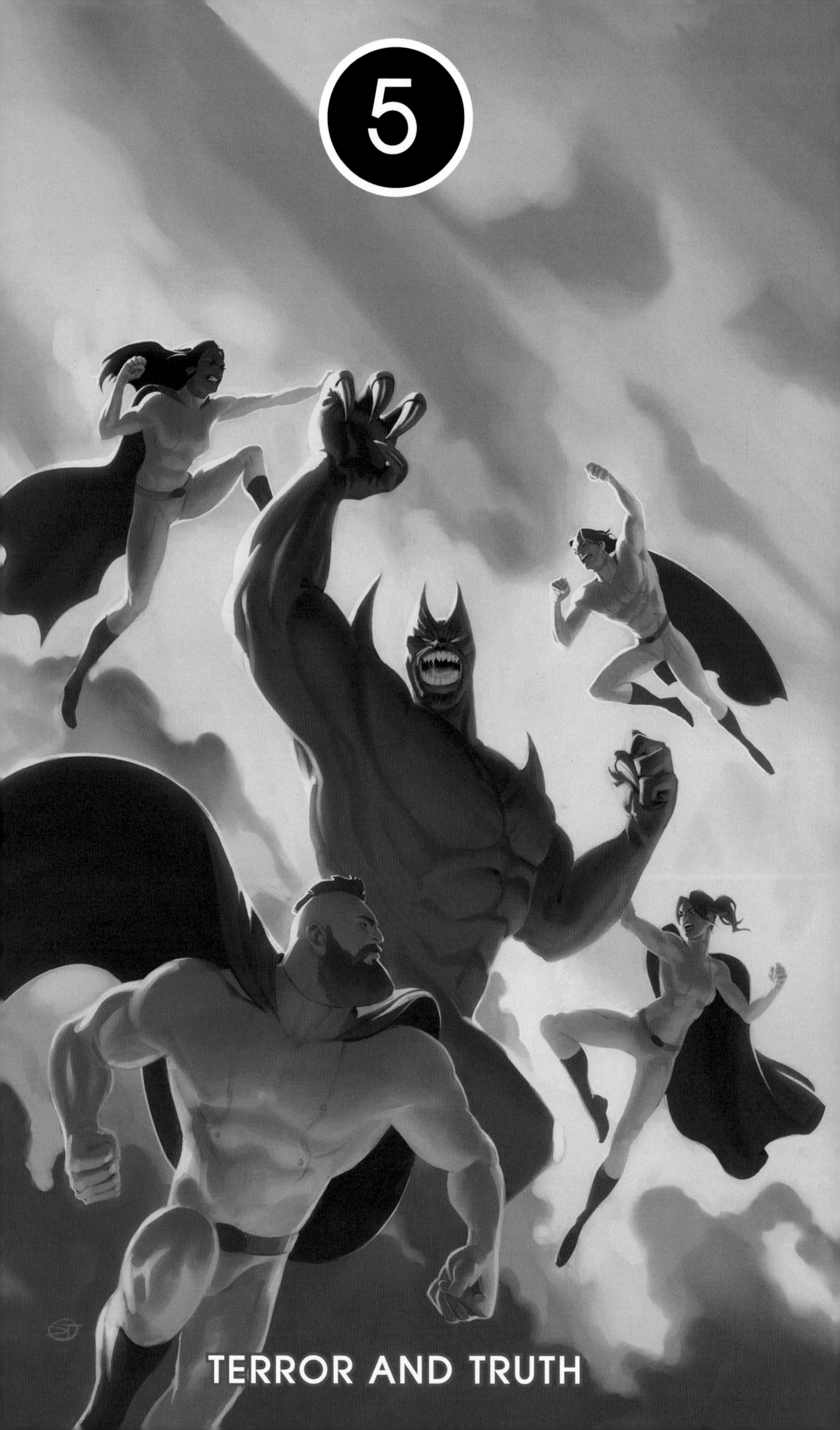
5
TERROR AND TRUTH

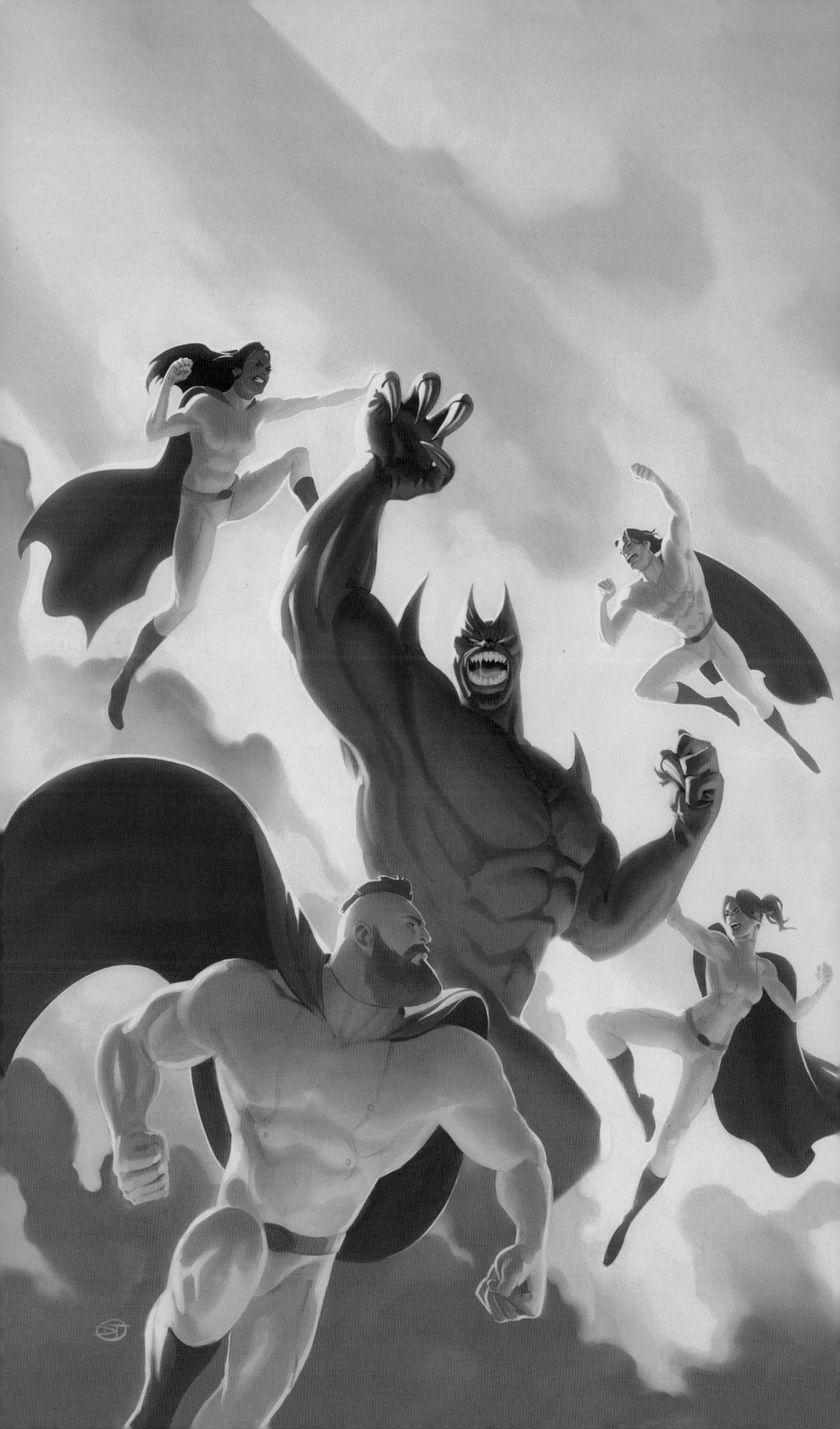

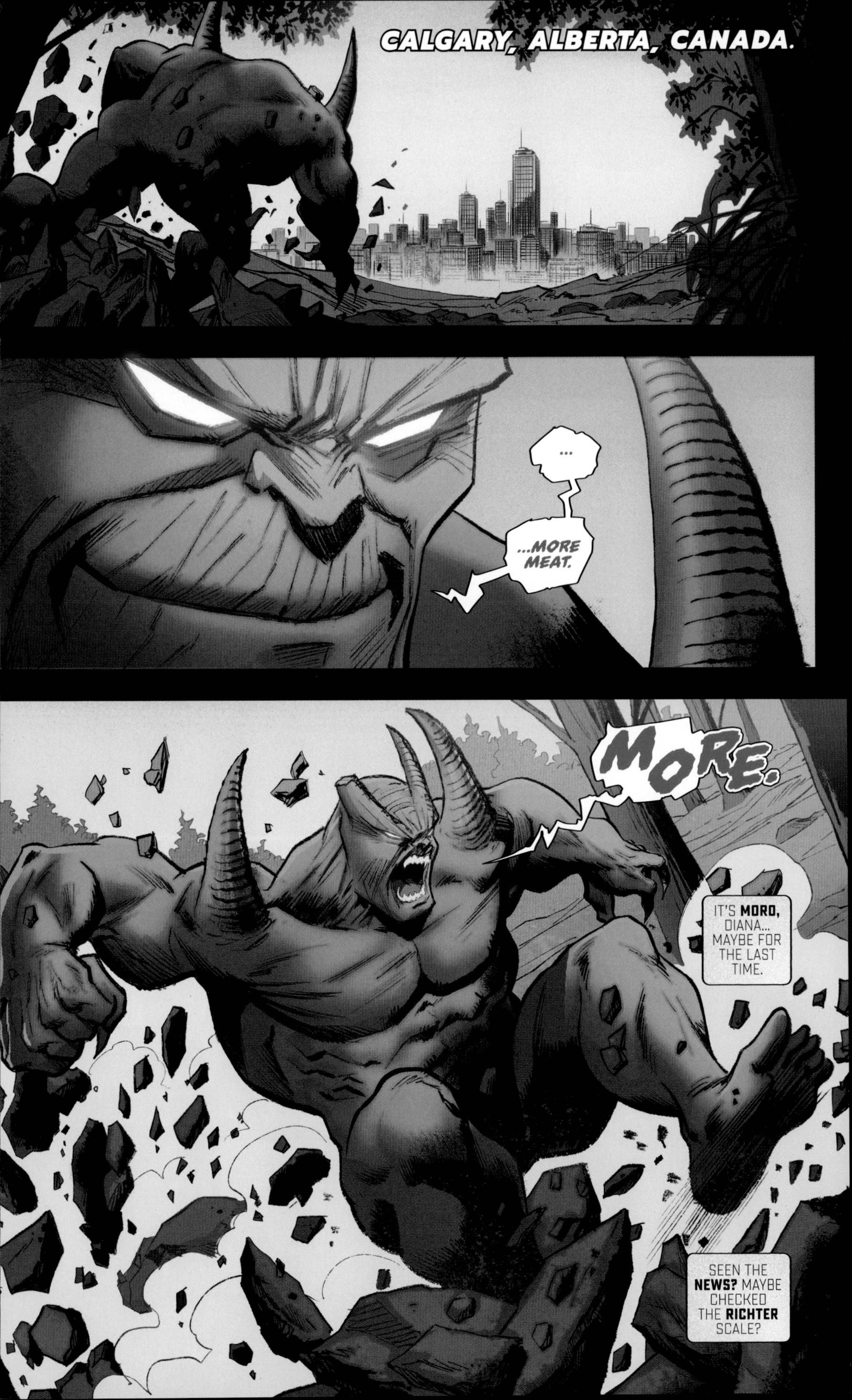
CALGARY, ALBERTA, CANADA.
...
...MORE MEAT.
MORE.
IT'S MORO, DIANA... MAYBE FOR THE LAST TIME.
SEEN THE NEWS? MAYBE CHECKED THE RICHTER SCALE?

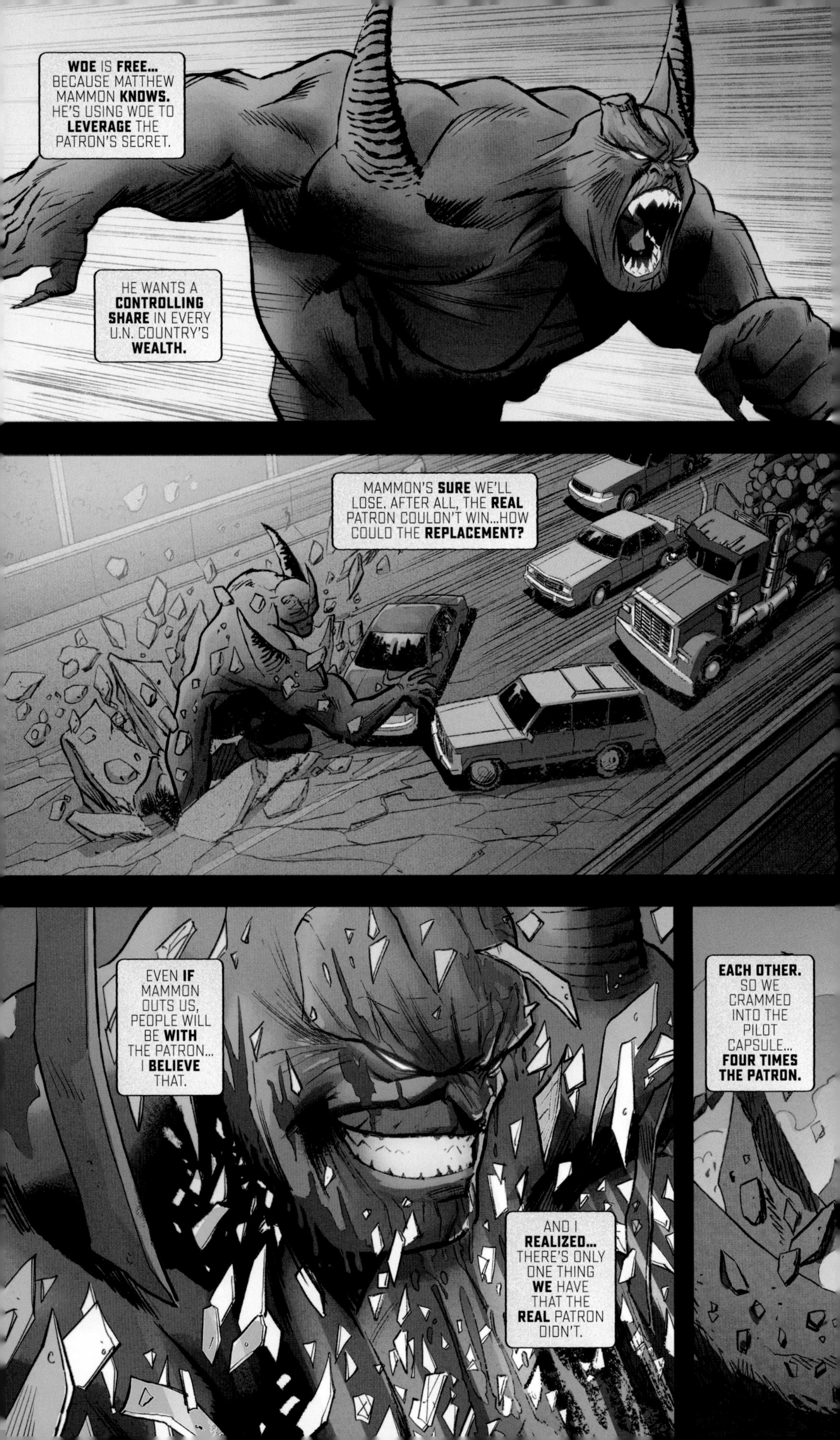
WOE IS FREE... BECAUSE MATTHEW MAMMON KNOWS. HE'S USING WOE TO LEVERAGE THE PATRON'S SECRET.
HE WANTS A CONTROLLING SHARE IN EVERY U.N. COUNTRY'S WEALTH.
MAMMON'S SURE WE'LL LOSE. AFTER ALL, THE REAL PATRON COULDN'T WIN...HOW COULD THE REPLACEMENT?
EVEN IF MAMMON OUTS US, PEOPLE WILL BE WITH THE PATRON... I BELIEVE THAT.
AND I REALIZED... THERE'S ONLY ONE THING WE HAVE THAT THE REAL PATRON DIDN'T.
EACH OTHER. SO WE CRAMMED INTO THE PILOT CAPSULE... FOUR TIMES THE PATRON.

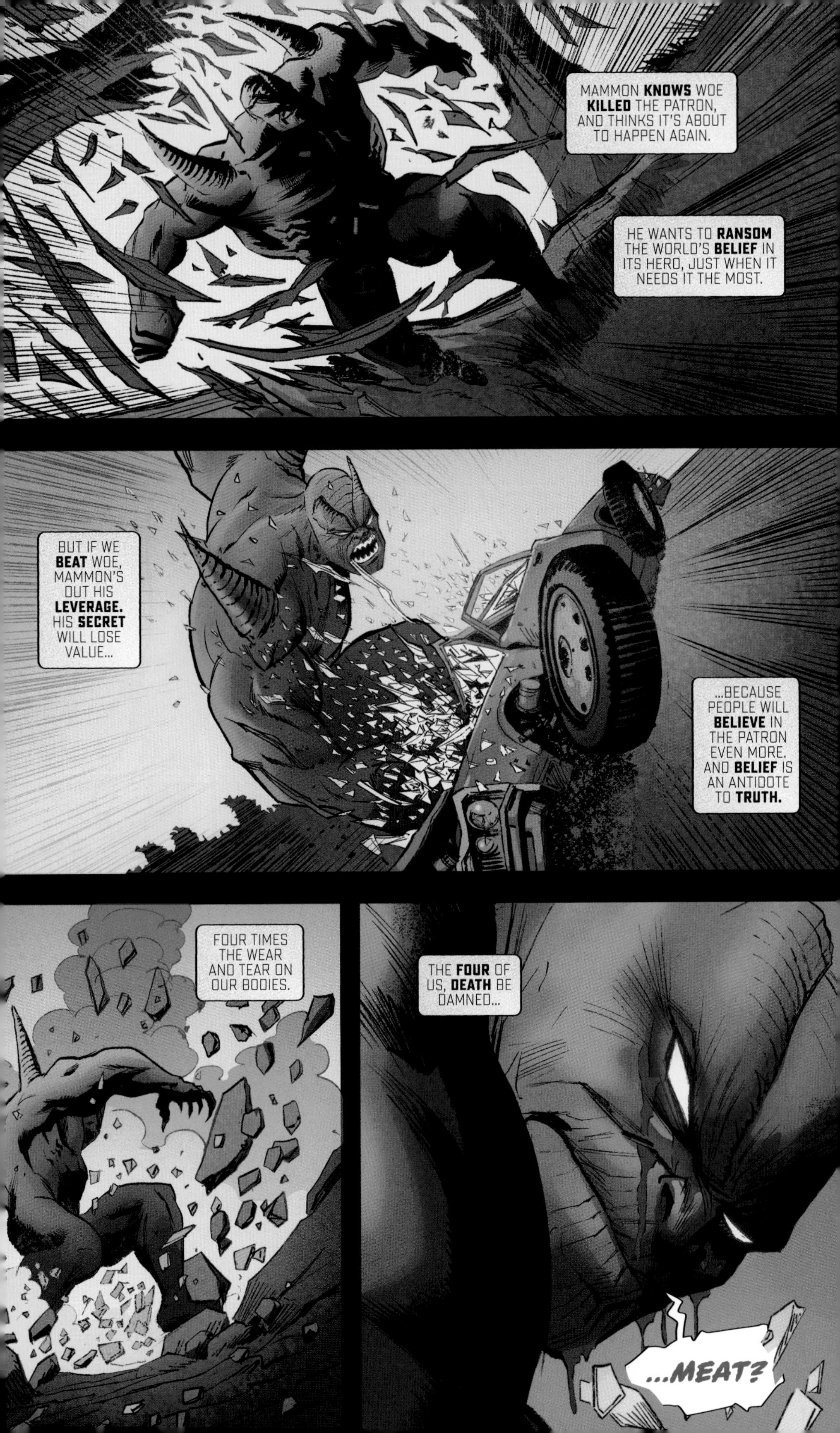
MAMMON KNOWS WOE KILLED THE PATRON, AND THINKS IT'S ABOUT TO HAPPEN AGAIN.
HE WANTS TO RANSOM THE WORLD'S BELIEF IN ITS HERO, JUST WHEN IT NEEDS IT THE MOST.
BUT IF WE BEAT WOE, MAMMON'S OUT HIS LEVERAGE. HIS SECRET WILL LOSE VALUE...
...BECAUSE PEOPLE WILL BELIEVE IN THE PATRON EVEN MORE. AND BELIEF IS AN ANTIDOTE TO TRUTH.
FOUR TIMES THE WEAR AND TEAR ON OUR BODIES.
THE FOUR OF US, DEATH BE DAMNED...
...MEAT?

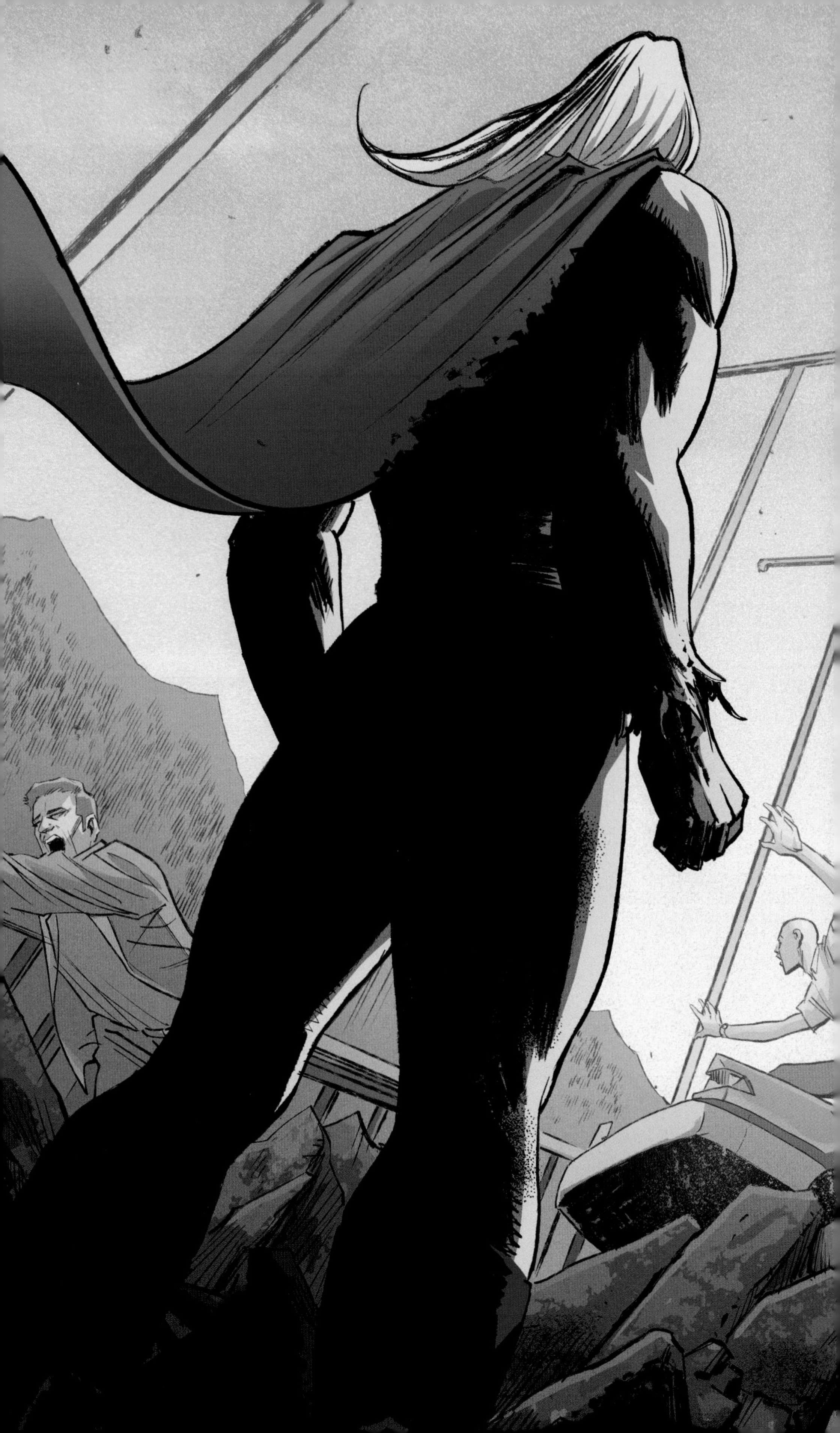

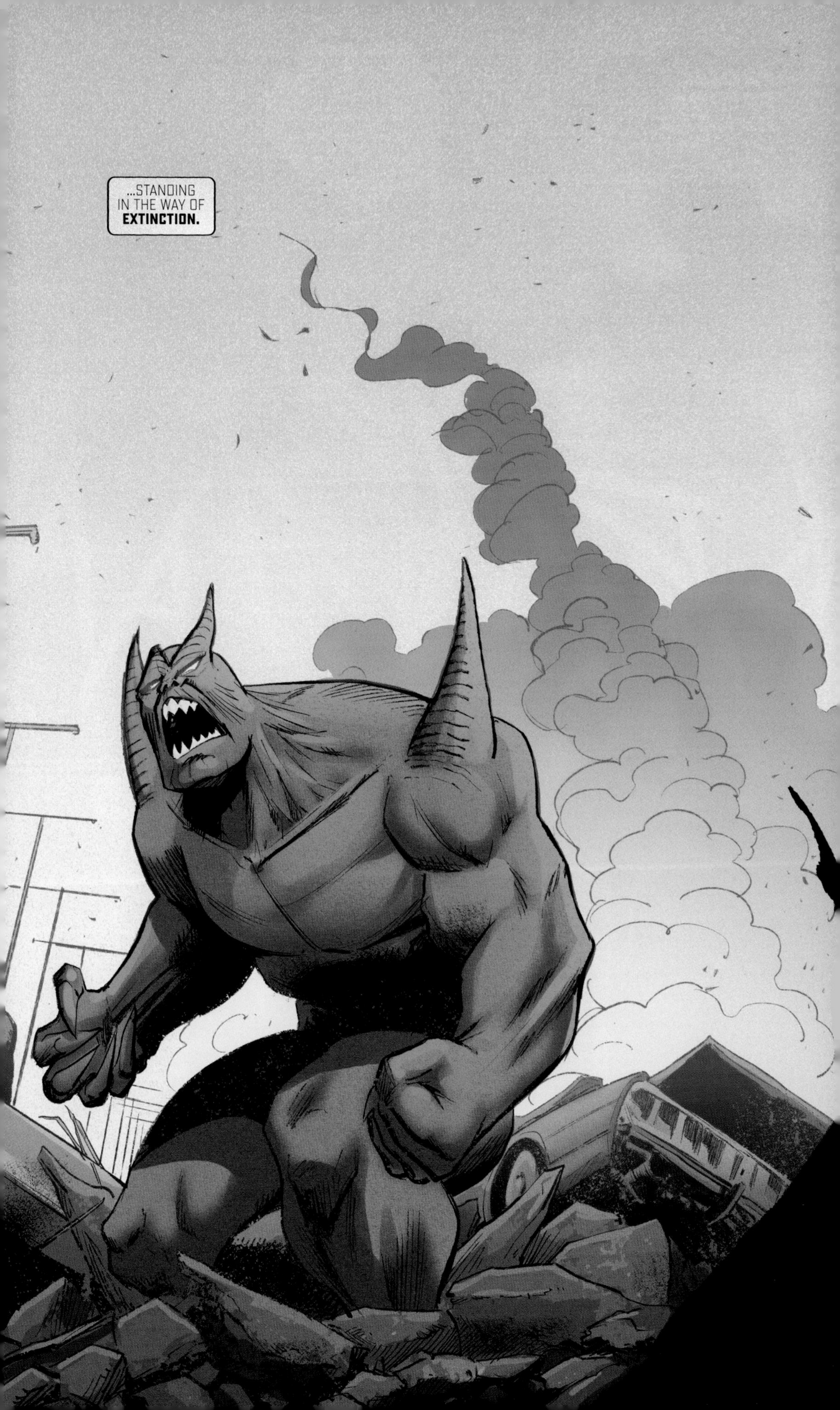
...STANDING IN THE WAY OF **EXTINCTION.**

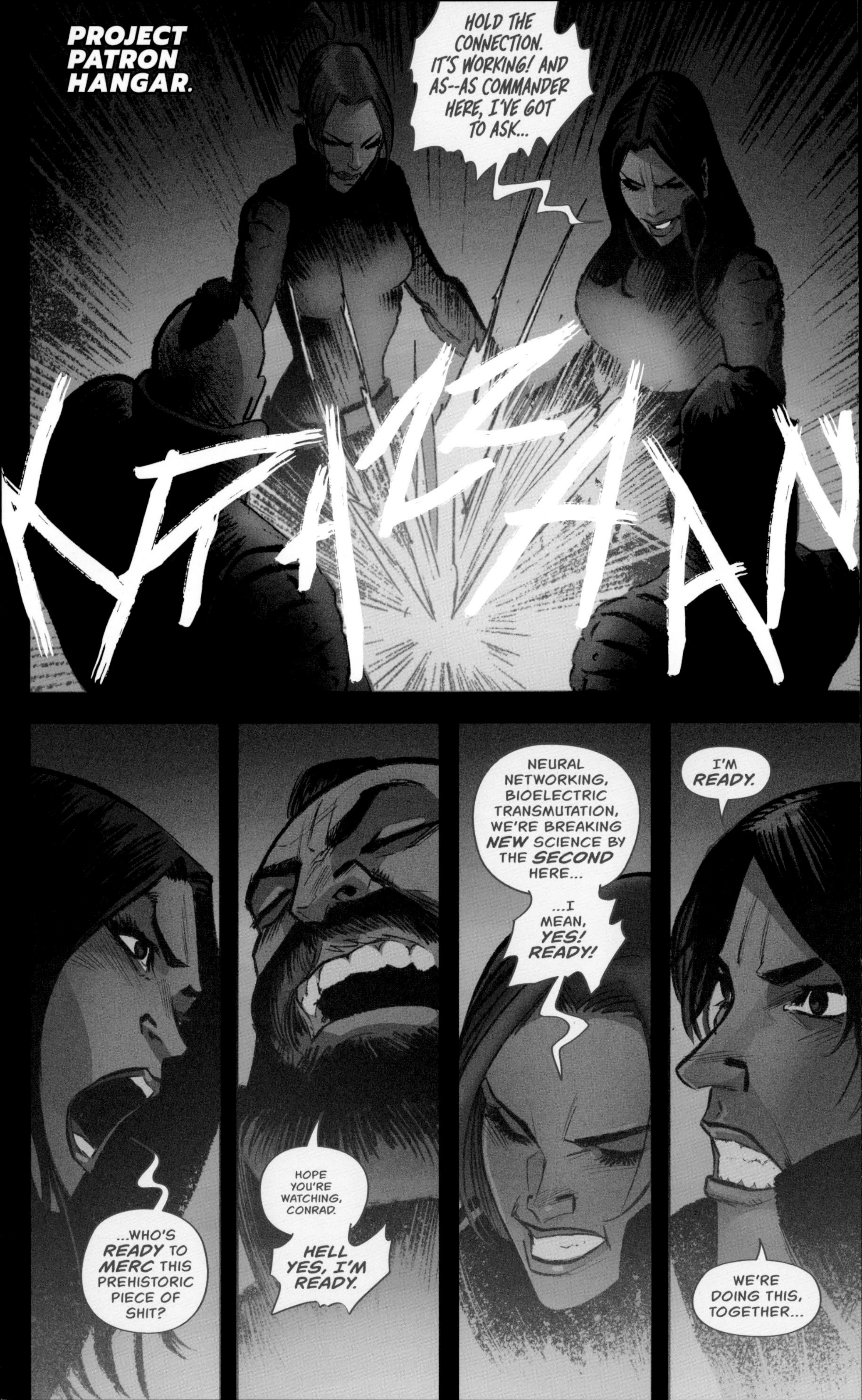
PROJECT PATRON HANGAR.
HOLD THE CONNECTION. IT'S WORKING! AND AS--AS COMMANDER HERE, I'VE GOT TO ASK...
...WHO'S READY TO MERC THIS PREHISTORIC PIECE OF SHIT?
HOPE YOU'RE WATCHING, CONRAD.
HELL YES, I'M READY.
NEURAL NETWORKING, BIOELECTRIC TRANSMUTATION, WE'RE BREAKING NEW SCIENCE BY THE SECOND HERE...
...I MEAN, YES! READY!
I'M READY.
WE'RE DOING THIS, TOGETHER...

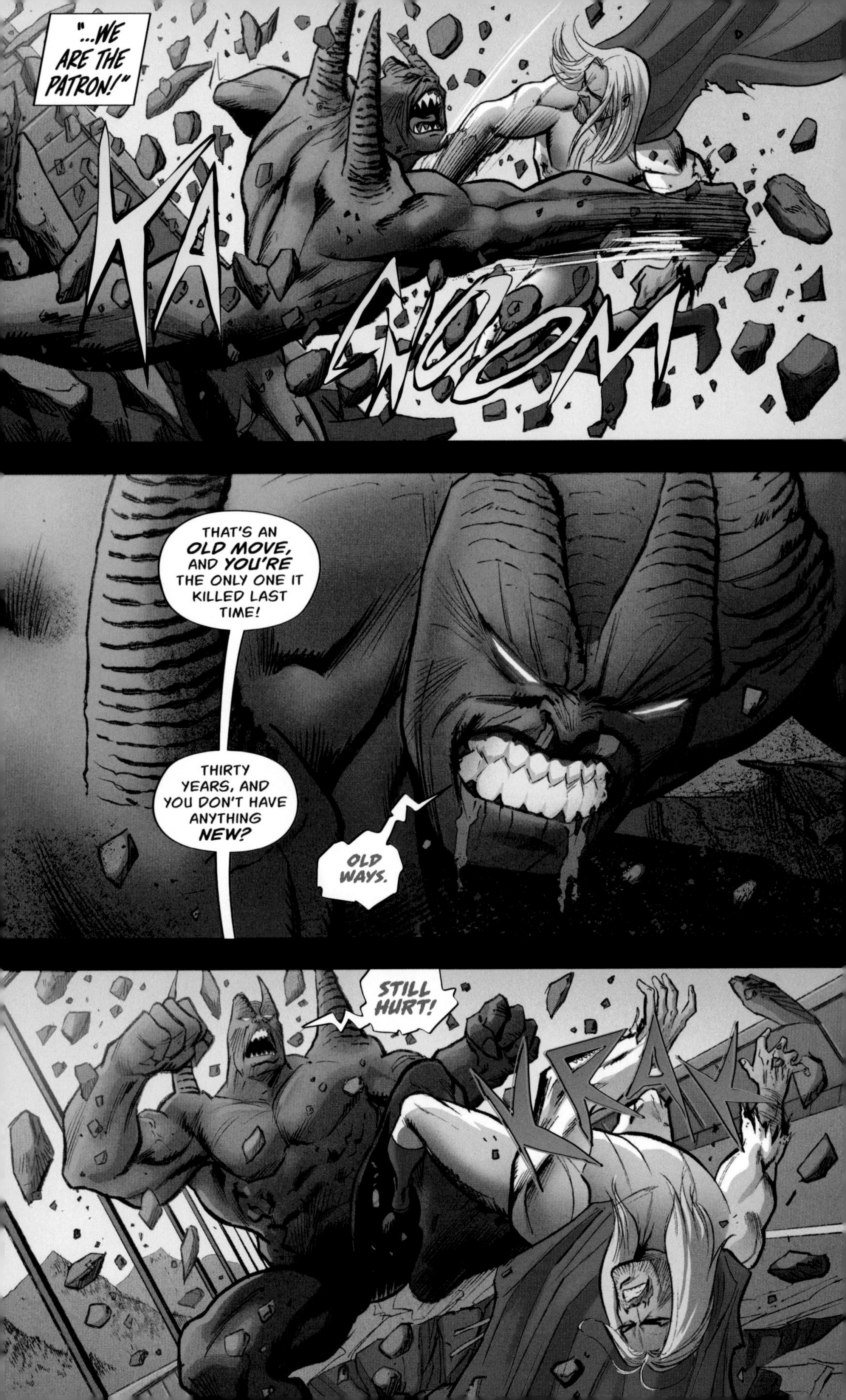
"...WE ARE THE PATRON!"
KA WOOM
THAT'S AN OLD MOVE, AND YOU'RE THE ONLY ONE IT KILLED LAST TIME!
THIRTY YEARS, AND YOU DON'T HAVE ANYTHING NEW?
OLD WAYS.
STILL HURT!
KRAK

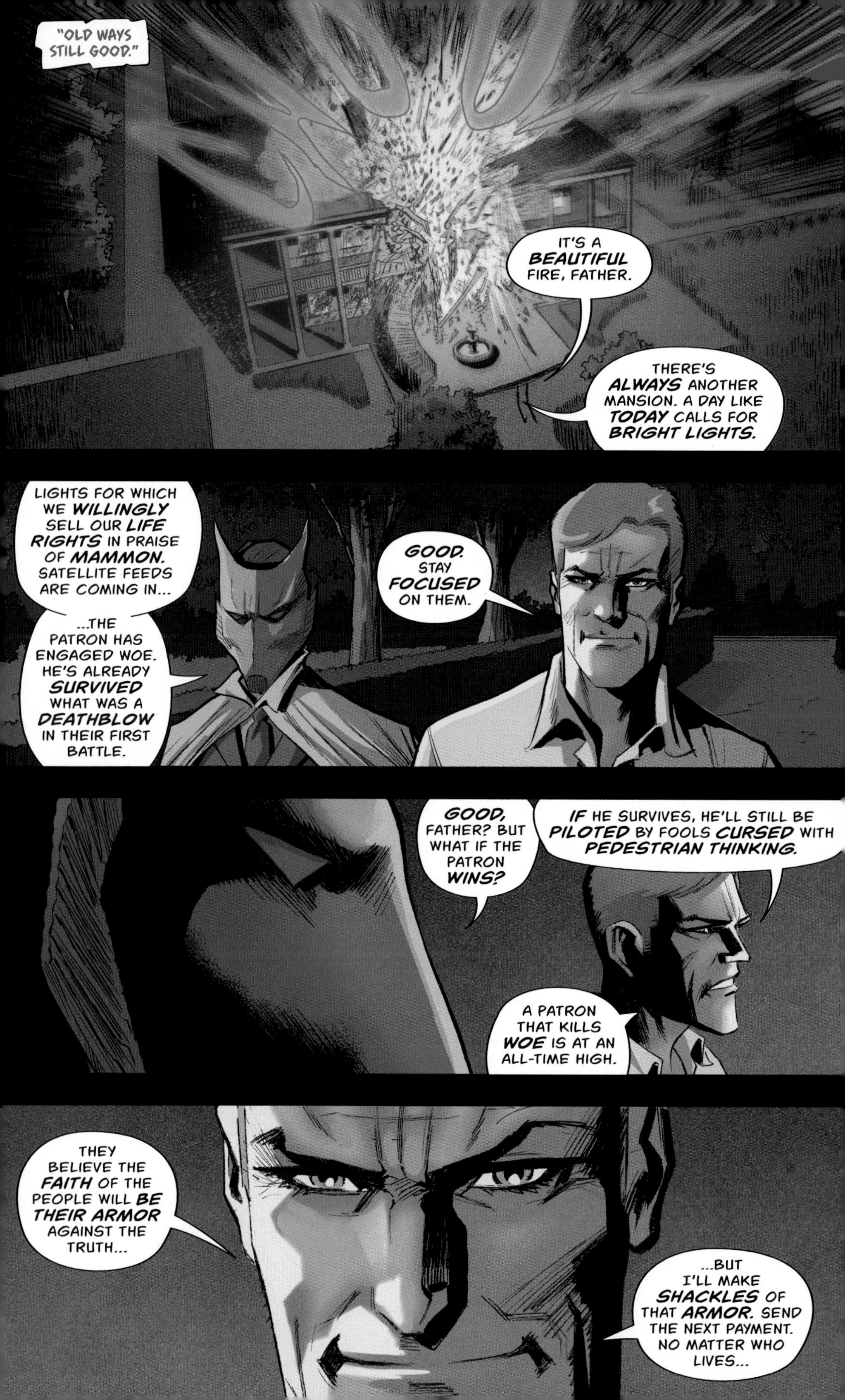
"OLD WAYS STILL GOOD."
IT'S A BEAUTIFUL FIRE, FATHER.
THERE'S ALWAYS ANOTHER MANSION. A DAY LIKE TODAY CALLS FOR BRIGHT LIGHTS.
LIGHTS FOR WHICH WE WILLINGLY SELL OUR LIFE RIGHTS IN PRAISE OF MAMMON. SATELLITE FEEDS ARE COMING IN...
...THE PATRON HAS ENGAGED WOE. HE'S ALREADY SURVIVED WHAT WAS A DEATHBLOW IN THEIR FIRST BATTLE.
GOOD. STAY FOCUSED ON THEM.
GOOD, FATHER? BUT WHAT IF THE PATRON WINS?
IF HE SURVIVES, HE'LL STILL BE PILOTED BY FOOLS CURSED WITH PEDESTRIAN THINKING.
A PATRON THAT KILLS WOE IS AT AN ALL-TIME HIGH.
THEY BELIEVE THE FAITH OF THE PEOPLE WILL BE THEIR ARMOR AGAINST THE TRUTH...
...BUT I'LL MAKE SHACKLES OF THAT ARMOR. SEND THE NEXT PAYMENT. NO MATTER WHO LIVES...

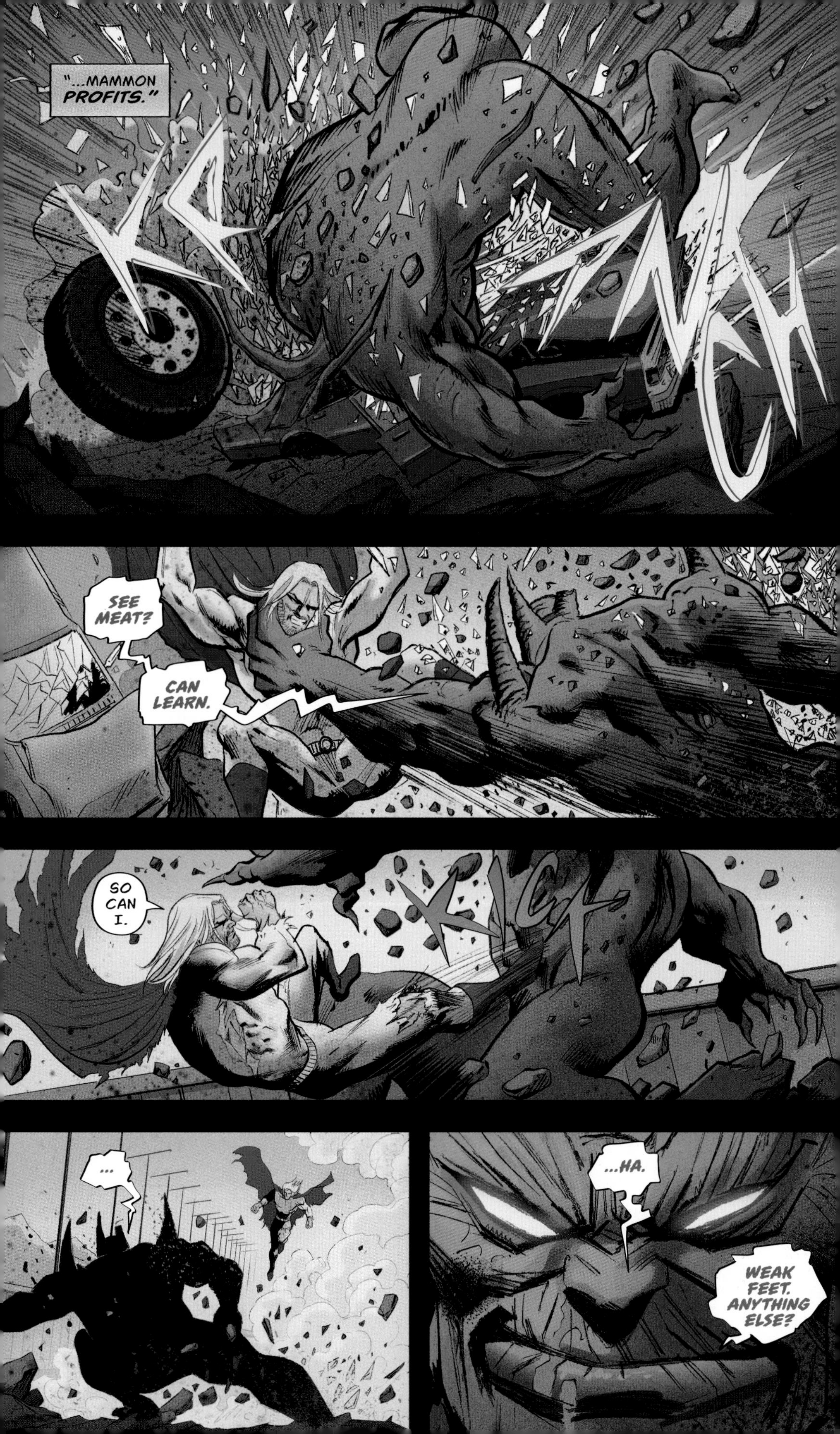
"...MAMMON PROFITS."
KRANCH
SEE MEAT?
CAN LEARN.
SO CAN I.
KICK
...
...HA.
WEAK FEET. ANYTHING ELSE?

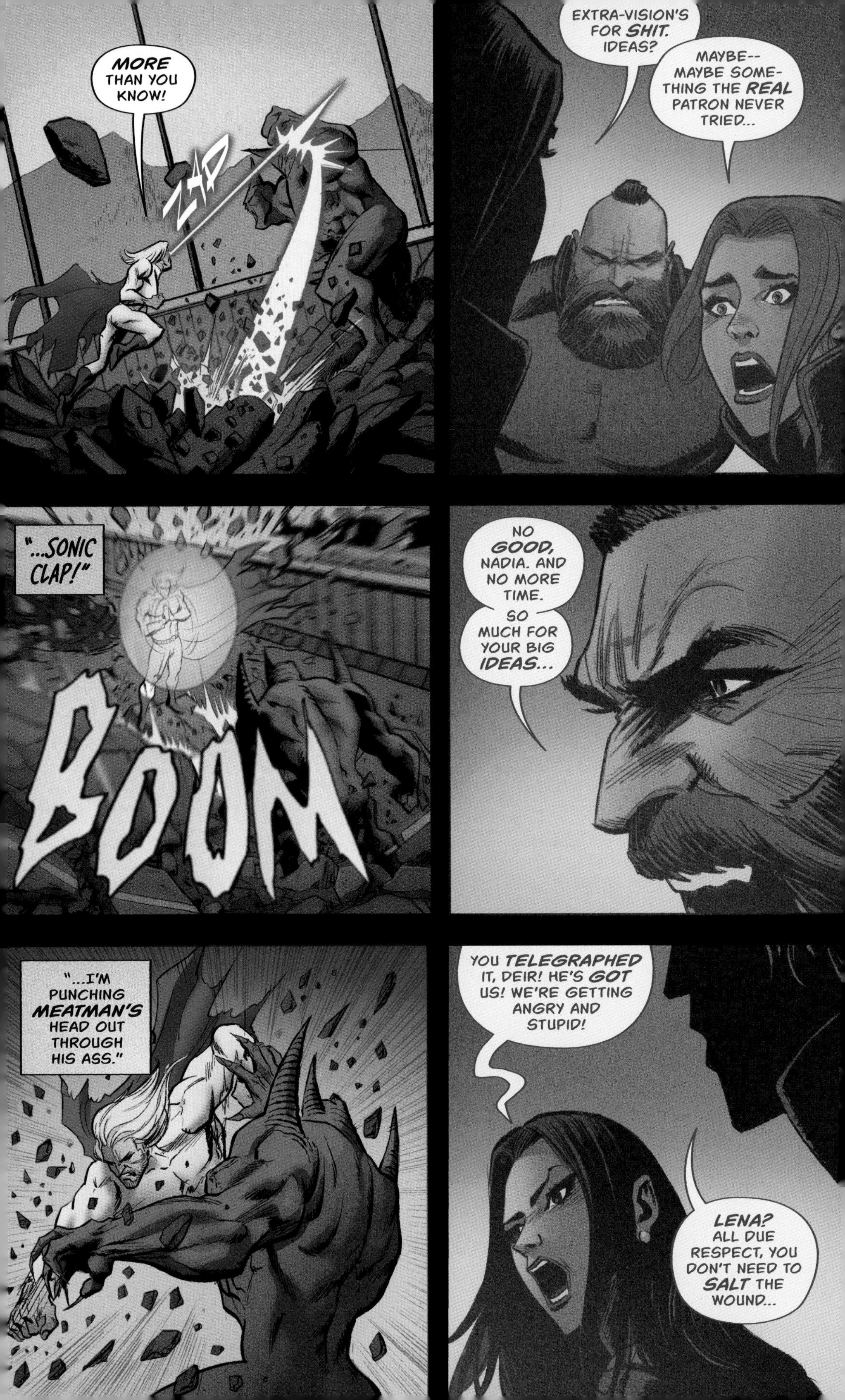
MORE THAN YOU KNOW!
ZAP
EXTRA-VISION'S FOR SHIT. IDEAS?
MAYBE-- MAYBE SOME-THING THE REAL PATRON NEVER TRIED...
"...SONIC CLAP!"
BOOM
NO GOOD, NADIA. AND NO MORE TIME.
SO MUCH FOR YOUR BIG IDEAS...
"...I'M PUNCHING MEATMAN'S HEAD OUT THROUGH HIS ASS."
YOU TELEGRAPHED IT, DEIR! HE'S GOT US! WE'RE GETTING ANGRY AND STUPID!
LENA? ALL DUE RESPECT, YOU DON'T NEED TO SALT THE WOUND...

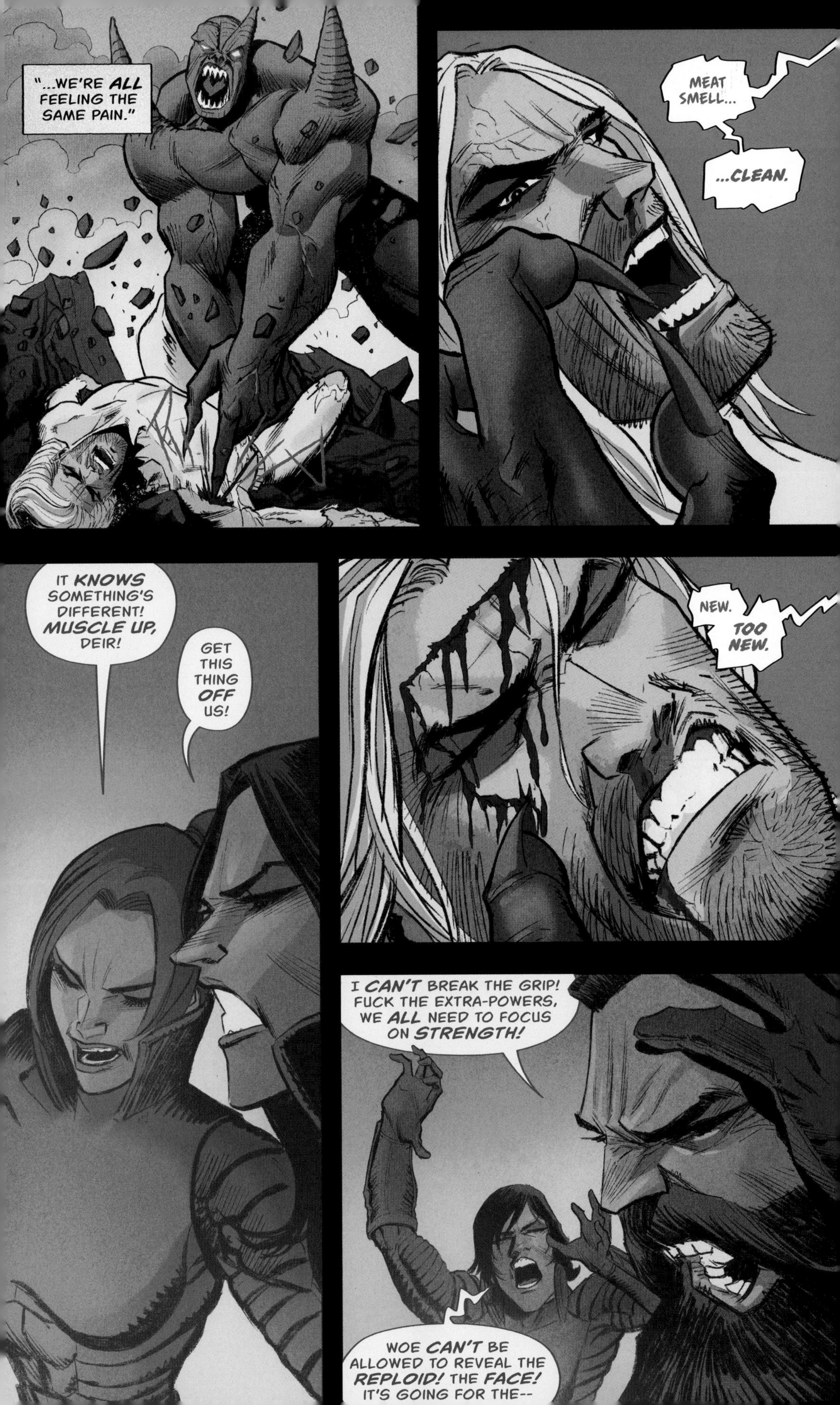
"...WE'RE ALL FEELING THE SAME PAIN."
MEAT SMELL...
...CLEAN.
IT KNOWS SOMETHING'S DIFFERENT! MUSCLE UP, DEIR!
GET THIS THING OFF US!
NEW.
TOO NEW.
I CAN'T BREAK THE GRIP! FUCK THE EXTRA-POWERS, WE ALL NEED TO FOCUS ON STRENGTH!
WOE CAN'T BE ALLOWED TO REVEAL THE REPLOID! THE FACE! IT'S GOING FOR THE--

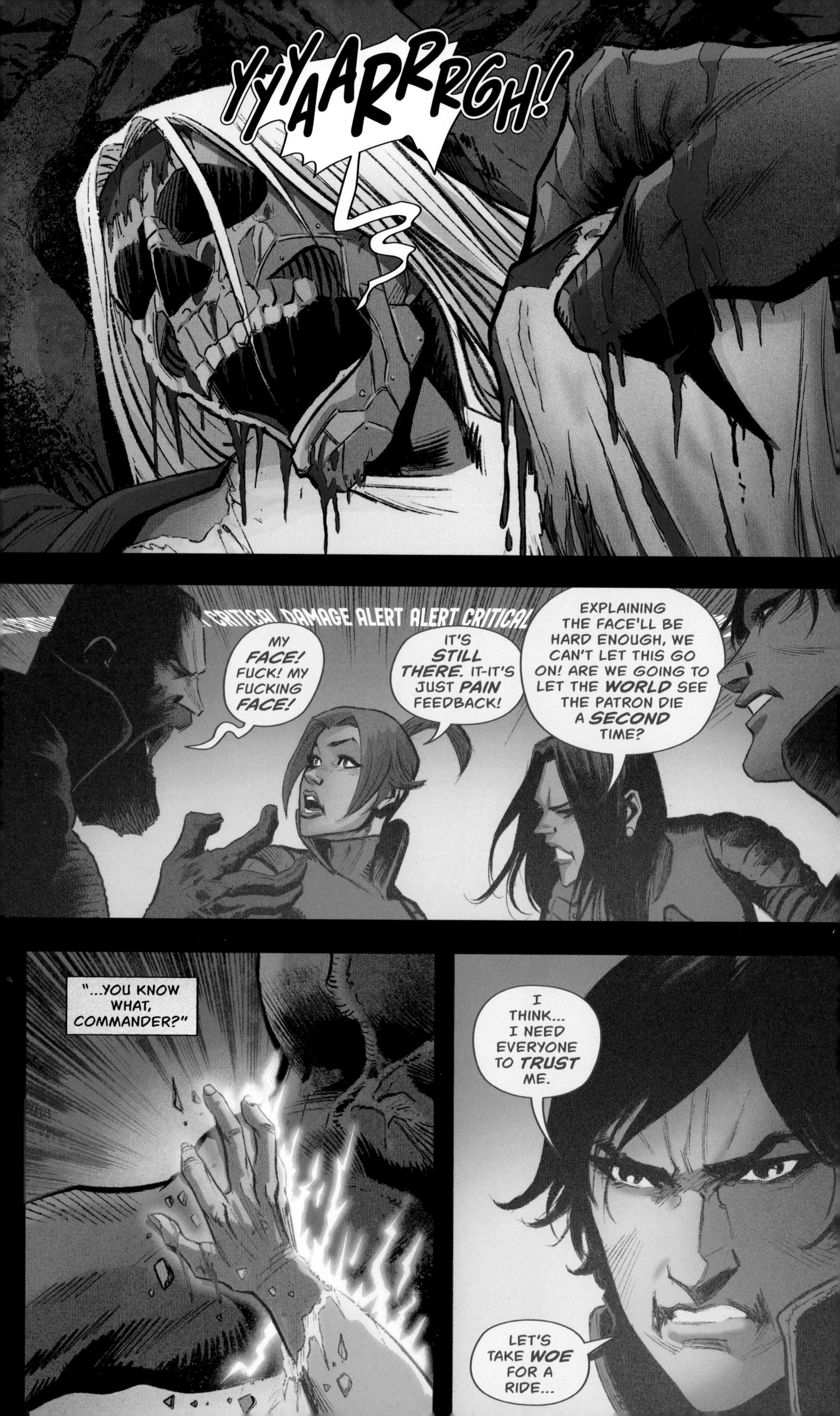
YYYAARRRGH!
CRITICAL DAMAGE ALERT ALERT CRITICAL
MY FACE! FUCK! MY FUCKING FACE!
IT'S STILL THERE. IT-IT'S JUST PAIN FEEDBACK!
EXPLAINING THE FACE'LL BE HARD ENOUGH, WE CAN'T LET THIS GO ON! ARE WE GOING TO LET THE WORLD SEE THE PATRON DIE A SECOND TIME?
"...YOU KNOW WHAT, COMMANDER?"
I THINK... I NEED EVERYONE TO TRUST ME.
LET'S TAKE WOE FOR A RIDE...

"...UP, UP AND AWAY."

"IGNATZ? WHAT ARE YOU *DOING?*"

"WHAT THE PATRON DID, COMMANDER..."

"...THE *LAST* TIME HE BEAT WOE."

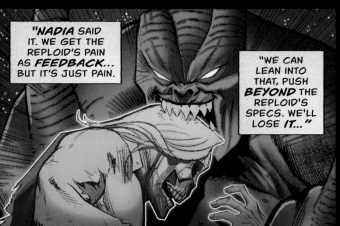

"*NADIA* SAID IT. WE GET THE REPLOID'S PAIN AS *FEEDBACK*... BUT IT'S JUST PAIN.

"WE CAN LEAN INTO THAT, PUSH *BEYOND* THE REPLOID'S SPECS. WE'LL LOSE *IT*..."

...BUT *NOT* OUR BODIES. IT'LL HURT *MORE* THAN WE COULD IMAGINE...

"...BUT WE KNEW PAIN WAS PART OF THE DEAL.

"THE *PATRON* WASN'T HUMAN. HE WASN'T USED TO *HURTING.*"

"HE FOUGHT OUT OF *FEAR*...

"...AND *SELF-PRESERVATION.*"

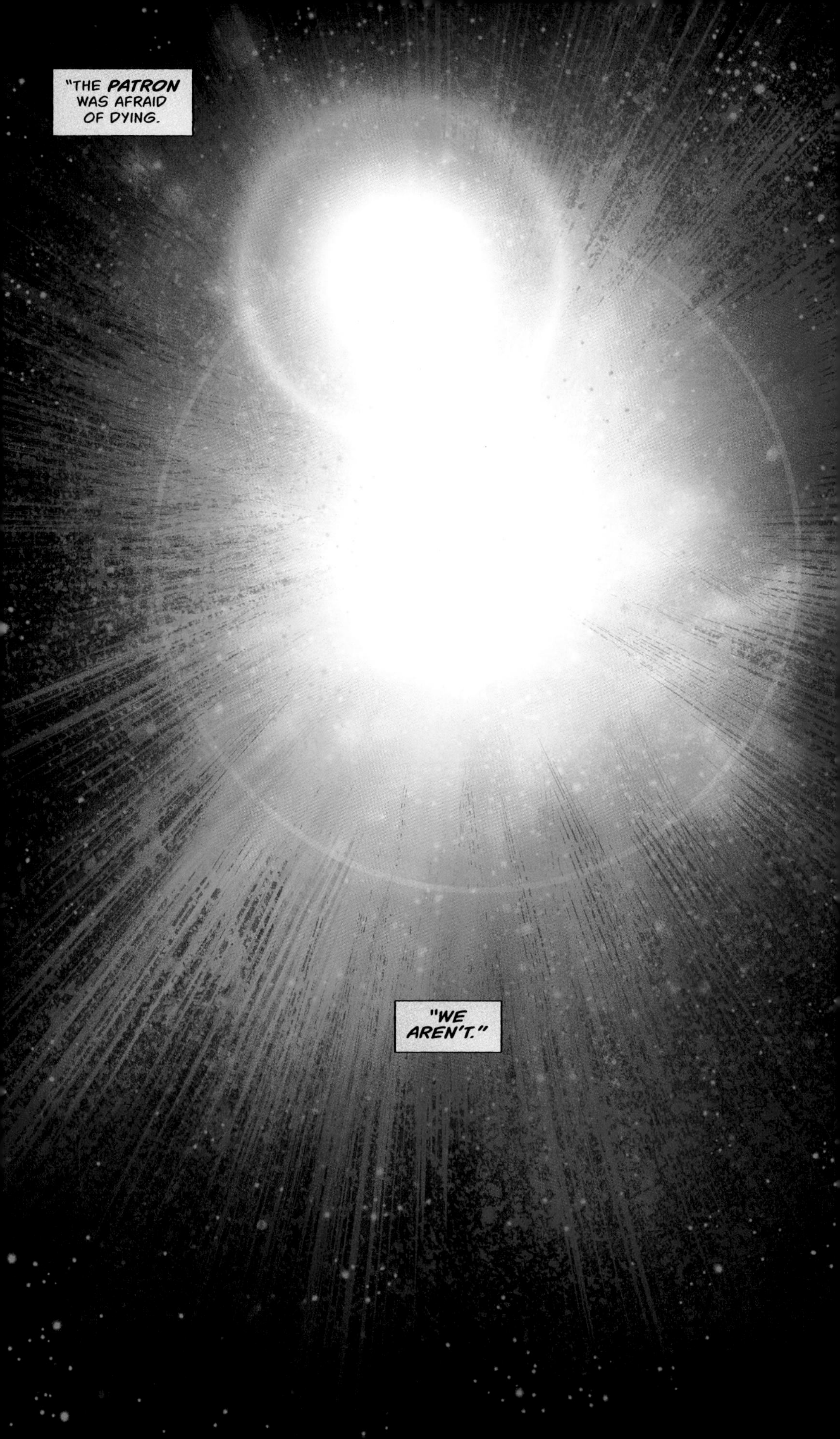
"THE PATRON WAS AFRAID OF DYING.
"WE AREN'T."

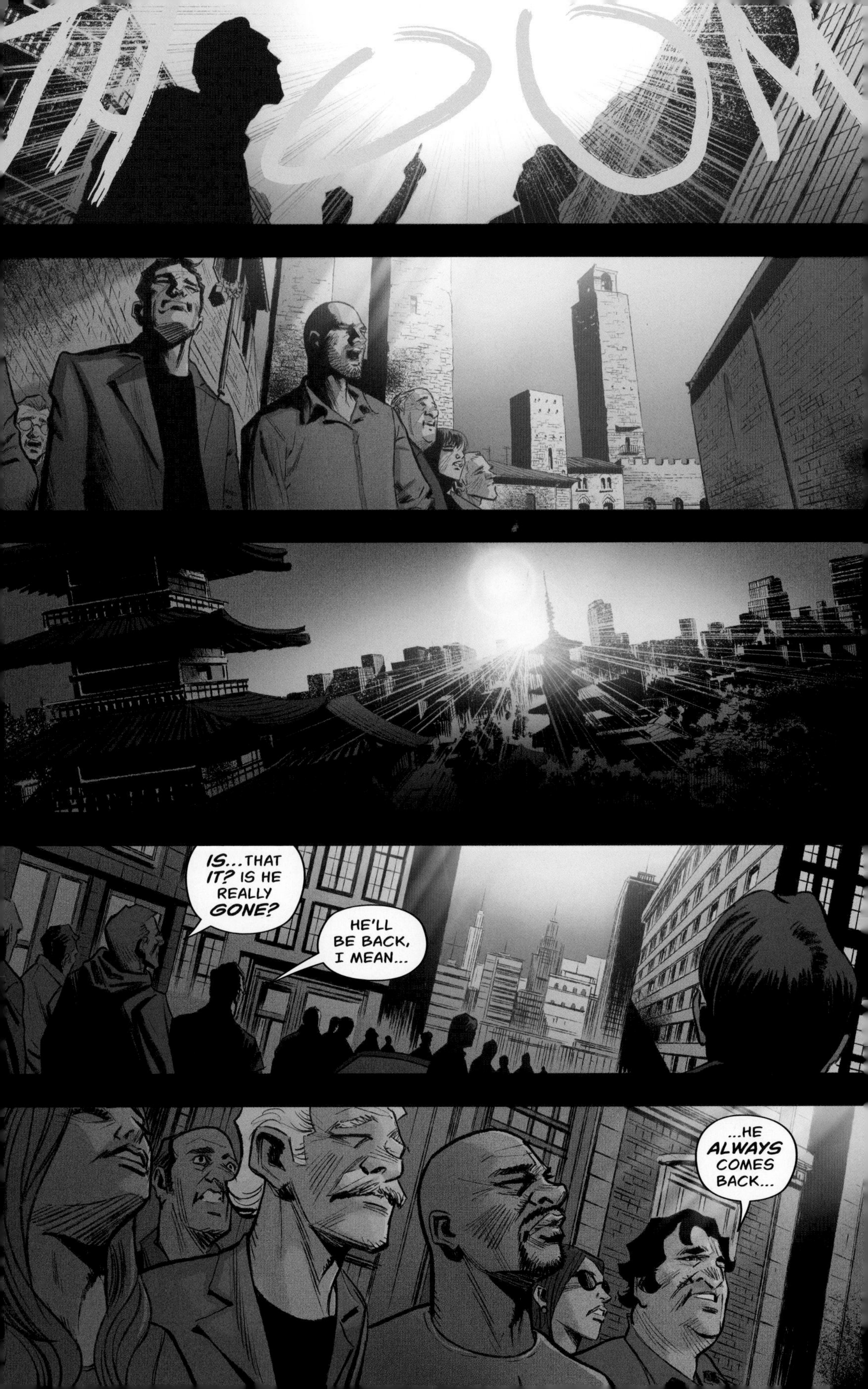
IS... THAT IT? IS HE REALLY GONE?
HE'LL BE BACK, I MEAN...
...HE ALWAYS COMES BACK...

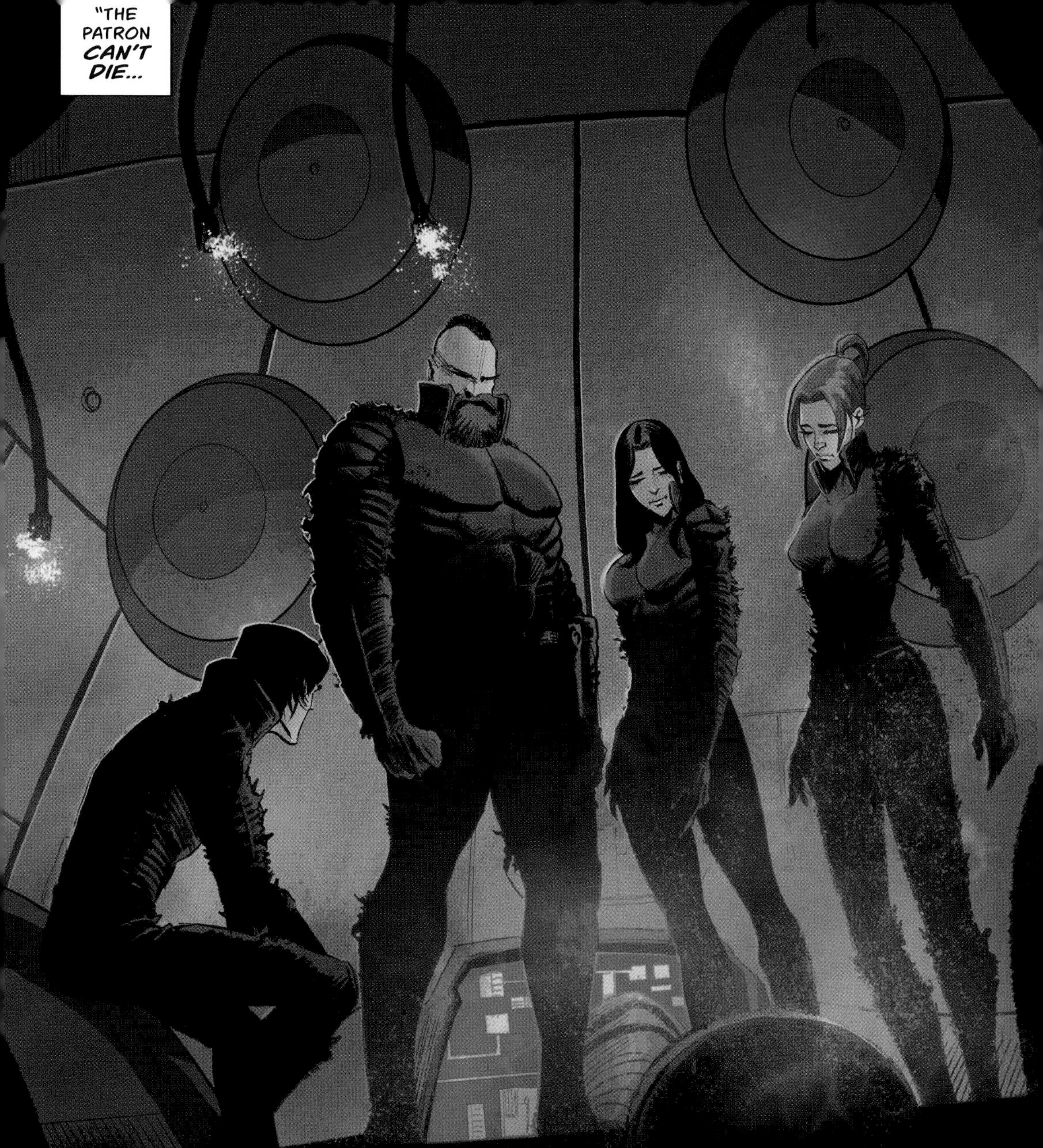
"THE PATRON CAN'T DIE...

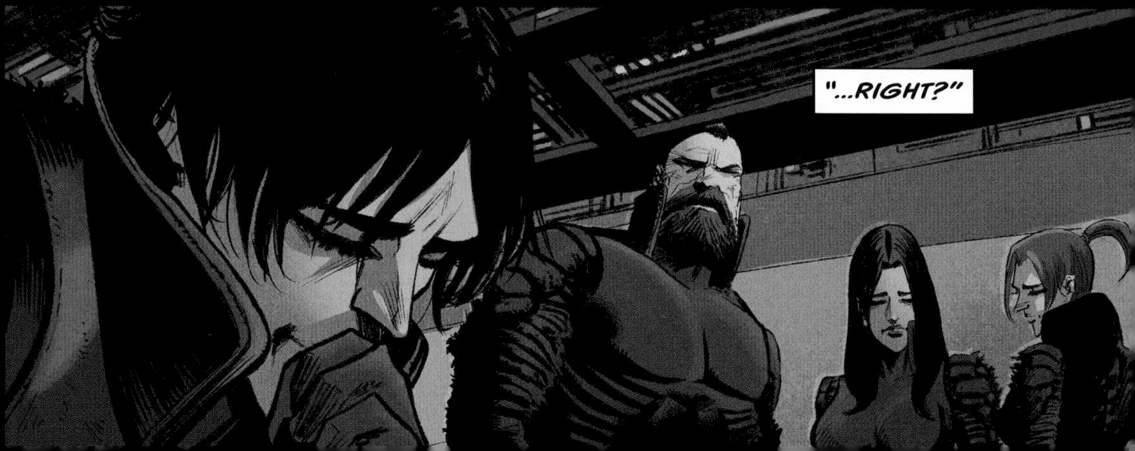
"...RIGHT?"

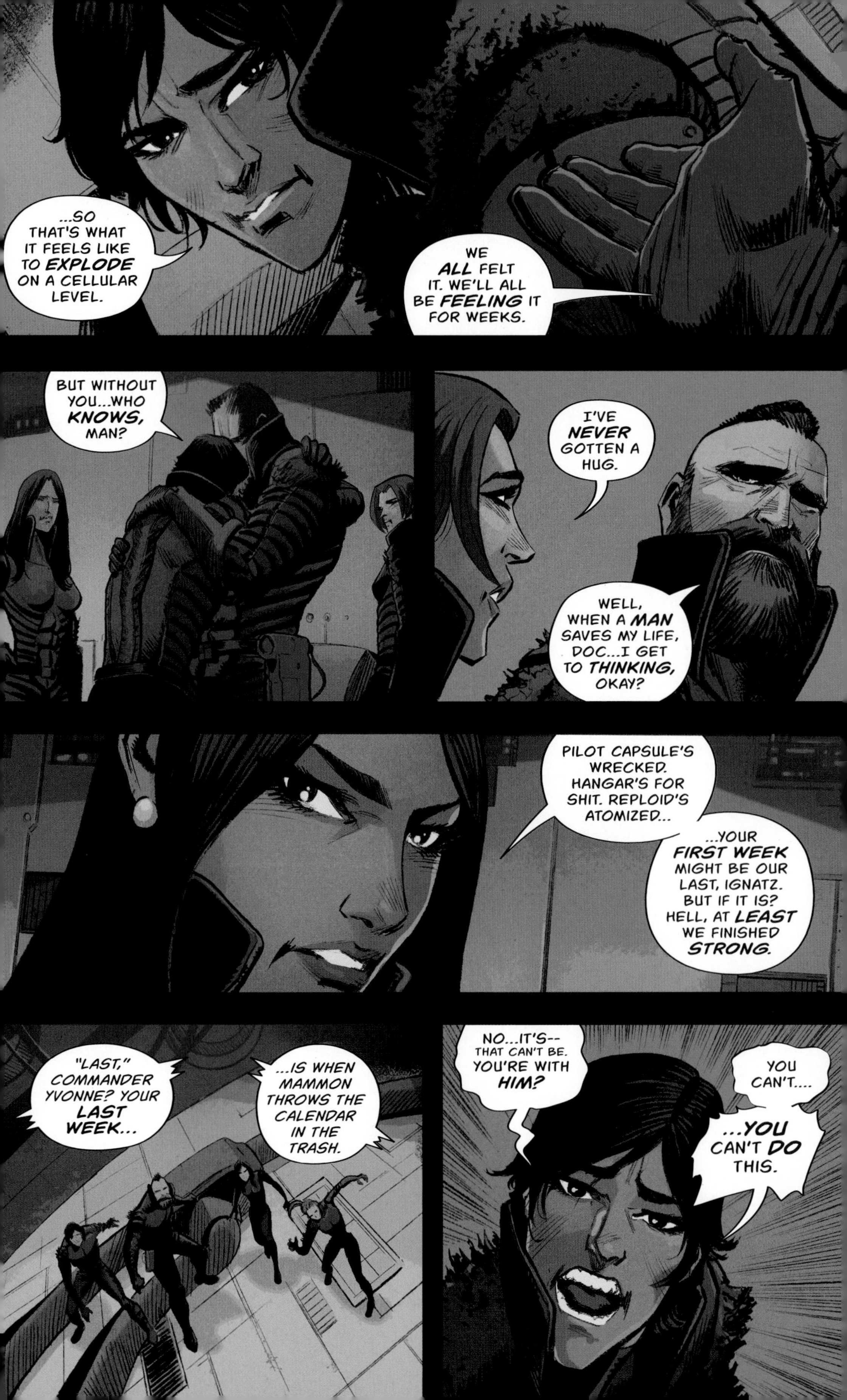
...SO THAT'S WHAT IT FEELS LIKE TO EXPLODE ON A CELLULAR LEVEL.
WE ALL FELT IT. WE'LL ALL BE FEELING IT FOR WEEKS.
BUT WITHOUT YOU...WHO KNOWS, MAN?
I'VE NEVER GOTTEN A HUG.
WELL, WHEN A MAN SAVES MY LIFE, DOC...I GET TO THINKING, OKAY?
PILOT CAPSULE'S WRECKED. HANGAR'S FOR SHIT. REPLOID'S ATOMIZED...
...YOUR FIRST WEEK MIGHT BE OUR LAST, IGNATZ. BUT IF IT IS? HELL, AT LEAST WE FINISHED STRONG.
"LAST," COMMANDER YVONNE? YOUR LAST WEEK...
...IS WHEN MAMMON THROWS THE CALENDAR IN THE TRASH.
NO...IT'S-- THAT CAN'T BE. YOU'RE WITH HIM?
YOU CAN'T....
...YOU CAN'T DO THIS.

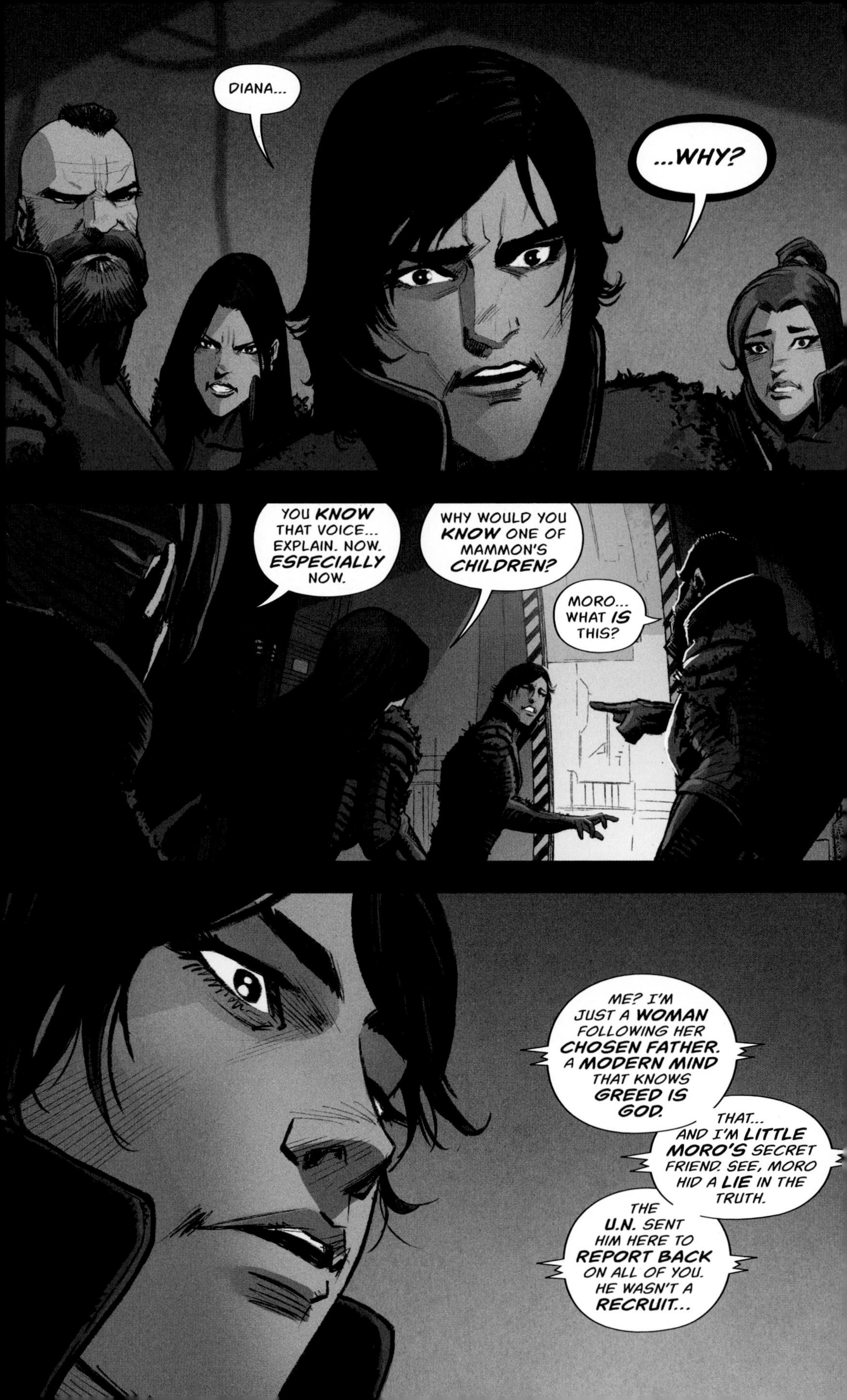
DIANA...
...WHY?
YOU KNOW THAT VOICE... EXPLAIN. NOW. ESPECIALLY NOW.
WHY WOULD YOU KNOW ONE OF MAMMON'S CHILDREN?
MORO... WHAT IS THIS?
ME? I'M JUST A WOMAN FOLLOWING HER CHOSEN FATHER. A MODERN MIND THAT KNOWS GREED IS GOD.
THAT... AND I'M LITTLE MORO'S SECRET FRIEND. SEE, MORO HID A LIE IN THE TRUTH.
THE U.N. SENT HIM HERE TO REPORT BACK ON ALL OF YOU. HE WASN'T A RECRUIT...

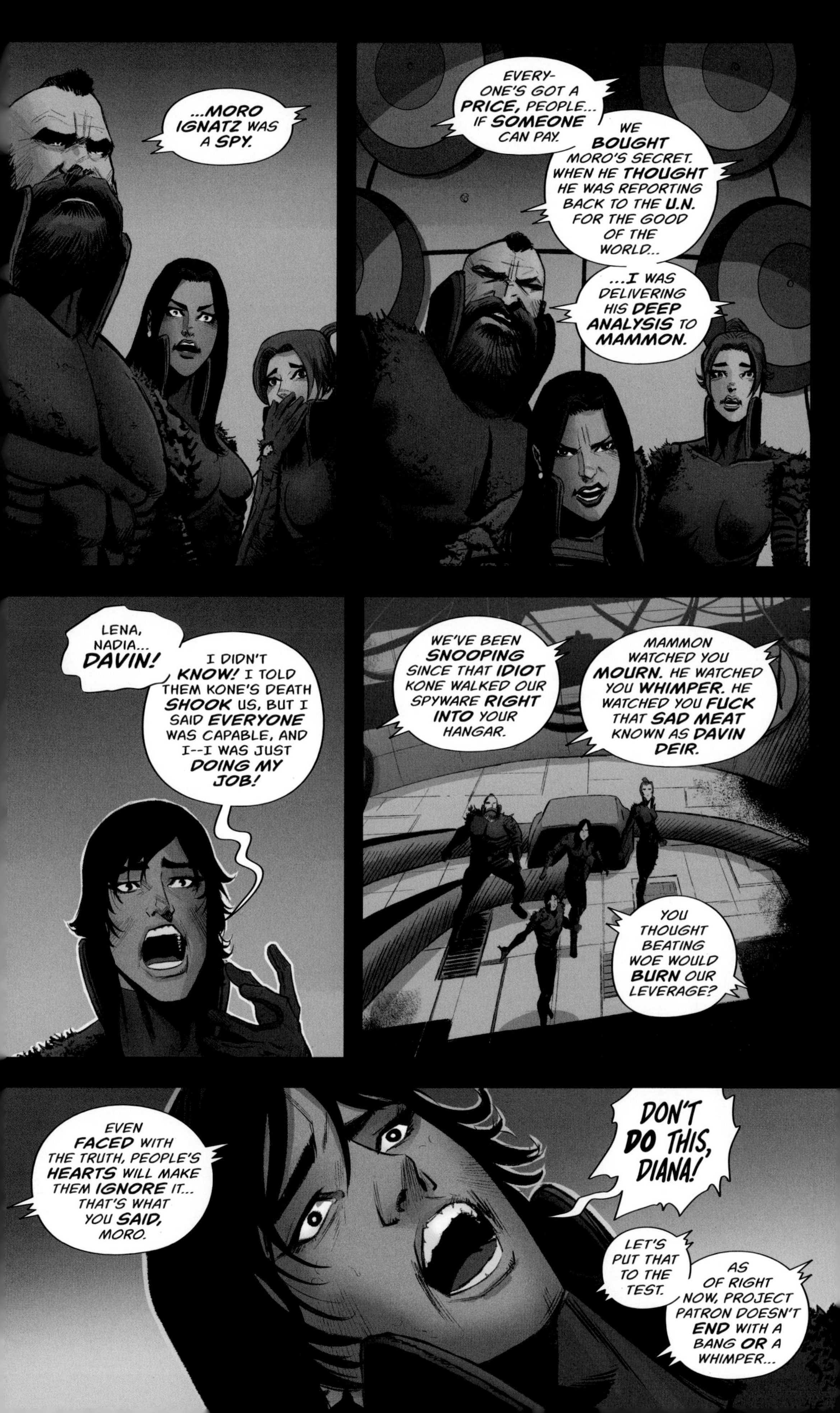
...MORO IGNATZ WAS A SPY.
EVERY-ONE'S GOT A PRICE, PEOPLE... IF SOMEONE CAN PAY.
WE BOUGHT MORO'S SECRET. WHEN HE THOUGHT HE WAS REPORTING BACK TO THE U.N. FOR THE GOOD OF THE WORLD...
...I WAS DELIVERING HIS DEEP ANALYSIS TO MAMMON.
LENA, NADIA... DAVIN!
I DIDN'T KNOW! I TOLD THEM KONE'S DEATH SHOOK US, BUT I SAID EVERYONE WAS CAPABLE, AND I--I WAS JUST DOING MY JOB!
WE'VE BEEN SNOOPING SINCE THAT IDIOT KONE WALKED OUR SPYWARE RIGHT INTO YOUR HANGAR.
MAMMON WATCHED YOU MOURN. HE WATCHED YOU WHIMPER. HE WATCHED YOU FUCK THAT SAD MEAT KNOWN AS DAVIN DEIR.
YOU THOUGHT BEATING WOE WOULD BURN OUR LEVERAGE?
EVEN FACED WITH THE TRUTH, PEOPLE'S HEARTS WILL MAKE THEM IGNORE IT... THAT'S WHAT YOU SAID, MORO.
DON'T DO THIS, DIANA!
LET'S PUT THAT TO THE TEST.
AS OF RIGHT NOW, PROJECT PATRON DOESN'T END WITH A BANG OR A WHIMPER...

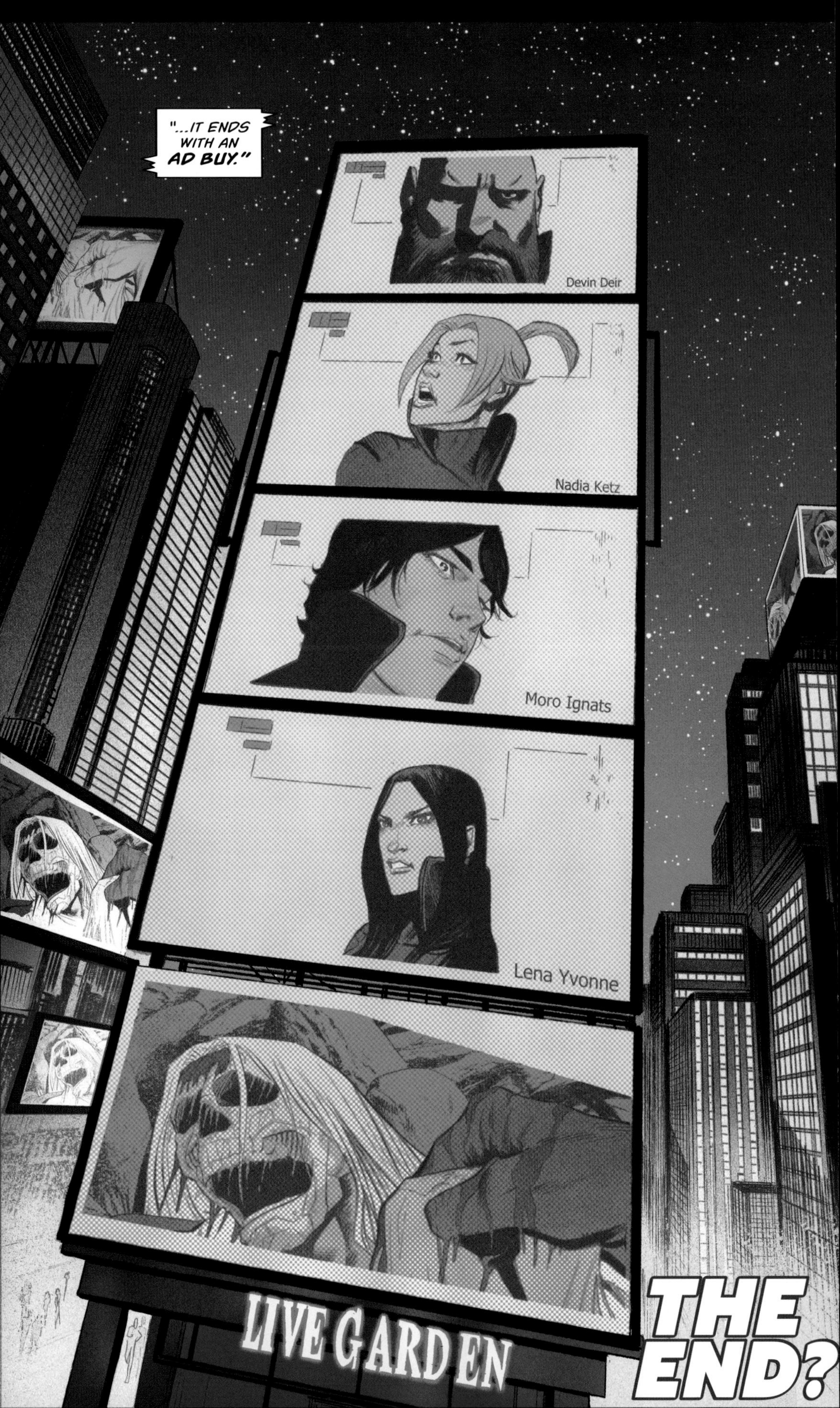
"...IT ENDS WITH AN AD BUY."
Devin Deir
Nadia Ketz
Moro Ignats
Lena Yvonne
LIVE GARDEN
THE END?

PROJECT: PATRON ™

BEHIND THE SCENES

Issue 1
AARON LOPRESTI
Incentive Cover

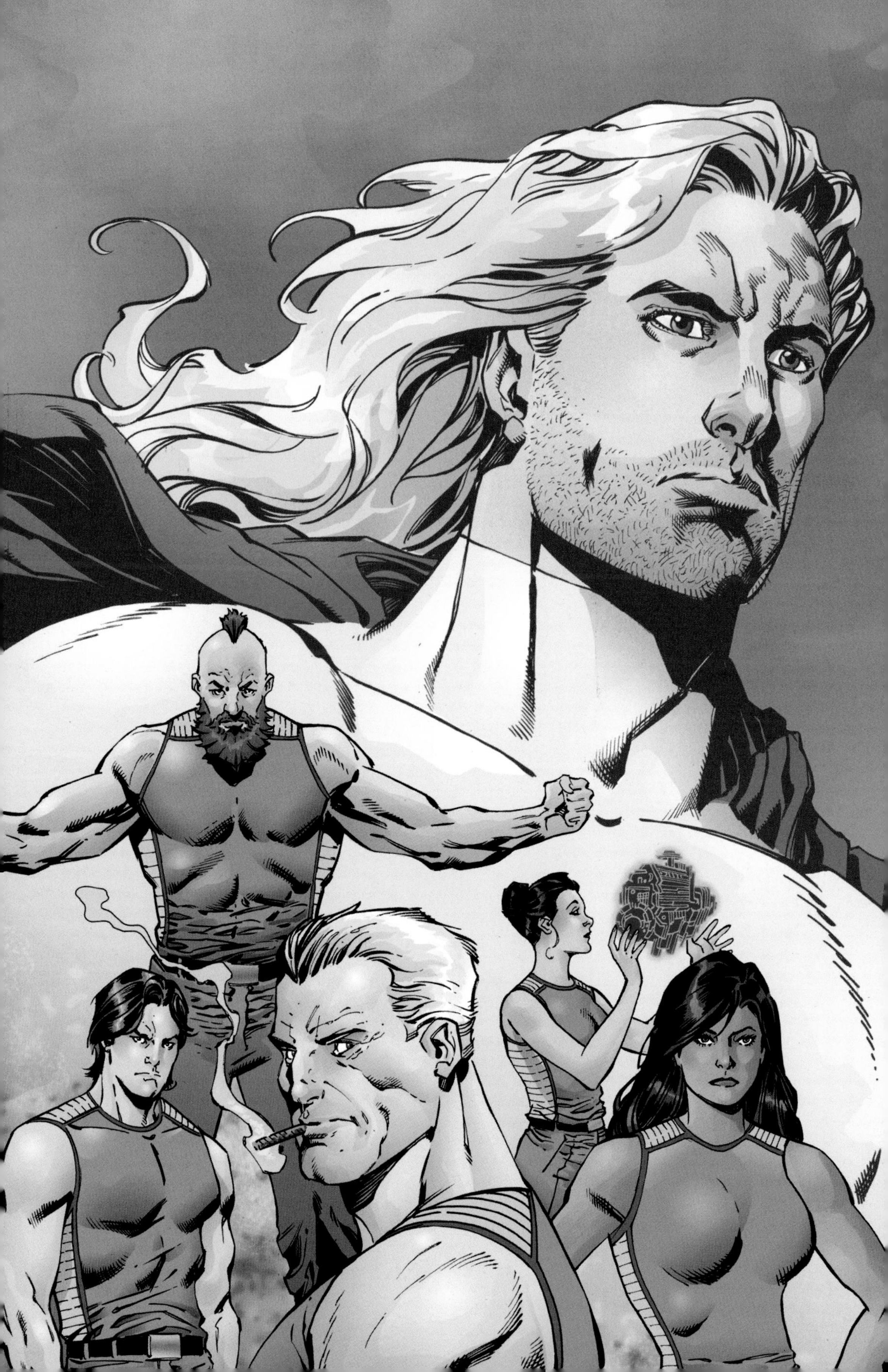

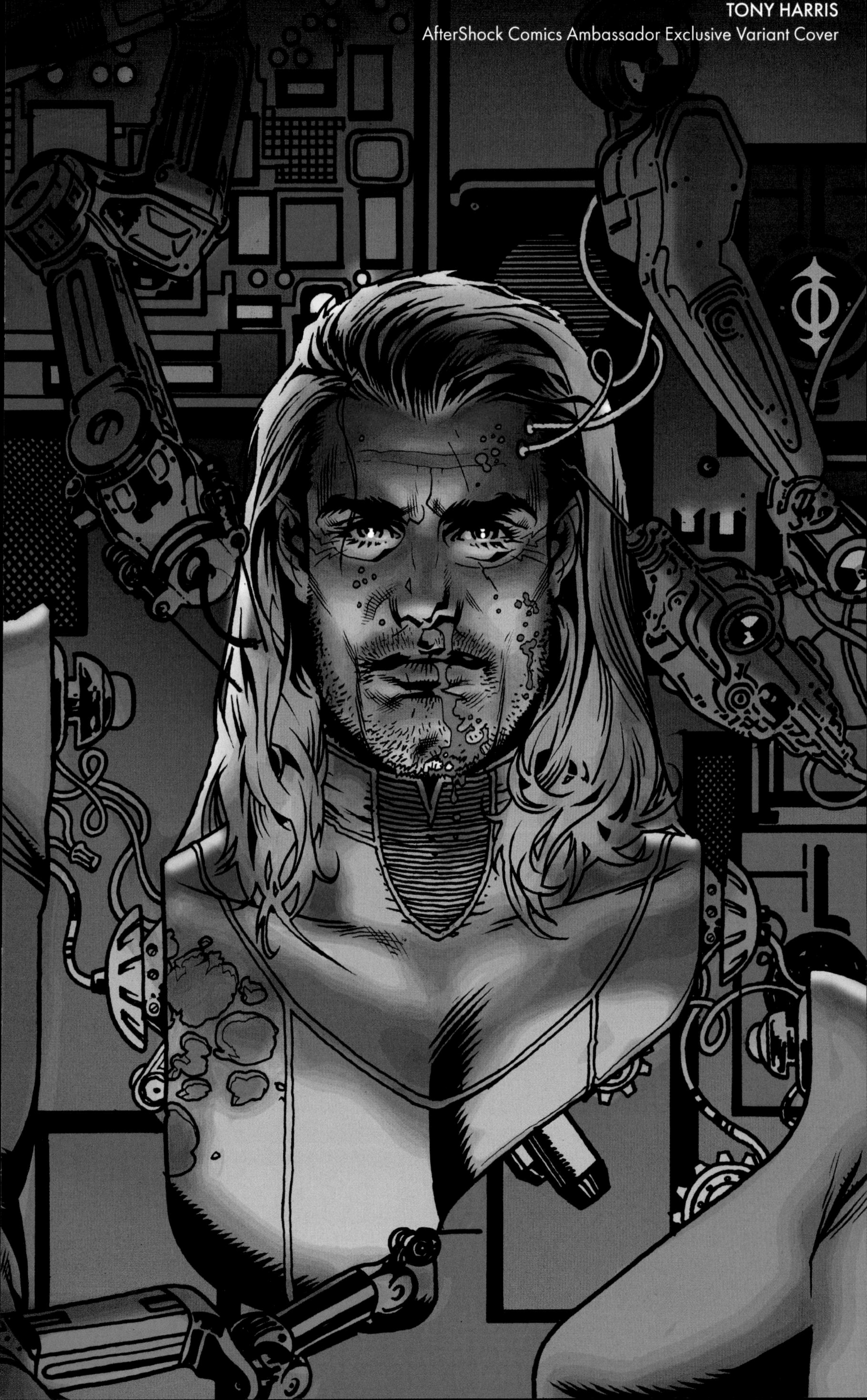

TONY HARRIS
AfterShock Comics Ambassador Exclusive Variant Cover

THROW OUT THAT

VHS

/ TAKE A BAT TO THAT

LASERDISC

AND GET READY FOR THE DEFINITIVE EDITION OF THE ICONIC DOCUMENTARY IN

HD!

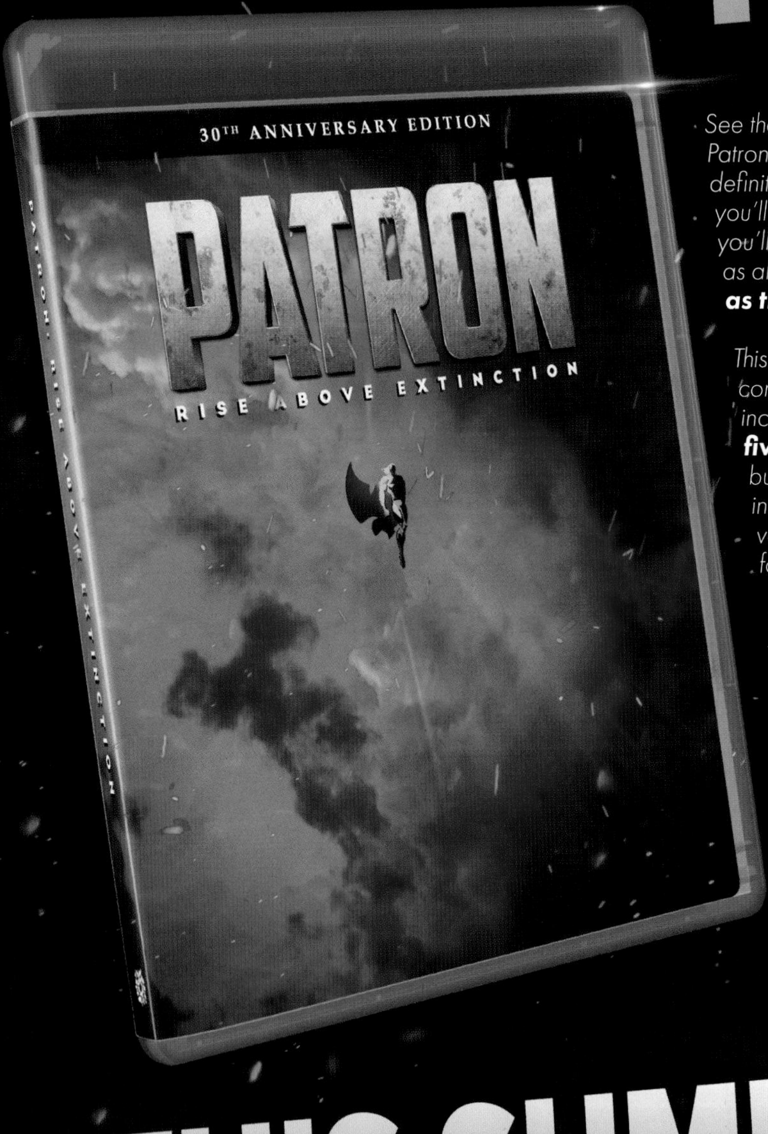
30TH ANNIVERSARY EDITION
PATRON
RISE ABOVE EXTINCTION
PATRON: RISE ABOVE EXTINCTION

See the fall and rise of the Patron like never before, in high definition! You'll feel each blow, you'll cheer for each rally, and you'll want to comfort your friend as all seems lost... ***then cheer as the Patron rises again!***

This ***30th Anniversary*** *commemorative edition includes not just the original* ***five-hour documentary,*** *but never before seen interviews with producers, voice actors, historians and forensic specialists!*

Take your celebration of the Super-Service community's most famous representative to new heights with reactions not just from those who were there, but the filmmakers who fought through their raw emotion all those decades ago to tell this ***award-winning story!***

THIS SUMMER!

IT'S THE SUPER-SYMBIOPSYCHOTAXIPLASM!

King City Courant

THE ONLY NEWS YOU NEED TO KNOW

Weather
Fair today. Warmer tomorrow. Moderate winds from the East.

VOL. XII   NO. 3289   WEDNESDAY, APRIL 7ᵀᴴ   PRICE $1.25

OPINION

LOOKING DOWN FROM ABOVE

Three Decades on, the Patron and Super-Service are still anything but friends.

BROWNE STEVENSON

We all remember where we were all those years ago, as the Patron fell. And likewise, we all remember news of his rise breaking through on every channel days later. But now, on the anniversary of the Patron's most iconic battle, how many of us are willing to reflect on those events with a lens other than awe? Thirty years after his near sacrifice cemented him as the world's most prominent Super-Service hero, just what is the Patron's true legacy?

There's no doubt we're all thankful for the Patron's ongoing aid to the world. The vast majority of us are too young to remember just how dubious the world was when he first arrived on our planet. While he wasn't the first personality to step out into Super-Service, every hero we'd seen so far was of terrestrial origin.

The Patron was different, blinking into reality in 1964 and saving the World's Fair from sabotage. It was a grand gesture, a grand display of power and it frightened as many has it heartened. His unbelievable story didn't help. Were we supposed to simply take the Patron's word that he was sent to Earth from a Utopian dimension as humanitarian aid? Where was his proof? The least he could of-

fer the world was a rocket ship. But, instead, he simply appeared one moment where he wasn't the moment before, with only a tall tale in hand. All the Patron could offer was a smile, and the promise that whether we believed in him or not, he believed in us.

From that day on, the Patron would appear in times of great need, proving his story more and more with every heroic rescue. Over decades, he earned the trust he asked for in his first appearance. By the 1980s, questions about his motivations were all but

sidelined by the adoring public. Polls at the time showed that the majority of citizens didn't care where he came from or why, as long as he kept working for their benefit. As long as the Patron kept making the world a safer place, to Joe Public, questions from the past were secondary. But while the world raised their hearts and minds to the sky, after the Patron's iconic fall and rise, other members of the Super-Service community took notice.

In the time immediately after this first appearance, the Patron was known to associate with the greater Super-Service community. Though he never officially added his name to any known rosters, he was regularly photographed aiding groups like The Truth Underground and Justice Direct. The Patron's summer partnership with the Carter-Era Son of '76 was a cultural sensation. But even

during those high times, the Super-Service workers were quoted as saying the Patron kept to himself, and had few interests besides the work. Heroes at the time quickly concluded he had no secret identity, no life to return to, no interest in being anything other than the Patron. While these reports lent credence to the incredible backstory he'd always told the world, it also created distance between him and his fellow heroes. The Super-Service workers of the world knew they could count on the Patron when the world was at stake, but new little else about him. In time, they too came to agree with the public. Maybe there wasn't more to the Patron than his fight for world safety and equity, and maybe there didn't need to be.

But the Patron's battle with Woe seems to have changed that. Woe's rampage hit the Super-Service community hard. Here was a threat with a story as unbelievable as the Patron's. And like the Patron's, Woe's story was proven by his actions. Few were ready to believe it could've been Woe that crashed to Earth long ago and massacred the dinosaurs before entering hibernation. Those minds changed after Woe's first battle against Justice Direct, a war that toppled the city of Buffalo and cost the lives of a team that had protected the world for years. When the Patron finally halted Woe's trudge towards extinction, the latest Son of '76 lay mutilated and American infrastructure was dealt a near-fatal blow. But the Patron did kill Woe, almost dying himself in the process.

Since the Patron's rise, his approval ratings have held steady across all key demographics. But the Super-Service community continues to raise questions about his behavior. While the Patron always kept his distance, Super-Service workers claim he now refuses to associate with them altogether. Collaborations with other heroes—be them the current Son of '76, a frequent guest on my show, or the returning Truth Underground—have become all but nonexistent. Heroes claim the Patron simply appears from the sky, paying them no greater mind than those in need, only to zip away again into mystery with no regard for camaraderie or a shared goal. What was once an idiosyncratic distance has now become a gulf between the Patron and the other heroes of the world. Is this simply a personality change after a near-death experience? The Patron has long refused to comment. Since the battle with Woe left every hero that previously knew him dead, there is no one left to confirm just how much the Patron has changed.

On the anniversary of the Patron's greatest battle, should we be listening to our Super-Service workers? Has the Patron been inching closer and closer to elitism, to a god complex, looking down on us from above with judgment? Did the failure of the world's super-service workers to stop Woe show the Patron he was the only hero that matters? Why cut ties with this new generation of he-

roes, instead of fostering their growth? Why disappear completely other than when the world is too panicked to ask questions? Has the Patron become too detached? Can we afford for that to be true? It's been thirty years, and much like looking in a mirror every day and not noticing the changes in our appearance, have we become so familiar with him that we've missed gradual changes in his personality?

I know these questions may be frightening. Perhaps we've all been too comfortable to ask them for too long. But on the upcoming season of my show, we won't be shying away. We'll be celebrating the Patron's anniversary the way it should be celebrated. We won't be offering blind faith, we'll be questioning power, interrogating the choices of gods, and giving a platform to super-service workers who have been sounding the alarm to deaf ears for decades.

Has the Patron changed before our eyes? What if, in the decades he's spent looking down from above, his compassion slowly changed to pity? What if that pity changed to disgust? What would we do? What could we do?

This year, to celebrate the Patron, let's finally ask for the one thing he might still be vulnerable to: the truth. □

PROJECT: PATRON

main cover sketches:
DAVID TALASKI

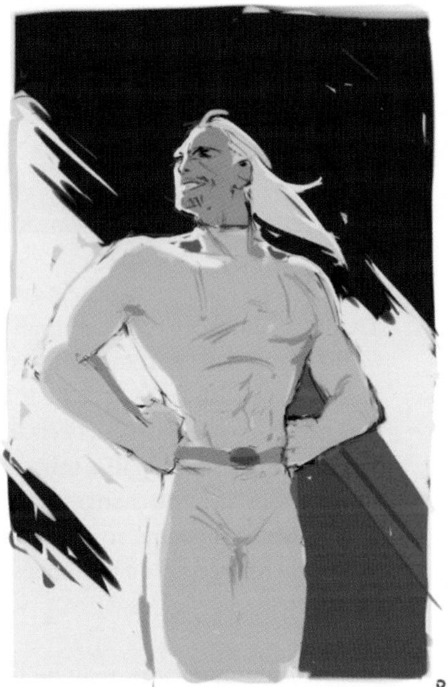

A

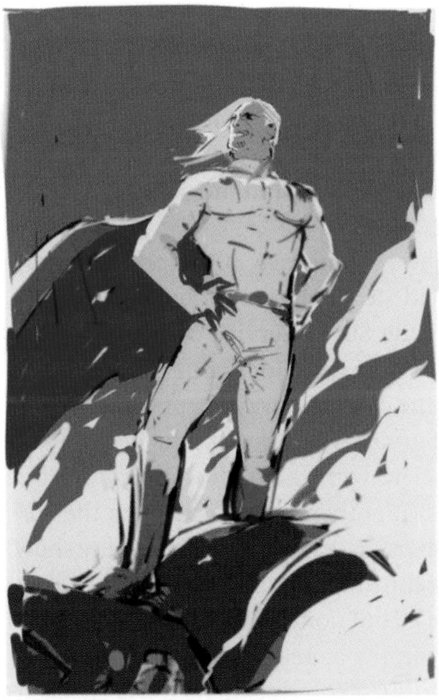

B

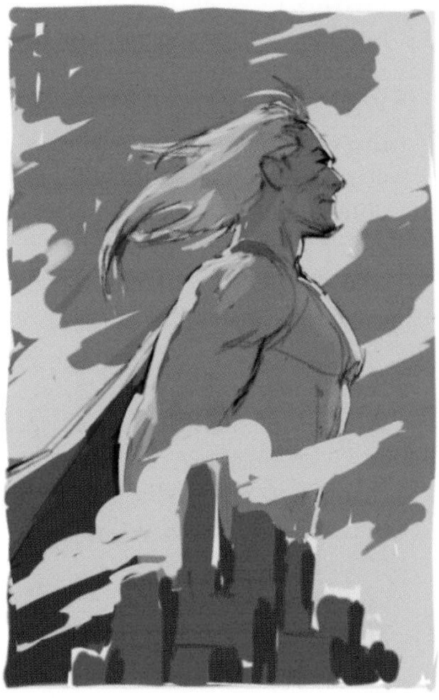

C

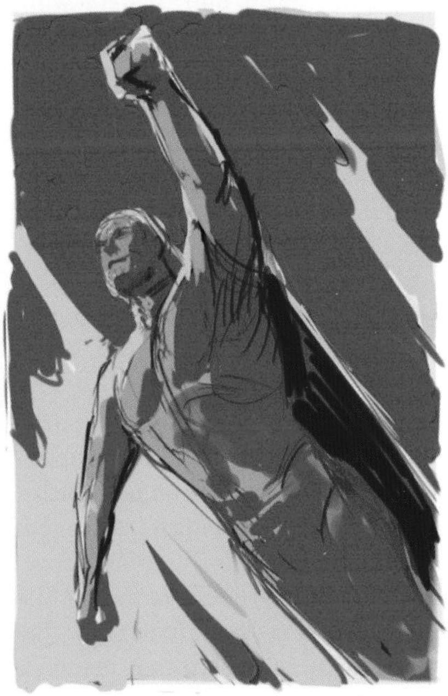

D

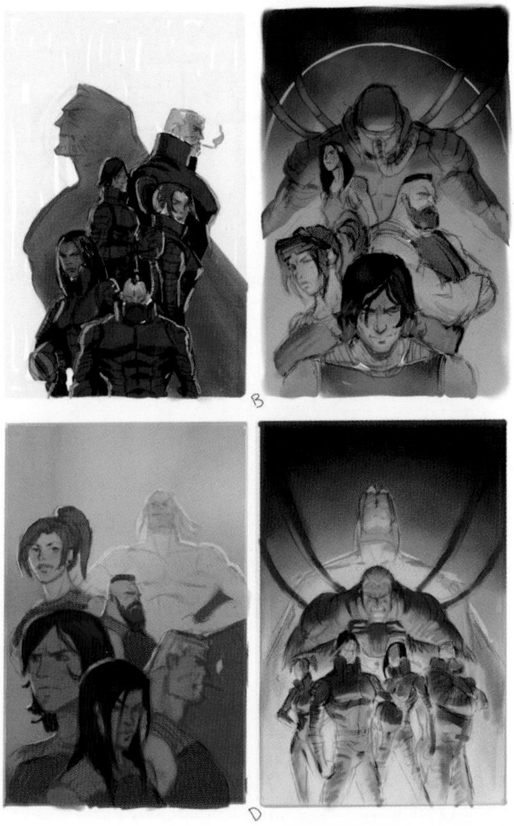

issue #2

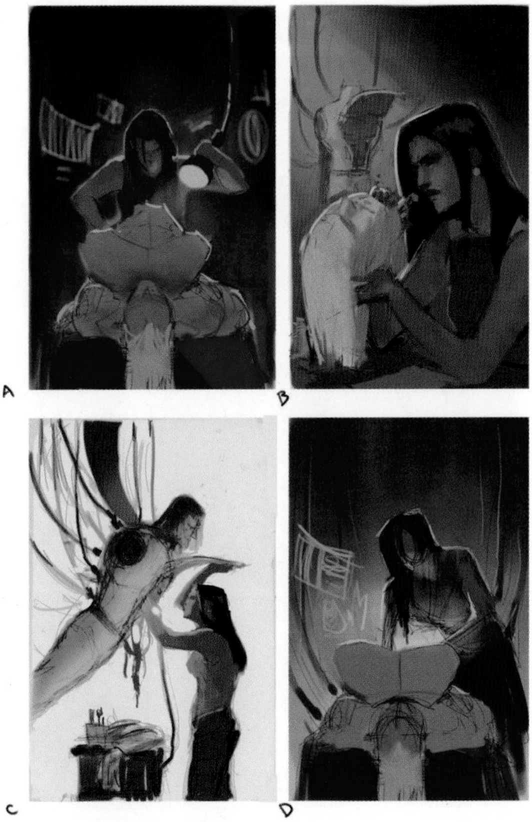

issue #3

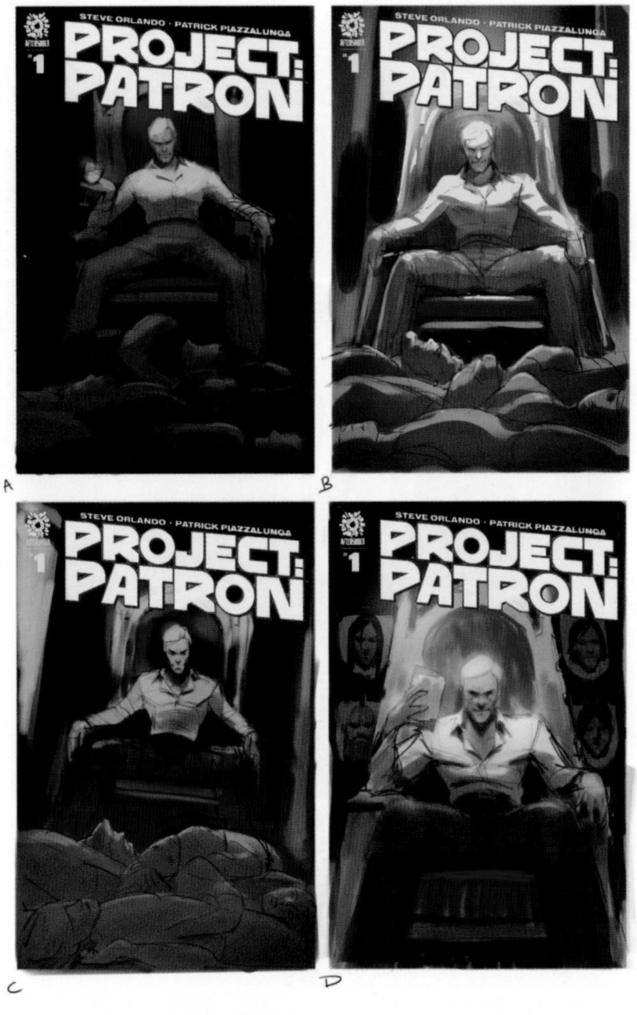
STEVE ORLANDO · PATRICK PIAZZALUNGA
#1
PROJECT: PATRON
STEVE ORLANDO · PATRICK PIAZZALUNGA
#1
PROJECT: PATRON
STEVE ORLANDO · PATRICK PIAZZALUNGA
#1
PROJECT: PATRON
STEVE ORLANDO · PATRICK PIAZZALUNGA
#1
PROJECT: PATRON

issue #4

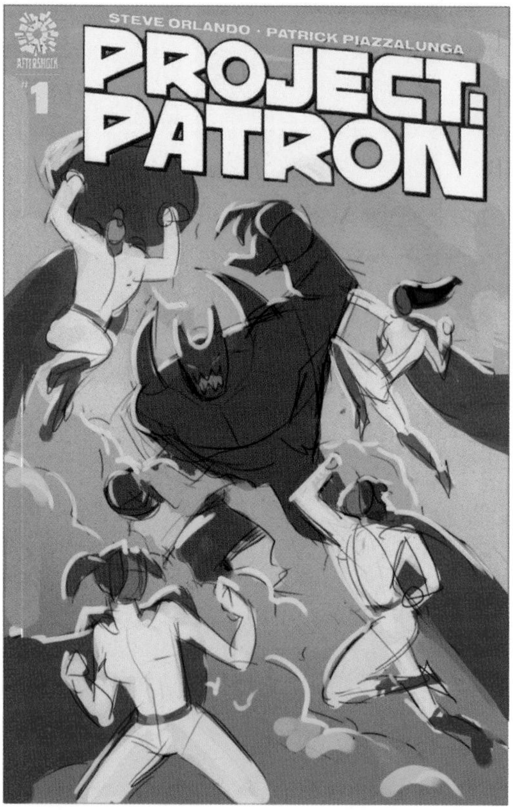
STEVE ORLANDO · PATRICK PIAZZALUNGA
PROJECT: PATRON
#1
AFTERSHOCK

A

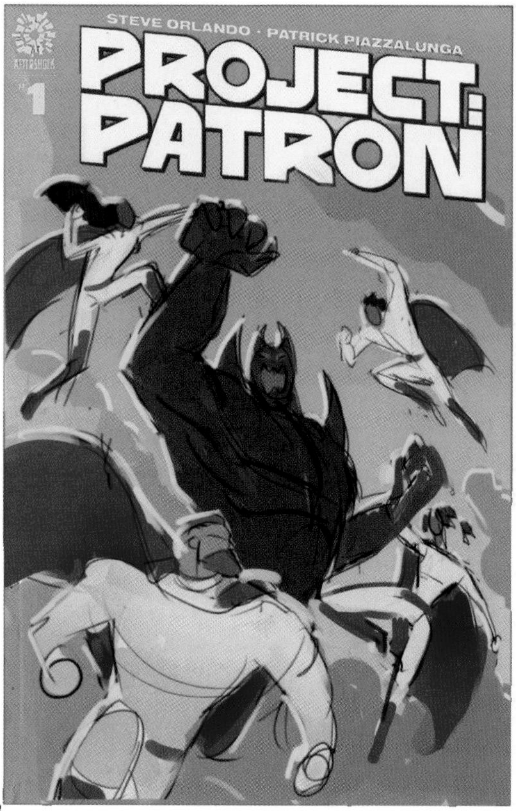
STEVE ORLANDO · PATRICK PIAZZALUNGA
PROJECT: PATRON
#1
AFTERSHOCK

B

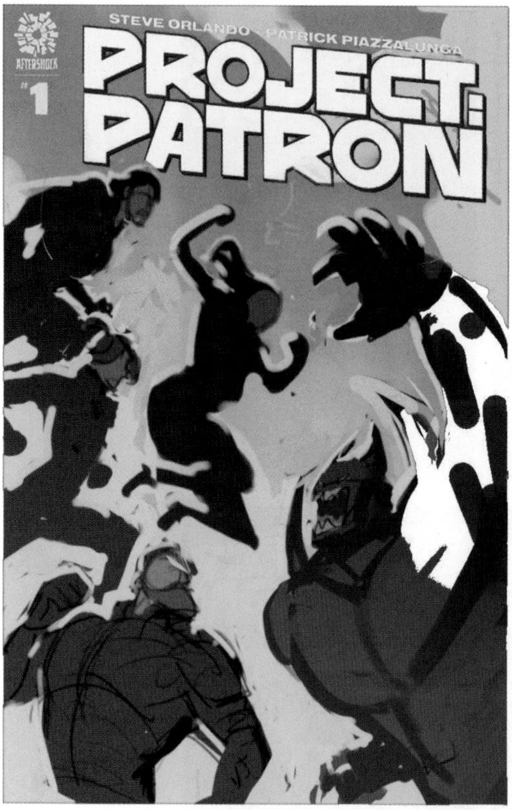
STEVE ORLANDO · PATRICK PIAZZALUNGA
PROJECT: PATRON
#1
AFTERSHOCK

C

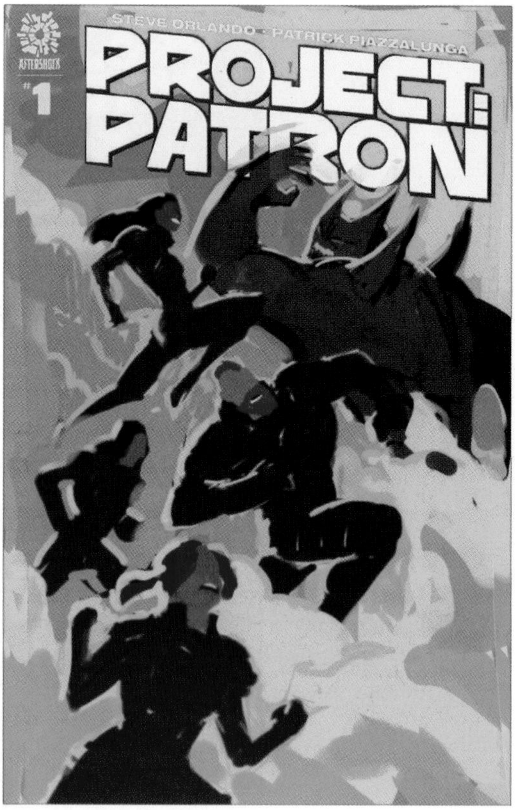
STEVE ORLANDO · PATRICK PIAZZALUNGA
PROJECT: PATRON
#1
AFTERSHOCK

D

PROJECT: PATRON

artist interview:
PATRICK PIAZZALUNGA

AFTERSHOCK COMICS: What was your favorite part about illustrating
PROJECT: PATRON?

PATRICK PIAZZALUNGA: I enjoyed drawing the hangar parts. I wanted to illustrate a
very dark atmosphere, like the first *Alien* or *The Thing*, with many shadows and mystery.

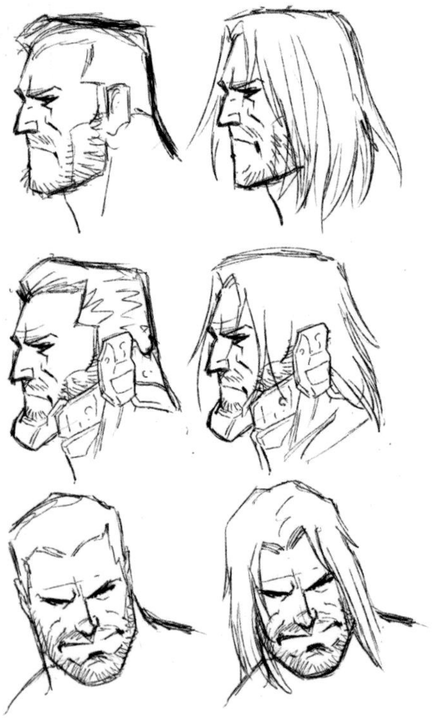

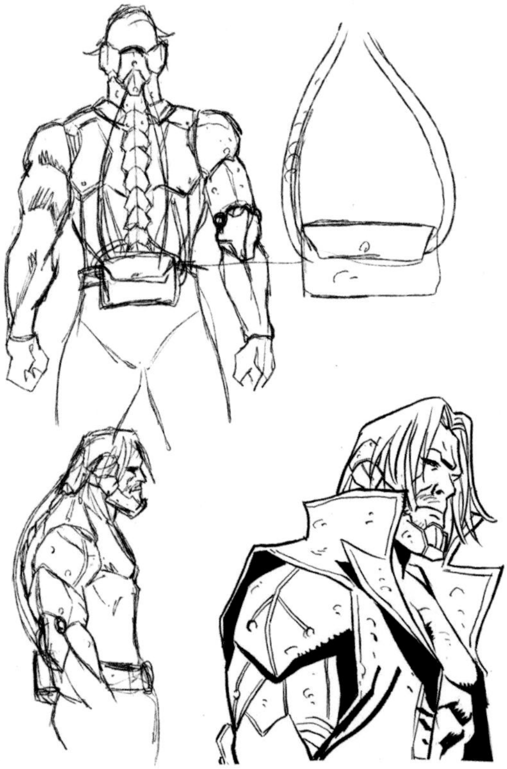

AFTERSHOCK COMICS: **What was the most challenging aspect for you when illustrating PROJECT: PATRON?**

PATRICK PIAZZALUNGA: The fight scenes between Woe and Patron.

AFTERSHOCK COMICS: What is your advice to creatives trying to get started in the comic book industry?

PATRICK PIAZZALUNGA: Dedication to drawing. Never give up on the first difficulties. Never be satisfied with your work, but always improve. Learn to draw and ink on paper. Digital might speed up your work but learn pencil, brush and paper! Have the great desire to do this job...the first contract will come!

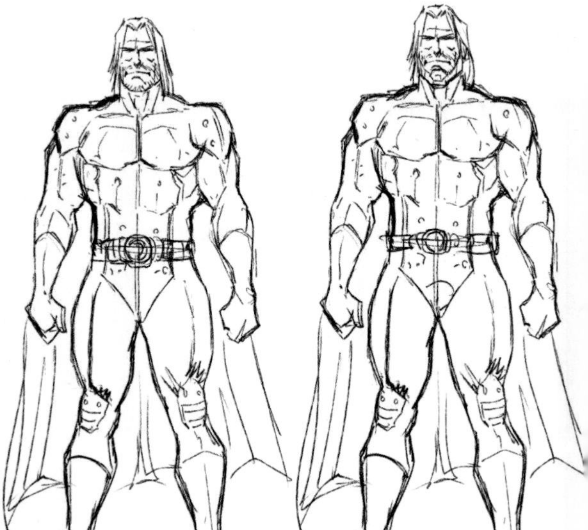

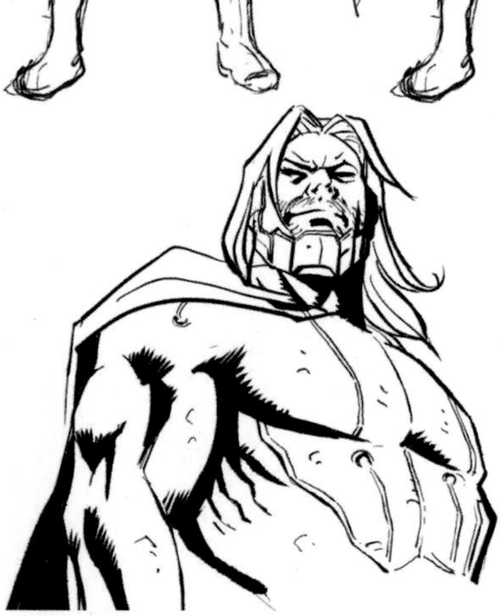

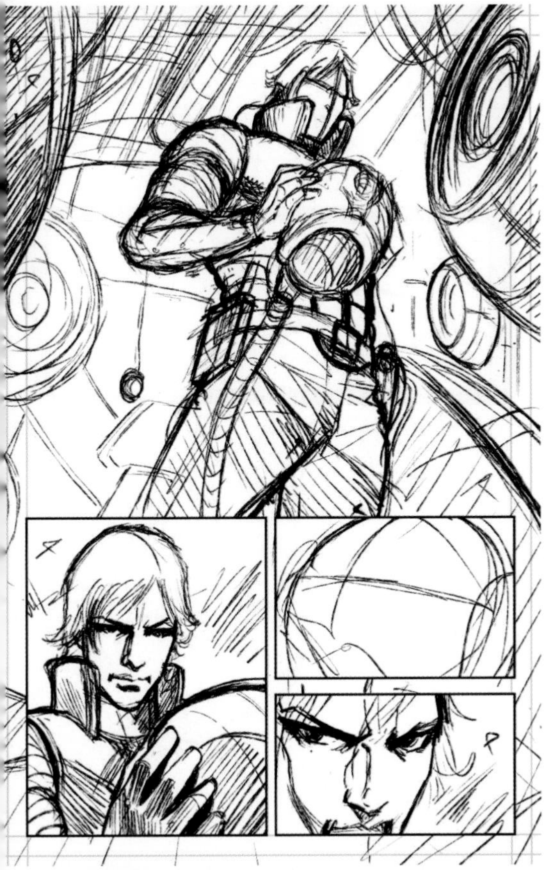

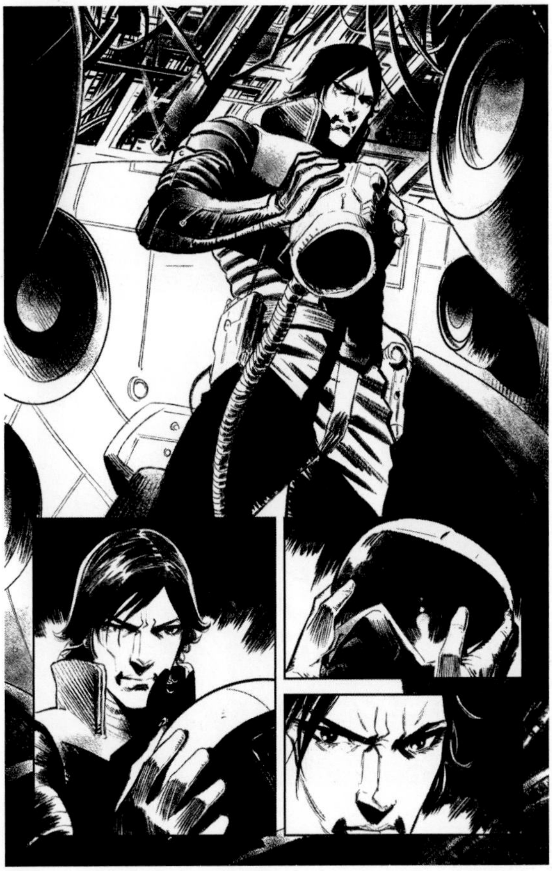

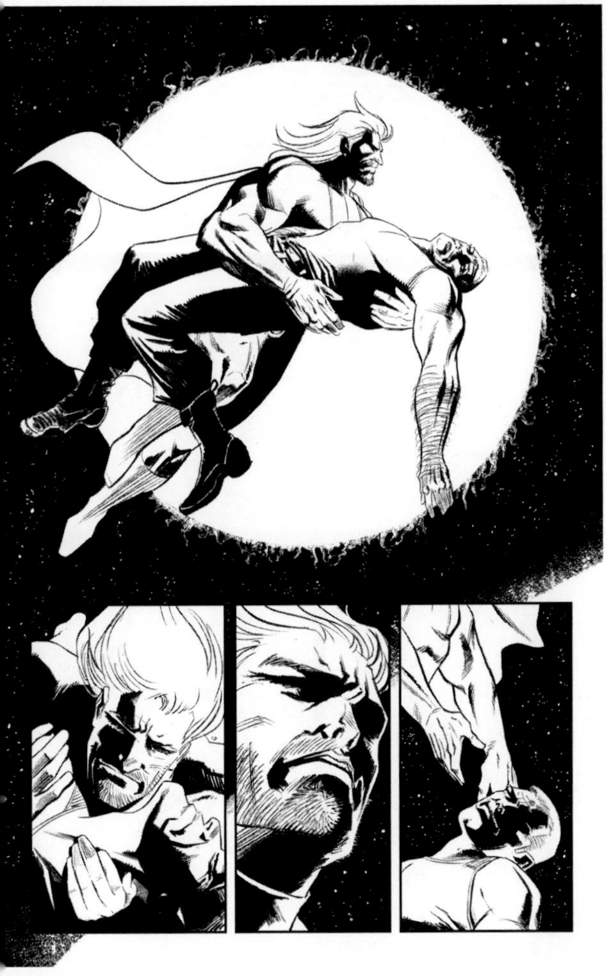

AFTERSHOCK COMICS: If you woke up and could choose one super power to have for the rest of your life, what power would you choose?

PATRICK PIAZZALUNGA: Good question — teleportation! I could travel anywhere in the world in a second, and at zero cost!

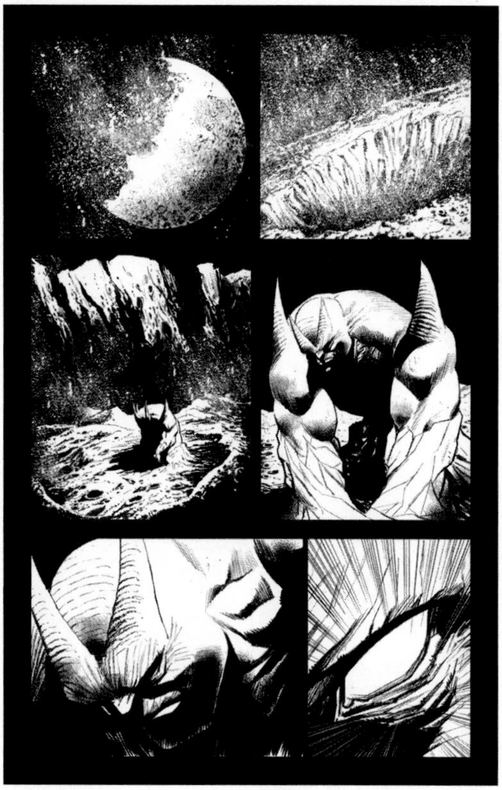

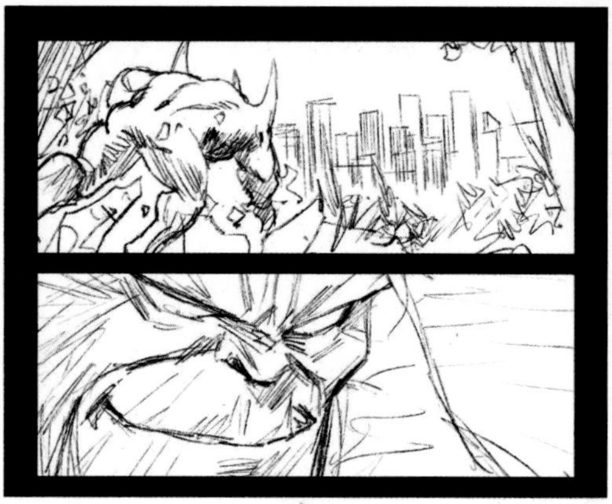

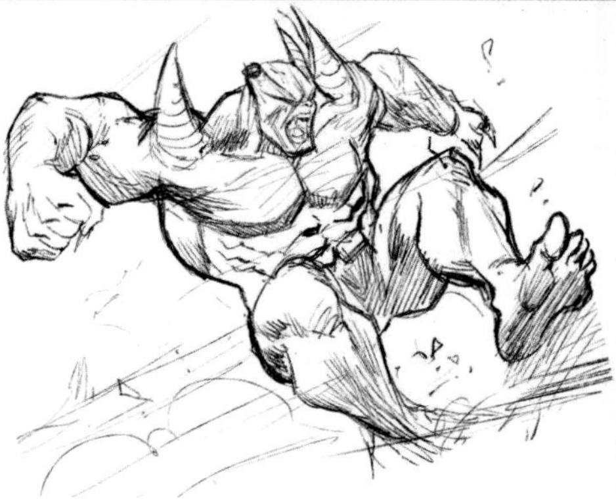

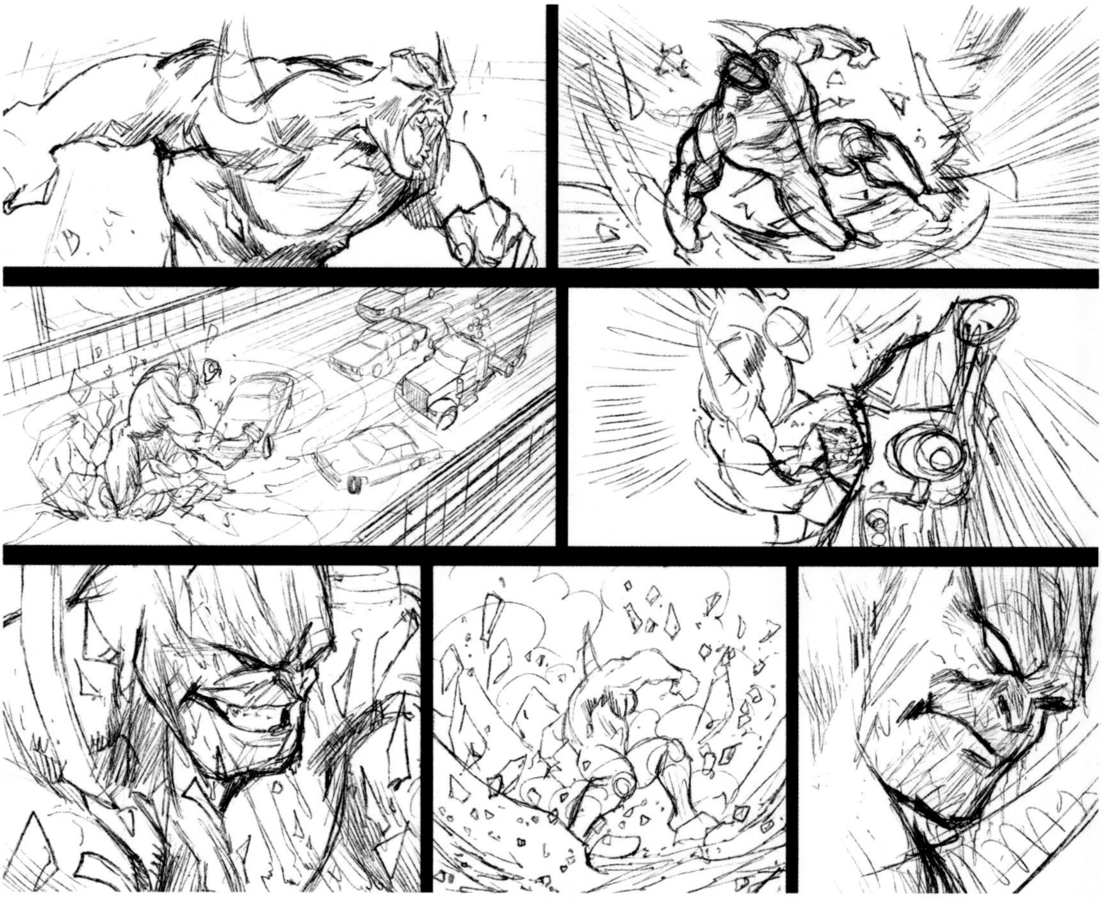

PROJECT: PATRON™

PROJECT: PATRON hit harder than I ever imagined, folks...and that wouldn't have been possible without all of you who gave us a shot. I couldn't be more thankful for your engagement and support! We started with a quirky idea of mashing up a Silver Age and Modern Age take on a Superman Robot, with the interrogative lens to fit the moment. In addition, it was a chance to write a love letter to a moment that shook not just my childhood, but the industry as a whole, with *The Death of* and *Return of Superman*.

This is a true comics love letter to the moments that molded me as a creator, but thanks to all your support, it's become more than that. It's evolved into a bold, provocative piece of work that I'm intensely proud of, and I am so thankful for each and every one of you that went on that journey with me. The Project: Patron hangar is open, folks!

Whatever hope looks like for the future—only one thing's for sure—it can never look like before.

Steve Orlando
July 2021

MORE FROM STEVE ORLANDO

KILL A MAN OGN
Steve Orlando / Phillip Kennedy Johnson
Al Morgan / Jim Campbell

DEAD KINGS VOL. 1
Steve Orlando / Matther Dow Smith
Lauren Affe / Thomas Mauer

RAINBOW BRIDGE OGN
Steve Orlando / Steve Foxe
Valentina Brancati / Manuel Puppo
Hassan Otsmane-Elhaou

PROJECT: PATRON™

STEVE ORLANDO writer

@TheSteveOrlando

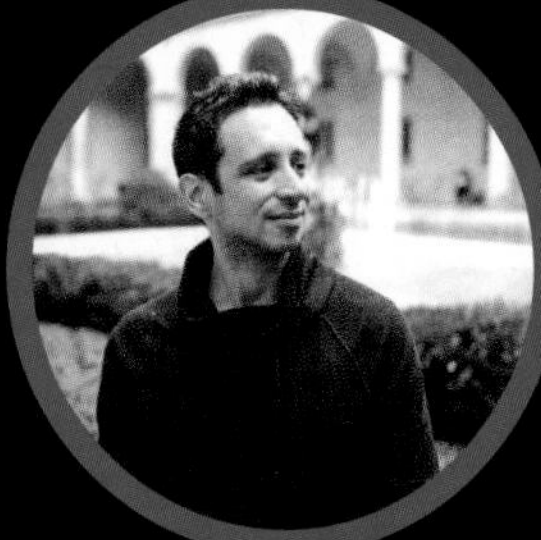

Steve Orlando writes and edits, including *Virgil* (IGN's best Graphic Novel of 2015), *Undertow* and stories in the Eisner Award-Nominated *Outlaw Territory* at Image Comics. He has also launched 2015's *Midnighter* and 2016's *Midnighter and Apollo*, both nominated for GLAAD awards, and took part in *Justice League of America*, *Batman and Robin Eternal* and most recently *Wonder Woman*, *Supergirl*, and *Batman/The Shadow* for DC Entertainment, as well as *The Shadow/Batman* for Dynamite Entertainment, *Namesake* for BOOM! Studios, *Crude* for Skybound Entertainment, and DEAD KINGS for AfterShock Entertainment. Outside of comics, he has been featured in *Hello Mr* and *National Geographic*. His 2018 sold-out launch *Martian Manhunter* was one of Tor's Best Single Issues of 2018. In animation, he's worked with Man of Action Studios on season four of *Ben 10*, and in translation, has produced localizations for Arancia Studios Best-Selling *Unnatural* and *Mercy* at Image Comics.

PATRICK PIAZZALUNGA artist

@Piaha86

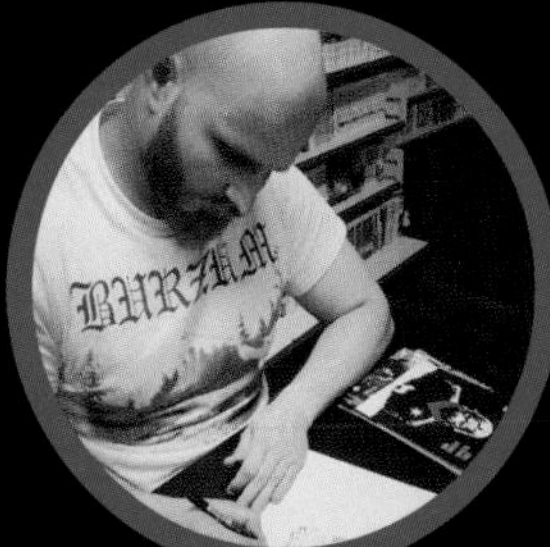

Patrick Piazzalunga lives and works in Tuscany. He broke into the industry at the age of 17, where he inked the comic strip *John Doe*, published by Eura. In 2008, he took part in a motion comic that tied into *The Dark Knight*, written by Dennis O'Neil and with pencils by Giuseppe Camuncoli. From there, Patrick moved on to collaborating with Marco Santucci on *X-Factor Siege: Spider-Man* and *Captain America: Forever Allies*. In 2018, Patrick worked with Alessandro Ginori on their creator-owned project, *Il Paese Dei Ciechi* (published by It Comics).

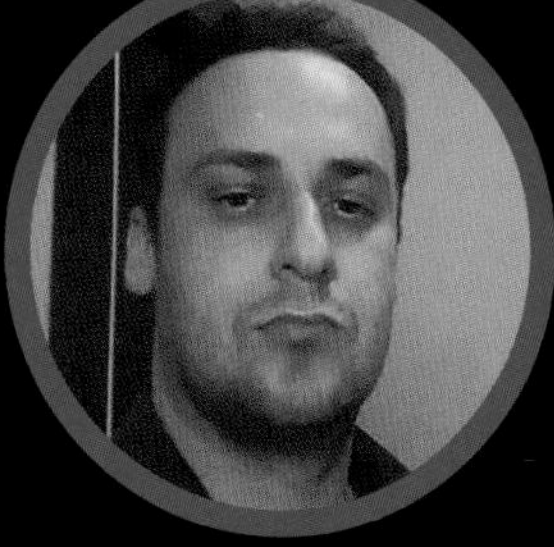

CARLOS LOPEZ colorist

@co_carloslopez

Born and living in Brazil, Carlos Lopez has been working in the comics industry since 2009. He has contributed to many titles and worked with publishers such as AfterShock, Marvel, Dynamite Entertainment, Disney and Top Cow.

HASSAN OTSMANE-ELHAOU letterer

@HassanOE

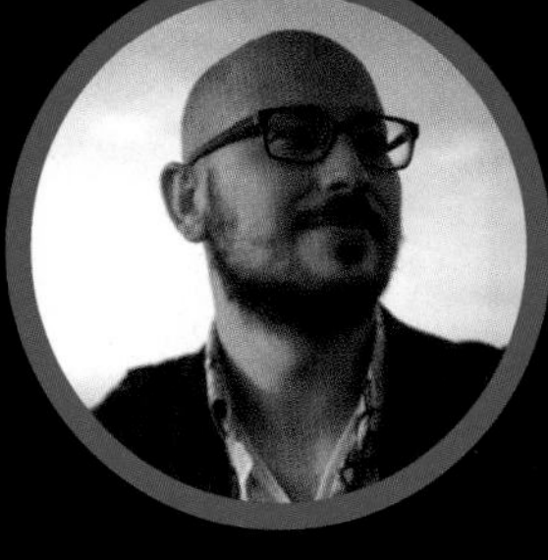

Hassan Otsmane-Elhaou is a writer, editor and letterer. He's lettered comics like *Shanghai Red*, *Peter Cannon*, *Red Sonja*, *Lone Ranger* and more. He's also the editor behind the Eisner-winning publication, *PanelxPanel*, and is the host of the *Strip Panel Naked* YouTube series. You can usually find him explaining that comics are totally a real job to his parents.